AF651267

SOCIAL AND CULTURAL TRANSFORMATION IN INDIA

Social and Cultural Transformation in India

M.H. Syed

ANMOL PUBLICATIONS PVT. LTD.
NEW DELHI - 110 002 (INDIA)

ANMOL PUBLICATIONS PVT. LTD.
4374/4B, Ansari Road, Daryaganj
New Delhi - 110 002
Ph.: 23261597, 23278000
Visit us at: www.anmolpublications.com

Social and Cultural Transformation in India

© Reserved

First Published, 2006

ISBN 81-261-2561-6

[Responsibility for the facts stated, opinions expressed, conclusions reached and plagiarism, if any, in this volume is entirely that of the Author. The Publishers bear no responsibility for them, whatsoever.]

PRINTED IN INDIA

Published by J.L. Kumar for Anmol Publications Pvt. Ltd., New Delhi - 110 002 and Printed at Arora Offset Press, Delhi.

Contents

Preface

Since the time immemorial, Indian society has been undergoing a sweeping socio-cultural transformation. The ancient India was a tolerant nation, which welcomed and absorbed the outsiders along with their culture. Even when the visitors turned to be invaders, the people of this country adopted the positive side of their cultural aspects and tried to enhance their life-style. The Mughals and the Britishers significantly contributed towards the making of socio-cultural fabric of India. Indians have a perennial talent in retaining their own cultural ethos and accepting that of others'. So Indians are still efficient and are speedily capitalising on the revolutionary change taking place, across the globe.

This work is based on detailed and analysed collections of information, regarding India's Cultural Transformation from a very remote past till today. This study comprises the chapters like: Impact of Buddhism and Jainism, Exposure to Outside World, Expansion of Hinduism, Impact of Islam, Mughal Culture, Impact of Christianity, The Renissance. Hopefully, this work is bound to make an interesting reading and serve the purpose, as a good reference book.

—Editor

1

Introduction

History is the product of two great forces, environment and personality; the course of action that the famous figures of history can take, must of necessity take into account the surroundings in which they are placed. In other words, the physical features of a country its normal conditions, its climate, hills, coast lines, rivers, borders, etc. have always influenced the course of its political, social and economic history. They go a long way in moulding the life and character of the people. It was well said by Richard Hakluyt that geography and chronology are the sun and the moon, the right eye and the left eye, of history. The History of India, like that of other countries, cannot be understood without a careful study of its physical features.

Various Names

The subcontinent of India stretches from the Himalayas to the sea. It is known as *Bharatvarsha,* or the land of Bharat. He was a king famous in the Puranic traditions. Bharatvarsha was said to form a part of a larger unit called *Jambu dvipa* that was considered to be the innermost of the seven concentric island continents into which the earth, as conceived by the Hindus, was supposed to have been divided. But early Buddhist evidence points out that *Jambu dvipa* was a territorial name actually in use from the third century B.C. It was applied to that part of Asia, outside China, throughout which the power of the great imperial family of the Mauryas made itself felt.

The present names, India and Hindustan, can be traced back to the early invaders of the country, the Persians and the Greeks. Their progress towards this country usually stopped short at the Indus or the *Sindhu*. Hence, they called the country "the land of the Sindhu." Since the Persians pronounce the letter's as 'h', they pronounced the word Sindhu as Hindu. The word India corresponds to the Sindhu (the Indus) or the Hindu of the old Persian epigraphs. Closely connected with "Hindu" are the latter designations "Hind" or "Hindustan" as used by the medieval Muslims. Most of these names still survive.

India is a vast subcontinent in Asia. It is a peninsula, having the shape of an irregular quadrilateral. Its area is 32,87,782 sq km. (including Sikkim), its length (North South) is 3,214 km and breadth (East West) is 2,933 km.

The 1981 census indicates the total population 68,90,10,051. As regards population it is the second biggest country in the world, the first being China.

Splendid Isolation

Walled off by the impenetrable Himalayan range in the north and flanked on the sides by lesser ranges, India is practically isolated from Tibet, China and the rest of Asia. Both in the west and the east, these mountain ranges are pierced by many passes more or less open thus forming the only gates of India. On the east, west and south its shores are washed by the Bay of Bengal, the Arabian Sea and the Indian Ocean respectively. With the waters of the ocean separating her from Africa on the one side and Malaysia and the islands of the Indonesian Archipelago on the other, and cut off by mountains on her land frontiers in the north, east and west, India was, from the beginning of her history, isolated to a large extent in her evolution and was individual in her life and development. This splendid isolation enabled her to develop peculiarities and special characteristics which constitute the differentiating marks of a distinct type of civilization and culture. Her civilization is distinct in important respect from the civilization of the rest of the world. To a very large extent the habits, the dress, the religion, the laws and learning of the Indians have been that they have themselves evolved and found to be suitable for themselves. No doubt, a few traces of foreign influence on Indian learning and art of the Greeks and the Arabs in ancient and medieval times and of the Europeans in modern times can be perceived. But they are comparatively small when considered along with the vast panorama of India's historical development and her civilization and culture.

Though India was isolated largely, yet her vast dimensions, variety of racial elements, wide differences of climate, great diversities of sod and different physical characteristics not only prevented her from being a stagnant pool but gave it a continental character. It enabled her to generate the forces of action and reaction which lead to the development of civilization. Thus, the continental character of India is an essential factor in her history.

Divisions Based on Geographical Divisions : India is divided primarily into the following four distinct regions geographically:

The Hilly Country of the North : It stretches from the jungles of the Tarai to the crest of the Himalayas. It embraces not only the upland tern tones of Kashmir, Kangra, Tehri, Kumaun, Nepal, Sikkim and Bhutan, but the greatest and highest mountain, the Himalayas, which forms a sort of wall about 2,450 km in length in the north of the country. This northern wall though pierced by many openings has not been used by immigrants or invaders due to the high elevation of the Himalayan range and its snow covered passes. Similarly, the north-eastern ranges comprising the Patakai and the Naga hills running down to the Bay of Bengal have offered tremendous difficulties to the invaders. This protective wall of the Himalayas has given to India the continuity of its civilization and social structure from the earliest to the present times. The Society described in the great Indian epics is not essentially different from what holds its sway today in India. Religious doctrines and beliefs, the rules of marriages, the ritual of burial and the organization of social relationship are not basically different even today. The continuity of Indian life is the supreme gift of the Himalayan range.

Unfortunately, there are a few openings in the north-western side of this Himalayan wall. Owing to their low elevation and the absence of forests, they have offered an easy access to the invaders of the country from times immemorial. The Aryans, Persians, Scythians, Turks, Tartars, Mongols, etc., all poured in through these openings, called the Khyber, Gomal, Bolan, Kuram and Tochi passes. They form regular gateways to India. For the security of the country, it becomes imperative that these gateways must always be kept well guarded. Indian history is not wanting in instances to show that whenever the Government of India neglected the defence on this side, it invariably came to grief.

However, it should also be noted that these mountain passes or gateways were not mere gates of expedition, invasion and conquest, but they fostered also a more pacific inter course with the outside world. The mountain roads from Nepal to Tibet have carried for ages peaceful missionaries of culture and religion. These mountain passes and roads brought to India "the pious pilgrims and the peaceful traders and constituted highways for the diffusion of Indian culture and civilization throughout the greater part of the Asiatic continent." "The natural frontiers of India thus gave security, but not immunity from invasion and while they ensured definite individuality to her people by separating them from the rest of Asia by well marked boundary lines, they never isolated them from the rest of the world."

The Great Northern Plain : It embraces the valleys of the Indus and its tributaries, the sandy deserts of Sind and Rajasthan, as well as the fertile regions watered by the Ganges, the Jamuna and the Brahmaputra. It has always been the core of the Indian continent. The whole of Sindh and nearly half of the old Punjab are now included in Pakistan. This plain is formed by the deposit of rich soil washed down during countless centuries from the vast Himalayan ranges on the north and from the hills and uplands of the Deccan on the south. Again, the river system of Northern India, namely, the Indus and its tributaries (the Sutlaj, the Ravi, the Beas, the Chenab, and the Jhelum), the Ganges and its affluents (the Jamuna, the Chambal, the Gomti the Ghagra and the Sone), and the Brahmaputra and its feeders irrigate this wide plain. These rivers, played an important part in the evolution of Indian culture.

It was in the valley of the Indus that the earliest civilization of Indian history (Mohenjodaro and Harappa) flourished. The rivers of the Punjab and the Ganges determined also the nature and course of the Aryan colonization in India. The vast natural resources of well watered plain explain the fertility and density of population in this region. The richness and fertility of land here also account for the multiplicity of big towns, centres of trade, and the capitals of ancient and modern empires in one or another part of this plain. All these have made this 'plain the lure of one invader after another. Again it is this plain, known in ancient times as *Aryavarta, that* has been the main seat of Indian civilization and culture, and the scene of the events most interesting to the outer world.

It was also the centre of great religious movements, like Jainism and Buddhism, and the core of Indian life whose gradual expansion to cover the whole continent is the central fact of Indian History. In fact, it has truly made India. But the climatic conditions of this region have been exercising an adverse effect upon the fortunes of the people living therein. While the abundance of leisure and the absence of keen struggle for existence made it always possible for the intellectual people to devote themselves to the progress of thought and culture, a luxurious and easy going life, on the other hand, enervated the masses and their wealth and riches tempted numerous invaders.

Division of Northern Plain : This extensive northern plain is broken in three divisions by wedges projecting northward from Rajasthan towards the west and the Santhal Parganas farther east. The Santhal Parganas separate the region of Bengal from the main Gangetic plain. Then in the south of Delhi lies the waterless tract. This creates a narrow corridor known in ancient times as *Kurukshetra,* running between the desert of Rajasthan and the Himalayas. It has been the cockpit of India; for owing to its strategic importance the fate of the country has been decided here on innumerable occasions. The history of the Aryan and the Muslim invasions illustrates this truth. The invaders from Central Asia passing through the Punjab to the Gangetic Valley had no alternative but to go through the narrow bottle necked plain of *Kurukshetra,* less than 320 km in width, to gain entrance into the heart of Northern India. This fact explains why all the decisive battles for the defence of the kingdoms in the Gangetic plain have been fought at one or another place in narrow region. The battle fields of Tarai, Kamal and Panipat are all within this corridor. Today it forms a part of the Haryana State.

The Deccan Plateau : It stretches south of the Gangetic plain and is separated from it by the *Vindhyas* and the *Satpuras.* It is shut in from the rest of the Deccan Peninsula by the western *Vindhyas,* the *Sahyadri* range on the Western Ghats and the *Mahendra* on the Eastern Ghats. It is a triangular tableland rising abruptly in the west sloping away towards the east. Geologically the Deccan Peninsula is older than the Himalayas and much more so than the Indo-Gangetic plain. It is the most ancient part of India and was once probably linked up with an Austral continent stretching far to the east. With the exception of the Narbada and the Tapti which flow westward and fall into the Arabian Sea; all the important rivers of the Deccan the Mahanadi, the Godavari, the Krishna and its tributary the Tungabhadra flow eastwards into the Bay of Bengal. Unlike the rivers of the north the Indus, the Ganges, and their tributaries these rivers of the Deccan are not of much service as a means of communication. Beyond the Deccan plateau lie the Tamil land, the Mysore or Karnataka region, and the open country stretching below it up to the sea. This is known as the Far South.

The descent from the highlands of Mysore to this plain below has been a determining factor in making its own history. As the descent on the west, being more abrupt, is attended with insurmountable difficulties the regions of Cochin and Travancore have been less influenced by the political and military ambitions of the Mysore rulers. On the contrary, the approach to the eastern and southern plains being gradual and easy from its uplands, Mysore had dominated the history of the Karnataka region.

The far South had a historical individuality. The people of this land had developed their own civilization. The cultural accomplishments and political genius of the Dravidians found a true home in the Far South. There they could develop naturally and successfully without being hampered by the aggressive and triumphant North. No Hindu or Muslim Empire builder of the North could ever subdue the whole of the Far South and retain it under his control for a long time.

On the northern side of the Deccan plateau, the *Vindhyas* and the *Satpuras* with their outlying ranges, the valley of the Narbada and the Tapti rivers and the dense impenetrable forests south of the Chhota Nagpur not only separate the Deccan from the north but create great barriers difficult to cross.

In the Vedic and Epic days, these mountains and their dense impenetrable jungles were known as *Dandakaranya* and *Mahakantar* which the Aryan tribes found difficult to penetrate. This led to the conception of two different *countries Aryavarta* and the *Dakshinapath.* Consequently, the Aryan culture and civilization remained confined to the North. Though later on occasional attempts were made by Ashoka, Samudragupta,

Allauddin Khilji, Muhammad Tughlaq and Aurangzeb to combine the North and the Deccan under one political unit, the two had only seldom been united in one political and cultural land. For centuries together the Deccan remained immune from the after effects of the Muslim invasions and the occupation of the north. Physical features, thus, have tended to isolate Southern India from the rest of the country and, consequently, it early developed a culture and thought essentially its own and has played only a secondary part in the history of the country.

However, there has been one great advantage of the Deccan. "In difficult and troublous times the culture of the north could always seek refuge in the Deccan. When Buddhism became dominant in the north, Brahmanical religion and culture made their way to the south, and thus were enabled to survive and later to regain power and ascendance in the north. Similarly, the Jains sought refuge in the south. The 'refugee' northern literature and culture were welcomed by the great Andhra, Chola, Chalukya, Yadava and Hoysala rulers of the south:" Today, since modern scientific inventions have been able to overcome the natural barriers and difficulties of communications, Northern and Southern India find themselves drawn more closely together.

The Eastern and the Western Ghats : The long and narrow maritime plains of the south extend from the eastern sea coast to the western sea coast containing the rich ports of the Konkan and Malabar as well as the fertile deltas of the Godavari, the Krishna and the Kaveri. The Deccan tableland is flanked on the west by a continuous high mountain wall, running parallel to the shores of the Arabian Sea for about 1120 km called the Western Ghats and on the east by the low Eastern Ghats. The Western Ghats, 900 to 2400 metres above sea level, are steep and have a number of flat-topped peaks, converted into impregnable fortresses which played an important role in the history of the Maratha nation. The narrow strip of land sometimes not more than 32 km. in width, stretching between the coast and foot of the Ghats is known as the Konkan and Malabar.

It has a rich soil and is evergreen with rice plants and coconut trees. It is highly productive and thickly populated. In the absence of modern means of communication and transport, it was hard and impossible at many places to climb or cross the Western Ghats. The people living in this coastal strip, particularly in the Southern parts, were, therefore, isolated from the rest of the Deccan for ages together. Even now some of them practise customs found nowhere else in India. On the other hand, in the far north on the Western Coast, the Narbada and the Tapti have broken through the western scrap and cut wide valleys across them. They, thus, formed easy paths leading to the north. It is in this region that great kingdoms and civilized people have lived from early ages. Again, from the earliest days the ports on the Western Coast from *Bhrigu Kachha* (Broach) to Cranganore formed the main outlet of Indian commerce with the west and were in close contact with the civilization of the Middle East.

On the eastern side, the coastal land which lies below the Eastern Ghats is much broader. The eastern scrap itself is of low elevation, much less steep and it is broken in many places by the valley of the Deccan rivers flowing eastwards. This made the communication on the east coast with the uplands of the Deccan easy. Consequently there, too, have been great kingdoms, famous flourishing cities and ,civilized people in the whole of this region. The ports of the eastern coast traded and maintained from times immemorial contacts with the nations of the east Java, Sumatra, Burma, Siam and Indo-China.

Indian History : Geographical Influence : The course of Indian History, like that of other countries in the world, is profoundly influenced by its geography. While the physical features were being described above, their influence was noted here and there. However, some general broad issues are mentioned below:

Different Local Zones, Political and Cultural Units : India is well known for her vast dimensions and the varied physical features. India contains winding chains of hills and the highest mountain ranges, lofty plateaus and vast plains, deep rivers and fertile river valleys dense forests and sandy deserts. There is also every variety of climate. "All these factors tended to separate India into different local zones, each with a regional spirit of its own. The natural barriers largely determined the different political and cultural units into which India was divided. The North India, the Deccan Plateau, the peninsular plains, the Ghats' region all have their marked political and social characteristics. The Aryan language and civilization could not sweep over the Deccan so successfully as it did in the Northern India, over a great part of the Deccan plateau and the far south, the non-Aryan languages together with older customs and ideas still prevail.

The Thar Desert rendered Indian Defence Weak : The Thar desert has affected the course of Indian history. This intervenes between the plain of the Indus valley and that of the Ganges. It separates these regions into two different units. This renders Indian defence weak. When the foreign invaders poured into India through the north-western mountain passes, "the bulk of the Indian plains being separated from this region by the great desert, the resources of North India, far less the whole of India, could seldom be employed to guard these gateways."

There is a narrow plain on the north of the Thar desert. The foreign invaders, being prevented from getting into the south by the desert, had to march along this bottle neck from the valley of the Indus to that of the Ganges. Many decisive battles were fought in this bottle neck. Geography has, thus, made this area a natural battle field. Those foreign invaders who won battles here occupied Delhi easily. They had the great advantage of forcing the main gateway of India and establishing their strong base within India, before they had to reckon with the main strength of Indian defence.

Primitive Indian Culture is maintained by the Forests, Deserts, and Mountain Valleys : The vast sandy deserts, the dense impenetrable forests and high ranges of mountains have provided regions difficult of access. They have offered shelter to the wild primitive tribes who were deprived of their belongings and driven away from the plains by the more civilized conquerors of India. This explains the existence of the Bhils, Kols, Santhals, Gonds, etc., in the desert, fastness of hills and forests of India. These aborigine tribes have maintained, almost intact, their primitive characteristics.

The Warrior Races of India : The hilly districts and impenetrable forests imparted a hardihood to their inhabitants and provided means of defence which are absolute in the plains. Consequently, the martial races of India have been chiefly bred in the dry, hilly districts of the north-west, Maharashtra and the deserts of Rajasthan, where a livelihood can only be wrested from the soil by intense efforts, and even then has to be supplemented by raids upon more favoured neighbouring regions. These martial races have imbibed from their environment love of freedom which sharply distinguishes them from their neighbours. They had carried on struggle for independence against heavy odds. The successful heroic struggle of the Marathas and the Rajputs against the imperial authorities of Delhi was to a large extent due to the geographical features.

The Isolationist Tendency and the Spirit of Local Autonomy : The Indo-Gangetic plain and the Deccan plateau have been divided into many local regions by the large rivers, their tributaries and ranges of the hills. Malwa, Bundelkhand, Oudh, Chhota Nagpur, Orissa, Northern Gujarat. Karnataka, etc., are such natural regions. Racial and linguistic factors have further stimulated the creation of such regions. These developed into separate distinct units retaining their individuality through ages. There developed gradually regional politics which "tended to keep alive the spirit of local autonomy in well marked political units", and the isolationist spirit was maintained there "even amidst political catastrophes and kaleidoscopic changes of rulers and dynasties."

The Growth of Fine Arts and Spirituality **:** The geographical features of India influenced the lives and habits of its inhabitants. The extreme heat and excessive cold have made the people of the country stay at home and ease loving. The numerous rivers and their tributaries offered easy means of communication. The productivity of the soil has made the struggle for existence less keen and provided cheap livelihood. It enabled the people to have abundance of leisure for intellectual pursuits and offered opportunities to consider the problems of life and death. This consequently developed a speculative frame of mind which attached more importance to mind rather than matter. Thus sprang up that mood of spirituality which still holds the Indian mind in its grip and saturates the whole life. "This at least partly explains why art, literature and philosophy flourished, but positive sciences made comparatively little progress in India.

Climatic Changes Affected Indian History **:** Like the mountains, rivers, and the sea coasts, the climate of India has also played a large part in Indian history. It has been often argued that the tropical climate has enervated the Indians and is responsible for their failure to resist the attacks of the foreign hardy mountaineers from colder regions. The destinies of a large part of India depend, to a considerable extent, upon the seasonal rainfall brought by the monsoons from the Arabian Sea. If the heavy rainfall in Uttar Pradesh, Bengal and Bihar accounts for the growth of rich and flourishing towns and happy peaceful life of abundance, the scanty rainfall in Rajas than and the Deccan explains the frequency of famines and raids of the roaming irregulars and the plundering armies.

It must also be borne in mind that a series of climatic changes, taking place in the north-western India (now Pakistan region), have materially affected the course of her history. The present arid wastes of Baluchistan once witnessed abundant cultivation and linked India with other civilizations of the west. Khotan, now a rainless desert, was once the seat of flourishing civilization as late as the 9th century and India was associated with it culturally. Sind, now arid, except where it is irrigated, was one time densely populated, with an equable climate and fertile soil. This is amply proved by the Indus valley seals, exhibiting rhinoceroses, elephants and tigers, all inhabitants of well watered forests, now unknown in Sind.

The Arab historians speak of Sind as an oasis surrounded by deserts, and Timur, as late as the 14th century, lost his horses at Multan due to heavy rains there. Strabo speaks of the vident monsoon rains of the spring and early summer of 326 B.C. in the Taxila district which hindered Alexander's operation. But now the face of this region has been considerably changed.

Maritime Activities, but Absence of Mighty Naval Power in India : India has a very long coast extending more than 6000 km. But the Indians never earned the reputation of being a maritime nation. However, it would be a mistake to think that the mystery of the sea never allured the Indian mind. The Dravidians of the pre-historic times navigated the seas in pursuit of trade and commerce. From the first century A. D to the fourteenth century commercial enterprise and the spirit of adventure led thousands of Indians from the harbours of the eastern coast across the eastern seas to Burma, Java, Sumatra, Malaysia and the neighbouring islands. The ancient Deccan kings patronized great sea faring activities. All this was responsible for the diffusion of Indian civilization and culture throughout eastern Asia in olden days.

The maritime activities of India were devoted to peaceful, cultural and commercial pursuits. Political aggression and annihilation or economic exploitation were never dreamt of by Indians. So the need for maintaining a powerful navy was never felt by them. More over, the Indian rulers had enough scope for their military enterprise and imperial ambition within India itself. The dubious chances of success afforded by the sea could hardly induce them to devote their energy time and resources to building a powerful navy in order to establish and retain an overseas empire.

General Features

Separate Histories of the Regions : The political history of India resolves itself into separate histories of the regions. The natural barriers of winding chains of hills and mountains, deep rivers, sandy deserts and impenetrable forests divided India into different territorial units. These divisions "favoured the growth of a local and regional spirit and fostered separatist tendencies." Consequently, there sprang up in different regions small political and social units whose divergences were accentuated by the infinite variety of local conditions. Each region had a distinct story of its own culture and civilization. The history of India, therefore is not one connected whole, but is the history of different parts following their own line of individual development. When we read or talk of the history of India, we generally take up the history of the central government and not that of the provinces or regions. This is the outcome of the diverse geographical conditions.

Dominance of the History of Northern India : Though geologically the peninsula of the Deccan is older than the Indo-Gangetic plain the history of the south does not go back to an earlier age. Northern India, on account of its physical features, plays a dominating part in Indian history. The excavations at Mohenjodaro and Harappa make us look to the north for commencement of Indian History.

Absence of Rigid Centralization : "The vastness of the Indian plains does not favour the 'city state' form of government as in ancient Greece." The Indian subcontinent has always been predominantly "a land of country states with the village as the primary unit." Though powerful and ambitious Indian kings frequently established an empire embracing nearly the whole of India, the vastness of the country and absence of rapid means of transport and communication rendered rigid centralization impossible. Whenever the king at the centre happened to be weak and vacillating, his feudatories and governors of the provinces utilised the opportunities for declaring their independence. This has been the normal course of the political history of India.

Monarchy the Normal Form of Government **:** Though some autonomous political clans and republics existed in the earlier ages, monarchy has been the normal form of government in India. As the representative system was not very common, a popular legislative body or Parliament of the whole of India was out of question.

Very Few Popular Revolts **:** Since the natural divisions of the country fostered local and regional spirit, local assemblies were very significant part of the body politic. The activities of the people were mostly predominated by local allegiance and local interest. Being accustomed to political subjection, people cared little about the central government. Politically they were indifferent. A change in the ruling dynasty or person did not such affect the activities of the people. It was simply 'a change of toasters' for them. Consequently, "popular revolts as distinct from the revolts of self seekers, have been remarkably very few" in India.

Absence of Chronological History **:** The history of India is marked with absence of chronological history and its gradual evolution. It does not develop from one centre. The history of India is a long account of many different personalities, political and cultural units. Therefore, we do not perceive an incessant and definite flow commencing from one tribe or unit and steadily continuing to others.

Unity in Diversity

India a Land of Varieties **:** India is well known as a land of varieties. It is described as "the epitome of the world". From geographical point of view there are endless varieties. The size of the country is enormous. It is as large as the whole of Europe excluding Russia and is nearly twenty times as big as Great Britain. But more remarkable than the geographical vastness and wide area of the country is the extreme diversity of its physical features.

India has winding chains of inaccessible lofty mountains, covered with eternal snow and flat plains, "and deserts almost untouched by the feet of men, as well as fertile river valleys maintaining a population of over 1170 persons to the kilometre." Every kind of climate is met within India, from the scorching heat of the desert of Rajasthan to the extreme arctic cold of the snowy heights of the Himalayan ranges; from the dry rocky tableland of Deccan to the moist tropical luxuriance of Bengal and Malabar. India offers all the three types of climate the Polar, the Temperate and the Tropical. As regards rainfall India enjoys equally wide range. It has the world's highest records of rainfall. It varies from 12,000 mm at Cherrapunji to less than 75 mm per year in Sind and Rajasthan. This amazing variety of latitudes and altitudes, temperature and moisture, produces a corresponding variety in flora and fauna. India possesses most of the types of flora and fauna known to natural sciences.

There is a great variety of racial types which India presents through her teeming millions. Smith rightly calls India an ethnological museum. The total number of the inhabitants in India amounts to about one-seventh of the whole world. As early as the 5th century B.C., Herodotus observed that "of all the nations that we know, it is India which has the largest population." This huge assemblage of human beings made up of diverse peoples the jungle tribes (like Kols, Bhils, Santhals), the Greeks, the Sakas, the Kusbans, the Huns, the Mongolians the Arabs, the Turks, the Afghans, etc. Today, India has the primitive tribesmen as well as the polished inhabitants of cities. Every phase of the social evolution is represented by the people of India.

There are in India no less than 14 separate peoples with their own languages. Each of these peoples has its own literature. More than 200 different dialects and languages are spoken in this vast sub-continent.

There is also to be found an equal variety of religions. All the world religions are found here Hinduism. Buddhism, Jainism, Sikhism, Islam, and Christianity. All have their sects and sub- divisions. The Hindu religion itself is split up in countless creeds the Vedic religion, the Puranic Hinduism, the

Sanatan Dharm, the Brahmo Samaj, the Arya Samaj, etc. The primitive tribes have their own peculiar cults.

Then, people differ considerably in the social habits, and cultural differences vary from state to State. Financially, too, we find men with barely an income of a few paise a day and others who *rank* among the richest of the world.

Conflicting and varying shades of blood, strains of culture, and modes of life all together build up rich and complex diversity in India. There is no wonder if "India is a museum of cults and customs creeds and cultures, faiths and tongues, racial types and social systems."

The vastness of the country, the extreme diversity of physical features, endless variety of races, and magnitude of its population, divided into countless castes, professing numerous creeds, speaking a variety of languages and dialects all these have made it difficult to establish an all India empire. This also accounts for the fact that political unity is not the normal characteristic of ancient and medieval Indian history. There was no political cohesion. In all the past ages India was divided into many principalities. They were from time to time brought under subjection and integrated into an extensive empire by powerful rulers like Chandragupta Maurya, Asoka, Samudragupta, Allauddin Khilji, Akbar and Aurangzeb. They exercised their sway over a large part of India. But, when internal weakness and disorder or foreign invasions or both shattered their empires, India relapsed once again into political disunity.

Again, not only the extreme south of the Indian peninsula ever remained independent of their paramount power, but India has also been mostly governed by her local provincial dynasties. In fact, India had never enjoyed supreme political unity till the nineteenth century. Politically a popular national feeling was almost absent. Calamity of the neighbouring province did not rouse much sympathy and support. In the people of another province. They had no urge to unite even in the face of common enemy or danger; this absence of political unity, no doubt, not only fostered the growth of varieties of Indian culture and civilization, but retarded also seriously the political progress of the country and hindered India from becoming a nation.

Fundamental Unity

In spite of the above mentioned bewildering diversity in the geographical features, the race, religion and language of the people, there is a deep underlying fundamental unity which is apt to be missed by the superficial observer. "He fails to discover the one in the many, the Individual in the Aggregate, the Simple in the Composite."

Sir Herbert Risley has truly observed, "Beneath the manifold diversity of physical and social type, language, custom and religion which strikes the observer in India, there can still be discerned a certain underlying uniformity of life from the Himalayas to Cape Comorin." This unity has undoubtedly been nurtured in recent times by a uniform system of administration and the spread of modern education. It is a mistake to suppose that it is wholly the result of recent events and the British rule and did not exist at all in early ages. The ideal of unity in India is not a recent growth or discovery. The founders of the Indian civilization were fully conscious of the geographical unity of the country and they tried to impress it on popular consciousness.

Geographical Unity : The first expression given to this sense of unity was their description of the entire land by the single name of *Bharatvarsha* or the land of Bharat. This very name is given to the whole country in the Epics and the Puranas :

"Uttaram yatsamudrasya
Himadres haiva dakshinam
Varsham tad Bharatam nama
Bharati yatra *santatih." Vishnu Purana,* (11, 3, 1)

"The country that lies north of the ocean and the south

of the snowy mountains is called Bharat; for there dwell the descendants of Bharat."

The name Bharatvarsha has a deep historical significance, symbolizing a fundamental unity. The term was not associated only with the geographical boundaries, but with the idea of universal monarchy also. This name together with the sense of unity that it imparted "was ever present before the mind of the theologians, political philosophers and poets who spoke of the thousand *Yojans* (leagues) of land that stretches from the Himalayas to the sea as the proper domain of a single universal emperor." They eulogized kings and emperors who endeavoured to extend their territories from the Himalayas in the north to the Cape Comorin in the south, and from the Brahmaputra in the east to the Indus in the west. The rulers of the medieval period also considered India as one geographical unit and sought to extend their sway over this whole land. Today, this geographical unity is reinforced by the conception of common motherland, *BHARATMATA*. The song *Vandemataram* characteristically embodies this sentiment of unity.

Political Unity : The sense of the unity of the whole country was promoted by politics also. The rulers of India established their sway over the whole country and consequently contemplated over it as a unit. The ideal of great rulers of India in various ages has been to become *Chakravarti* or to rule over the entire country. Chandragupta, Asoka and Samudragupta had established their suzerainty over the whole of India.

The institution of paramount sovereignty was a familiar political idea of the Hindus in ancient ages. The frequent use of the terms *Adhiraja, Rajadhiraj, Samraj, Eka* Raja, *Virat, Sarvabhauma,* etc., in the ancient sanskrit literature, and the repeated performances of such rites and sacrifices as the *Rajasuya, Ashwamedh, Vajapeya, Punarabhisheka, Aindra, Mahabhisheka* show that the idea of universal conquest and an all India overlordship was well known to the ancient Hindus.

In the medieval ages Allauddin and Aurangzeb sought to establish their overlordship over the whole of the country. The Mughals created an imperial system which deepened the conception of oneness of rule and sameness of political experience. Sir J. N. Sarkar rightly points out that the Mughals unified with such political bonds as a centralized administrative system, uniform laws and customs, common coinage, one official language, Persian extensive roads, etc. The British also achieved this political unity in India. After the political emancipation of India, the incorporation of the princely states in the Republic of India completed this political unity of the country.

Religious Unity : There is an undercurrent of religious unity among the various religious sects in the country. The worship of Vishnu and Shiva, though under different names is as widespread in the north as in the south. The temples in honour of Vishnu and Shiva have been constructed all over the country. They raise their spires not only in the snow covered Himalayas and Indo-Gangetic plains but in the deltas of the Tungabhadra, Kaveri and Krishna also.

The ancient epics the Ramayan and the Mahabharat, have been studied in the far south as well as in the Punjab, Kashmir and the Doab. The stories of Ram and Krishna are sung with as much devotion and respect in the Tamil and Kanarese regions as in the Indo-Gangetic Valley. The cow, the Vedas, the Gita the Puranas and other scriptures are respected equally throughout the country. The ancient religion of the Vedas and Puranas has been giving solace, even today, to the countless people. Monotheism, immortality of the soul, reincarnation, *Karma*, deliverance air *Moksha*, *Nirvana*, etc., are the doctrines believed in and followed by all the sects prevailing in the country. They have faith in the unseen Reality and a sense of the sacredness of all life, charity and tolerance. Religious rites and rituals have almost the same uniformity throughout the land. A permanent and characteristically Indian expression of this religious unity is the network of shrines and sacred places with which the country has been covered.

The most sacred places of Hindu pilgrim age, such as, Badrinarayan in the north, Dwarka in the west, Rameshwaram in the south and Jagannath Puri in the east, embrace the whole of the country and they speak of India, being one land. A visit to these holy places and sacred shrines is enjoined by Hindu religion upon every pious Hindu. The conception of pilgrimage was perfected as an expression of love for the motherland and as a means of acquiring an intimate knowledge of the land in ancient times. The list of the sacred places of the Hindus in Sanskrit books shows complete religious unity and familiarity with every part of India. The daily prayer of a Hindu includes the names of all the main rivers of the north and the south like the Indus (Sindhu), Ganga, Jamuna, Godavari, Saraswati, Narbada and Kaveri. They remind him not only of the vastness of his country, but also of the cultural and religious concepts and the fundamental unity of its people.

Cultural Unity : A peculiar type of culture and civilization, utterly different from any other type in the world, has been evolved among the diverse peoples of India. This culture has a fundamental unity. In spite of different languages, customs and political disunity, a uniform cultural stamp was printed upon the literature and thought of all the different units of India. There has been a basic unity of literary ideas, philosophy, conventions and outlook upon life through out the country. The fundamental basis of the social and cultural life of the whole country is one and the same.

The cultural unity and the homogeneity is also reflected in the social ceremonies and the religious rites, festivals and modes of life which are the same in both, the north and the south. The sanctity of the family, the rules of the castes, the *sanskars* (for example, the *Namakaran sanskar),* the rite of cremating a dead body, the cleanliness of the kitchen, etc., are common to all the communities and sects. They are much the same all over the country. The Rakshabandhan, Dasahra, Dewali, Holi and other festivals are celebrated throughout the length and breadth of the country in a uniform way.

Unity of Language : India enjoyed unity of language. Before the Christian era there was Prakrit. It was the common language of the people. The message of the missionaries of Buddhism was successfully carried in this language to the doors of the humblest of subjects. Later on Pali and Sanskrit took its place. Sanskrit has been acknowledged as the one sacred language by all sections of the people irrespective of their race, rank and creed. Different section and creeds have adopted Sanskrit as the sacred language of their scriptures. Again, Sanskrit has been the original source of the different languages of the country like Hindi, Marathi, Gujarati, Bangla, etc. Even Tamil and Telugu, the languages of the South, could not escape the far reaching influence of Sanskrit. What Sanskrit had done in the past, the English language tried to achieve during the British rule, and now Hindi has been doing the same.

Physical Uniformity : Various tribes Aryans, Sakas, Scythians, Huns, etc. have entered India. But they were so completely absorbed in the Hindu fold that they had lost their separate individuality. Even a large number of Muslims and Christians who have been living in India are the descendants of the Hindus who were converted to Islam and Christianity. All these different races and tribes have acquired, with the lapse of ages, physical uniformity. Sir Jadunath Sarkar points out that "there has been achieved some approximation also in physical type and mode of life among the various foreign races that have lived long enough in India, fed on the same crops, drunk of the same streams, basked under the same sun and submitted to the same rules in their daily lives.

Even the immigrant Indian Muslims have in the course of centuries received the imprint of this country and now differ in many essential points from their brethren living in other parts of Asia, like Arabia and Persia." An Indian character and a general Indian personality has gradually evolved. The Hindus all through the past ages have been maintaining fundamental unity in diversity. The non-Hindus have not been altogether unaffected by this sentiment of their Hindu surroundings. Saints, prophets and followers of different rival creeds have been associating freely throughout the country. Instances of their close friendship are abundant. Many followers of Islam in India, have shown profound interest in the science, philosophy and religion of their Hindu brethren.

Even to this day, in the villages of India, the votaries of different creeds and sects follow Hindu festivals, practices, customs and modes of life. Today, reformed and modernized Hinduism together with Christianity and Islam, having ideals of social democracy, have been doing much "to counteract these fissiparous tendencies of caste and creed, and check the centrifugal forces in Indian politics" and maintain the sentiment of unity in all spheres. Thus, in spite of the appalling diversity India is herself the great example of the doctrine of one in many. There is unity in diversity a unity far more profound than that produced either by geographical isolation or by political suzerainty that transcends the innumerable diversities of blood, colour, language, dress, manners, and sects."

Fostering Fundamental Unity and Uniform Culture : The following agencies have been fostering in the country uniform culture and unity:

Sages and Saints, Missionaries and Pilgrims : From the early Hindu times many *rishis* or Sages had set up their hermitages at different places in the country. They were the centres of the highest learning and promoted culture among the common folk. Later on the holy cities and the prosperous towns took their places. Varanasi, Taxila, Mathura, Kanchi, Nalanda, Avantika, Madura, Puri, Shringeri, etc., were such places. They were looked upon with veneration by the people who craved to visit them. The pilgrims who visited them or the students who lived there and returned after some years contributed substantially to the diffusion of Indian culture and fundamental unity. Sanskrit Scholars, saints and missionaries also fostered the sentiment of unity by travelling all over the country. If Shankara Charya had carried his message from the Cape Comorin to the Himalayas, Chaitanya spiritualized the environment from Bengal to Vrindavan and

Mira from Vrindavan to Dwarka in Gujarat. Thus, the devoted pilgrims, the zealous missionaries, wandering Saints or Sanyasis and keen Brahman students formed a connecting link between the different and distant units of the country and reinforced the sentiment of unity.

Imperial Conquerors and Soldiers of Fortune : Ambitious Emperors like Chandragupta, Samudragupta, Allauddin, Akbar, Aurangzeb, etc., conquered extensive territories and united distant provinces under their scepter. Similarly, soldiers of fortune or military adventurers, especially of the Rajput race (for example, Shivaji's ancestors), penetrated deep into backward and obscure provinces and there carved out their own destiny. In due course they served the purpose of a powerful engine for the spread of Indian culture and unity.

Uniform Administration : Uniform administration as set up all over the country during the rule of the Guptas, the Mughals and the British has been an agency for uniting the provinces of India.

Language and Religion : In the ancient times Sanskrit and Prakrit, and in modern times English and Hindi have been doing a good deal to encourage cultural oneness. Similarly, Hinduism which has been the fountain head of several sects and creeds has been fostering the growth of uniformity of spiritual life and thought.

Modern Means of Transport and Communication : Railways, telephones, telegraphs, wireless, radio, aeroplanes, bus, roads, etc., have reduced time and distance considerably and consequently aided in strengthening the sentiment of unity.

Common History and Nationalism : Common historical traditions and the subsequent rise of countrywide nationalism have successfully united the people of India. Thus, Indian culture and fundamental unity have been grounded together. A basic unity of religion, philosophy, customs, conventions, literary ideas, and cultural life have been fostered throughout India from the earliest times and it continues even today.

2

Impact of Buddhism and Jainism

The sixth century B. C. witnessed a great religious ferment in the world. It was during this age that there prevailed, in society, general, spiritual and moral unrest, and consequently, reformers all over the world raised their voice against the existing religious order, and endeavoured to reconstruct it on a new basis. In the Greek island of Ionia, Heraclitus preached his new doctrines; in Iran, Zoroaster launched his protest against the prevailing religious superstitions: and in China, people welcomed the philosophic' teachings of Confucius who gave them a higher conception of the duties of life.

It was an age when people in India were disgusted with old philosophical dogmas and were striving for simple methods of worship and easier means of escape from the ills of this mundane existence. New leaders of thought and religion sprang into vigorous activities and gave a new orientation to life in this country. It was an era of revolt an age of protest against the old order of things. The revolt was against the standardization of social patterns, the ritualistic form of religion, the absolute power of the priest craft and the deadweight of a dead culture. The new philosophy of revolt was anti-social in form and anti caste in spirit. It preached pure individualism and spiritualisation. It discarded the principle of social immobility, inequality and injustice; it upheld the sanctity of human intellect and its freedom. It stood for man and woman to achieve his or her salvation as human beings.

The ultimate aim of the revolt was not materialistic but spiritual, not the socialization but the spiritualisation of life. The spirit of times expressed itself in a number of reforming movements. Humanitarian and theistic movements gathered force and momentum as popular faith in animal sacrifice and barren rituals tended to diminish. These movements judged human progress in terms of spiritual advancement of man. Life was regarded not an end but a means and an idea for spiritualisation.

The thinkers of the new movements were pure intellectualists philosophers and conceived life as a philosophy of power and knowledge. Outside the Brahmanical Holy Law, spiritual leadership passed from the hands of priestly theologians and scarifleers to ascetics and wanderers *(Sramanas, Parivrajakas)* who laid the greatest emphasis on the cessation of craving for the things of the world. These ascetics and wandering teachers rejected the authority of the Vedas and Vedic priests, denounced blood sacrifices which constituted a very large part of the Brahmanic ritual and even denied the existence of God. Right conduct, they declared, was the only way of getting out of the meshes of *Karma* and *Samskara.*

The right conduct included, among other things, the practice of *Ahimsa* or non-injury to living beings. The greatest of these wandering teachers were Kshatriya princes Vardhaman Mahavir and Gautam Buddha. The philosophy and the ideologies of the former took the shape of a reforming movement known as Jainism, while those of the latter led to another movement called Buddhism. Like Luther and Calvin of Europe, Mahavir and Gautam Buddha protested against the corruption that had crept into Hinduism. Their movements Jainism and Buddhism—are Protestant Hinduism as Lutherism and Calvinism are Protestant Christianity. Jainism never went beyond the confines of India, but it still remains the religion of a wealthy community. Buddhism, extinct in the land of its birth after a glorious career of more than fifteen hundred years, remains to this day one of the greatest spiritual forces of the world.

Origin of Buddhism and Jainism : As noted above, Jainism and Buddhism were the reformation movements of Hinduism. They were to a creed, but "an appeal for holier living in the bosom of the existing Hindu religion and society." Both urged the common folk to give up their vices and follies and inspired them to practise purity of conduct in daily life. Both took their stand on certain aspects of the pre-existing religious systems. Vardhaman Mahavir emphasized asceticism and self-mortification, references to which are observed in the Vedas, the Aranyakas and the Upanishads. If the Upanishads recommend retirement into forests or hermitages to seek the highest divine knowledge, the *Smritis* lay emphasis on *sannyas* (renunciation and ascetism) as the last phase of a man's life.

Similarly, the basic doctrines of Buddhism as preached by Lord Buddha have their roots in the pre-existing Hindu philosophy of the Sankhya system and the later Upanishads. Jainism, Buddhism and the *Sankhya Yoga* philosophy, which goes back to the primitive currents of religious and philosophical speculation all the three share a kind of pessimism, a conviction that human life is full of misery, no trace of which is to be found in the optimistic attitude of the Vedic Aryans. The doctrine of transmigration, unknown to the early Drahmanas, suddenly emerges in Upanishads and forms an essential element in Jainism, Buddhism and *Sankhya Yoga*. This doctrine of transmigration is associated with the doctrine of Karma, and the most primitive ideas of Karma are found in Jainmeta physics. An atheistic attitude and a kind of dualism between spirit and matter characterize all these three systems of religious thought.

The *Ashtanga Marga* or the eight-fold path, enjoined by

Lord Buddha for extinguishing the earthly miseries of soul, caused by the cycle of births and deaths, is only a code of general ethics and not the special creed of a new revealed and distinct faith.! Instead of inventing a complete new code of morality, Buddha urged the people to follow the morals and virtues of the old *Rishis* or saints. Except certain prohibitions and duties that he laid down for monks and nuns, he adopted many articles of morality and pious customs of the Brahmanistic code. We are told in the *jatak* tales that Lord Buddha explained to the people repeatedly that true piety consists not in the performance of elaborate rituals or repetitions of the complicated prayers but in leading a pious life. Buddha did not lay down particular dogmas or special rituals for his followers. Even the doctrine of *Ahimsa* or the non-violence was known to the people in the post Vedic period.

Without admitting the existence of the soul, Buddhism accepted the Upanishadic theory of *Karma,* that is, the inevitability of the effects of deeds in regulating future births. The theories that the worldly existence is full of misery, and that the cessation of worldly existence must be sought for, were also inherited by the Buddhists from the previous thinkers.

Again, it is wrong to say that both Jainism and Buddhism instituted new orders of monks and nuns. There existed before Jainism and Buddhism organized groups of ascetics having their own codes of discipline as is evidenced from the Bhikshu Sutras. Both these reformation movements have been reputed for fostering the spirit of scientific inquiry and intellectual discussion before accepting a belief blindly. But this was not a new development in the later Vedic period. We have references to some famous discussions and debates in the Upanishads. Raja Janaka used to initiate such intellectual discussions. Thus, Jainism and Buddhism did not diverge from the main streams of Hinduism. In fact, they represent a significant phase in the religious life and cultural development, an important attempt to reform the spiritual life of India.

Circumstances which led to the Rise of the New Religious Movements : The following are the conditions that favoured the rise and growth of the new religious sects Jainism and Buddhism in this country.

Burden of the Ritualism : By the sixth century B.C., the Vedic philosophy and religion lost their original purity and had decayed in cumbrous, meaningless rituals. The rites and ceremonies were made so elaborate and expensive that they were no longer within the reach of the average man. People, therefore, groaned under the heavy burden of ceremonial rituals.

Belief in Mantras : If the Vedic religion had degenerated into ritualism, the spiritual outlook of the masses was burdened with superstition. The Vedic hyms were replaced by mantras formulae which were supposed to possess divine powers. It was popularly believed that the recital of the mantras could cure people of diseases, bring victory or defeat in wars, assure the prosperity of a state or the destruction of its enemies, silence the arguments of an opponent, even stop cough and promote the growth of hair, etc. In short, the mantras embodied in themselves the universe. There was no phase of daily life, great or small, which could not but be affected by them for better, or for worse.

Sacrifices : The Aryan belief in the divine power of sacrifice was much exploited by the priestly class. The actual killing and sacrificing of living animals and sometimes even human beings on certain ceremonial occasions created a feeling of revolt and contempt against such things in the minds of many. Besides the great public ceremonies like *abhisheka* and *asvamedha* which drained the coffers of the state, there were many household rites for which the services of the Brahmanas were necessary. These practices were 'very revolting. They turned the people against not only the Brahmanas but also the system that they represented.

Intellectual Confusion due to the Theory of Karma, Jnana and Tapas Margas : While people in disgust were eager to seek some solution for these ills, minds of many were stirred by complex problems of life and death, and they strove to find a means by which the soul could be rescued from that unending miserable plight of life. Different means were advocated to attain this end. The priestly classes emphasized the efficacy of the performance of several ceremonies and sacraments *(Samskaras)* for a person who wished to obtain the cherished deliverance of his soul. This was styled as *Karma Marga*. But the Karma Marga was not regarded as the only means of salvation. Soon there developed the doctrine of *Tapas* or self mortification as a means of self realization. The underlying idea was to enable a man to practise austerities in the forest, to subdue physical senses and develop the faculty of concentrating upon the realization of the Supreme Spirit. It was supposed that even the gods submitted to a person who subdued his passions and practised penance in the seclusion of forests.

While the *Karma Marga* and the *Tapas Marga* were growing popular with the average man, the intellectual section of the people convinced that deliverance or *Moksha* could be attained by the *Jnana Marga* (true knowledge). They emphasized utmost the doctrine that "he who knows God, attains to God, nay, he is God." Soul, in fact, is an integral part of God. It is from God, in God, and of God, and so it must merge in God. Its absorption in God was essential for man's spiritual salvation and eternal bliss. They, therefore, discarded the *Karma* and the *Tapas Margas*.

The Supremacy of the Brahmanas : These conflicting views for the attainment of *Moksha* (deliverance) created unrest and confusion in the moral and spiritual world. Besides this intellectual confusion, there was existing the growing monopoly of the unscrupulous and exacting priestly class. Their galling dominance disgusted the masses. They claimed to be the leading exponents of the Vedic tradition. There were endless and elaborate sacrificial rites which required their presence. They dominated every aspect of the life of the Aryans, right from birth to death. There was no escape from their guardianship and the priestly craft. Even the work of the government was executed by them. The Kshatriya princes or rulers of the age were guided and supervised by the Brahmana councillors who had monopolized all powers and offices in the state. They enjoyed special privileges and powers, and considered themselves superior over the rest of the people in society, and they required people to have blind faith in Brahmanism. But people were no longer in a mood to accept this.

The Caste System : The caste system had developed its rigidity and vigour and its fetters were becoming tighter. Change from one caste to another was becoming impossible. The members of the low caste had to face a very miserable plight. They were treated with contempt. Moreover, the current usage which forbade the depressed and downtrodden and the non-Brahmana castes from taking to the ascetic life or following the *Tapas Marga* added to the resentment of the people against prevailing Brahmanism.

Several leading teachers and scholars voiced the spirit of the time and founded religious sects, each of which sought to provide spiritual repast for all and find an easy, simple and practicable way to obtain deliverance for the soul from its unending pilgrimage. These sects or religious movements, according to the Pali works, were no less than sixty two, and according to the Jain texts their number was more than three hundred. The Buddhist canonical work, *Anguttara Nikaya* (fourth third centuries B.C.), refers to religious sects, such as, *Ajivika, Nigrantha* (Jain), *Munda Sravaka, Jatilaka, Parivrajaka, Magandika, Traidandika, Aviruddhaka, Gautamaka* (Buddhist), and *pevadharmika.* The *Mahaniddesa* and *Chullaniddesa* (Buddhist canonical commentaries of the second first centuries B.C.) refer to the *Ajivikas, Nigrantha, Jatiaka, Parivrajak* and *Aviruddhaka,* along with the worshippers of the elephant, horse, cow, dog, crow, Vasudeva, Baladeva, Pumabhadra, Mamibhadra, *Agni,* the Nagas, the Yakshas, the Asuras, the

Gandharvas, the Maharajas, Chandra, Surya, Indra, Brahma, Deva Dik. These lists indicate the existence, side by side with well known religious sects, of a bewildering variety of primitive faiths and popular cults. Of these sects, cults and movements, two alone Jainism and Buddhism survived, the rest had disappeared with the lapse of time.

Jainism

Antiquity of Jainism : The origin of Jainism is shrouded in mystery. In the Rigvedic *mantras* there are clear references to Rishabha and Arishtanemi, two of the Jain *Tirthankaras,* the former being the founder of Jainism. The story of Rishabha occurs also in the *Vishnupurana* and the *Bhagvatpurana* where he figures as an *avatar* (incarnation) of Narayana. All this indicates that Jainism is as old as the Vedic religion, if not order. The Jains believe that it is the outcome of the teachings of the twenty four *Tirthakaras* or prophets or saints, all Kshatriyas, coming one after the other. The first twenty two *Tirthankaras* are so legendary in character that it is hardly possible to say anything about them.

The twenty third *Tirthankara,* named Parsvanath, who lived 250 years before Vardhaman Mahavir, seems to have been a real historical personage. He was the son of King Asvasen of Varanasi, but he abandoned the royal state in favour of spiritual life. His main teachings were non injury, non lying (not to tell lies), non stealing and non-possession. Parsvanath seems to have left a well formed organization behind him. The parents of Vardhaman Mahavir and the members of his family were the followers of Parsvanath's religion and naturally Mahavir too was influenced by the Jain doctrines in his youth. The next and the last *Tirthankara* was Vardhaman Mahavir himself.

Vardhaman Mahavir (599 527 B.C.) : Vardhaman Mahavir was born in Kundagrama, a suburb of Vaishali (modern Muzaffarpur district in Bihar) in 599 B.C in a rich Kshatriya family. His father Siddhartha was the head of a Kshatriya clan called the Jnatrikas ; and his mother Trishala was the sister of Chetaka, the most famous 'Lichchhavi prince and ruler of Vaishali. As King Bimbisara of" Magadha had married Chellana, the daughter of Chetaka, Mahavir was related to the eminent ruling dynasty of Magadha. Vardhaman was educated to the highest perfection in all branches of knowledge and art, and was married to Yasodhara, had by her a daughter whose husband Jamali became the first disciple of Mahavir and subsequently the leader of the first schism of the Jain Church. In his thirtieth year, on the demise of his parents, Vardhaman renounced the world, left his home and became an ascetic in the search of truth.

During one of his visits to Nalanda, he made acquaintance of an ascetic called *Gosala Makkhaliputta*. He was so much impressed by Vardhaman that he attached himself to him, but left him after six years to establish a new religious order called *Ajivikas*. For thirteen years Vardhaman lived the life of self-mortification, severe austerities, and deep meditation. Then in the thirteenth year of his ascetism, on the tenth of Vaisakha, outside the town of *Jrimbhikgrama*, near the Parsvanath hills, he attained "intuitive knowledge". At this supreme knowledge and the subsequent final deliverance from pleasure and pain, in his forty second year of age, Vardhaman became known as Mahavir, the great hero, or Jaina (the conqueror who had subdued his passions) and his followers were named *Nirgranthas* (free from fetters or bonds). For the next thirty years he moved from place to place and preached his doctrines in Kosala, Magadha and further east. He paid frequent visits to the Kings, Bimbisara and Ajatasatru, who honoured him highly. He died at Pava (in the Patna district) at the age of seventy two in 527 B.C. Some modern scholars prefer 468 B.C as the date of his death. He was contemporary of Gautam Buddha and survived him by many years. He established a religious order which was open to all friars and nuns as well as laymen, both males and females. He accepted the teachings of Parsvanath as the basis of his faith.

Teachings of Mahavir : Mahavir believed in dualistic

philosophy and held that matter and soul are the only two ever existing elements. In other words, a man's personality comprises material and spiritual natures. The former is perishable while the latter eternal and evolutionary. According to him, on account of *Karma* (the accumulated effect of actions done in the past lives) the soul is in a state of bondage created by passions and desires collected through several previous births. It is by means of continued efforts through several lives that the *Karmik* forces binding the soul can be counteracted and the soul itself is rendered passionless.

The disintegration of the *Karmik* forces constitutes the final liberation of the soul *(jiva)*. By *tapas* or severe austerities and self-mortification and discipline of the body, the forming of fresh *Karmas* and their assimilations is prevented and the already deposited *Karmas* are lessened and finally shaken away. Side by side with this decay of the *Karmas* the internes qualities of the soul get expressed more and more and the soul shines in full luminosity and in infinite greatness and glory which represents final liberation of *Moksha*, and then the soul becomes *Paramatman* the pure soul, with infinite knowledge, power and bliss. *(The Cultural Heritage of India*, Vol. I, p. 207) "

Certain ethical code is assigned both for a householder and a homeless monk. Since the aim of life is to attain salvation, one has to avoid evil *Karmas*, then gradually prevent all kinds of fresh *Karmas* and destroy the existing ones. For this purpose, a householder is to observe five vows of non-injury *(ahimsa)*, speaking truth *(satya)*, non stealing *(asteya)*, non adultery *(brahmacharya)* , and non possession *(aparigraha)*. This comprises right conduct. Then he has to follow two more principles Right Paith and Right Knowledge the former means a belief in the Jinas and the latter means the knowledge of eventual liberation and of life in all existent things. More severe than this is the code laid down for a monk.

Mahavir did not believe that God created this world or exercises any control over it. According to him, there is no creation of the world, no supreme creative spirit, nor there is any creator necessary to explain the nature of the world. God, according to him, is only the highest, the noblest and the fullest manifestation of all the powers latent in man (the most perfect man).

He regarded all objects, animate or inanimate, as endowed with various degrees of consciousness. They possess life and feel pain on the infliction of injuries. So the greatest emphasis is laid on the doctrine of *Ahimsa* or non injury to any kind of living being, however low may be the state of its evolution.

He rejected the authority of the Vedas and objected to the Vedic rituals and the Brahmana supremacy. He advocated, as noted above, a very holy, ethical and elevating code of life and severe asceticism and extreme penance for the attainment of *Moksha* or the highest spiritual state. Modern Jainism embodies these very doctrines of Mahavir.

Unlike Buddha, Mahavir was more a reformer of an existing religion and possibly of a church, than the founder of a new faith. All the Pali canon shows that it regarded Mahavir not as a founder of a new sect, but merely as a leader of a religious community.

The Jain Church : Mahavir successfully founded the Jain Church. His severe asceticism and simple doctrines attracted many followers. He had eleven close disciples or apostles known as *Ganadharas* or "Heads of Schools", Only ,one of them, Arya Sudharman, survived Mahavir and became the Pontiff of the Jain Church after his death. Sudharman, the first *thera,* died twenty years after his master's death. His successor was Jambu who held the office for forty-four years. Three generations of Pontiffs passed after him and during the reign of the last, Nanda of Magadha the Jain Church was ruled by two *theras,* Sumbhuta vijaya and Bhadrabahu, who was the author of the *Kalpasutra* of the Jains. Nothing in detail is known concerning the fortunes of the Jain Church for about 150 years. For the history of the Jain Church from its inception to the fourth or third century B.C., we are indebted to the Jain *Kalpasutra* of Bhadrabahu who was the sixth *thera,* after

Mahavir, and was a contemporary of the Emperor Chandragupta Maurya.

It is reported that he died) 70 years after Mahavir's *nirvana.* The Jain *Kalpasutra* consists of three different sections the first section contains the biographies of the twenty-three Jinas or *Tirthankaras* who preceded Mahavir. The twenty-third Jina, *Parsvanath,* is said to have laid the foundation, upon which Mahavir, who followed him about 250 years after, set up the Jain Church. The main part of the first section is the detailed biography of Mahavir. The second section of the *Kalpasutra* consists of the Theravari, a list of schools *(ganas)* and their heads *(ganadharas).* As the list goes far beyond Bhadrabahu it seems that it was possibly written by others and not Bhadrabahu himself. The third section contains the *Samachari* or the Rules for the ascetics or Jain monks.

The First Jain Council and the Great Schism : The fourteen *Purvas,* the text books of the old Jain scriptures which Mahavir himself had taught to *Ganadharas,* were perfected by Sambhuta vijaya and Bhadrabahu. Sambhuta vijaya is said to have died in the same year in which Emperor Chandragupta Maurya ascended the throne. Towards the close of the fourth century B.C., a terrible famine, lasting for twelve years, broke out in South Bihar. When it led to the exodus of an important section of the Jains, headed by Bhadrabahu, to the Mysore region in the south, many Jains remained in Magadha under Sthulbhadra, a disciple of Sambhuta vijaya. They summoned a council at Pataliputra about 300 B.C to collect and revive the knowledge of the sacred texts which was passing into oblivion. Its result was the compilation of the twelve *angas* that are considered as the most important part of the Jain canon.

The followers of Bhadrabahu, on their return to Magadha, refused to acknowledge the canon as drawn up by their co-religionists in Bihar holding that the fourteen Purvas were lost. Moreover, there was already a wide gulf made between those who had emigrated and those who stayed in Magadha. The latter had become accustomed to wearing white garments and discarded Mahavir's teachings, whereas the former still continued going naked and strictly followed the teachings of Mahavir. This is how the first Schism split the Jain Church into the *Digambaras* (sky clad or naked) and *'Swetambaras* (clad in white).

The Second Jain Council at Valabhi (512 A.D.) : With the lapse of time the canon of *Swetambaras* was reduced to a disorderly condition, and it was in danger of being lost altogether. Therefore, in 12 A.D., a Council was held at Valabhi in Gujarat, presided over by Devardhi Kshamasra mana, a Ganadhara, to' collect the sacred texts and write them down systematically. At this time the twelfth *anga*, drawn in the first Council at Pataliputra, had already disappeared Jeavingonly the eleven *angas* in the recession that has come down to us; They were written in *Ardha Magadhi.*

During the centuries that "followed, furthermore splits took place amongst both the sections the Digambaras and the Swetambaras the "most 'important of them being one that renounced idol worship altogether and devoted itself to the worship of the scriptures. They are called *Terapanthis* among the Swetambaras and *Samaiyas* among the Digambaras. This sect came into existence not early than the sixteenth century A.D. Today the Jain Church with all its schisms is still existing and this religious order founded by Mahavir is still preaching his teachings all over the country.

Jain Philosophy : Jainism shows a close affinity with *Samknya system* of philosophy. It was called *Syadvada.* According to *Syadvada* or the theory of 'May be', seven modes of predication are possible. If the question is "Is there a soul?" it would admit seven answers to it : (i) is, (ii) is not, (iii) is and is not, (iv) is unpredicable, (v) is and is unpredicable, (vi) is not and is unpredicable and (vii) is, is not and is unpredicable. There is a sense in which there is a soul, and there is also a sense in which no soul exists and a third sense is not inconceivable in which one cannot describe soul, and so on: Knowledge is only probable.

Jainism has a theory of reality also. According to it the world consists of two eternal, uncreated, co- existing but independent categories, namely the conscious *(Jiva)* and the unconscious *(Ajiva)*. The conscious being or Jiva corresponds to the soul. It knows and feels. It acts and is acted upon. It suffers by its contact with matter and is born again and again only to suffer. Its highest endeavour is to free itself from this bondage. This is salvation which could be attained by higher knowledge and meditation upon the great truth. The Ajiva or the unconscious is not what we call matter. It includes matter, which is given the name *Pudgala*, but it also includes such things as space and time, virtue and vice, etc.

According to Jain philosophy there is no God or Creator. Man's salvation from suffering does not depend upon the mercy of any god or creator. Man is the architect of his own destiny. By leading an austere life of purity, virtue and noble thinking and acting, one can escape the ills of life. Life of renunciation is the shortest way to salvation.

Thus, Jainism is a moral code in the modern sense. It must be noted that Jainism did not dogmatize. According to its fundamental logic, no absolute affirmation or denial is possible. When all knowledge is probable and relative,' your opponent's view is as likely to be true as yours. As a result of this spirit of accommodation Jainism has survived in India till today.

Ascendancy or Jainism : The inspirational and literary evidence seems to indicate that, in its earlier stages, the success of Jainism was more remarkable than of Buddhism. The use of common dialect in place of Sanskrit by Mahavir and his preaching monks, the simple and homely moral precepts instead of subtle and unintelligible doctrines of God and soul, the free ministration of spiritual truths to the masses, the activities of the Jain monks, and royal patronage were the forces which helped in the spread of Jainism.

The incessant missionary efforts of a strongly organized religious order, that was left behind by Mahavir, made animal sacrifices fall into disuse and non-violence became firmly established as a rule of life even amongst those classes of people who did not embrace Jainism. The followers of Mahavir gradually spread over the whole country. Jain monks were to be seen on the banks of the Indus when Alexander invaded India. According to the Jain traditions, Udayin, the successor of Ajatasatru, was a devoted Jain. The 'Nandas were also probably jain. In the first century B.C., Ujjain became a great centre of Jainism as is evidenced from the legends of the Jain saint Kalakacharya and Gardabhilla and his son Vikram of Ujjain. By the close of the fourth century B.C., a team of Jain monks under Bhadrabahu migrated to the Deccan and spread Jainism throughout the South with Savanna Bengal in Karnataka as their central seat. A late inscription (900 A.D.) records that the summit of the Chandragili (Karnataka) is marked by the footprints of Bhadrabahu and Chandragupta Munipati (Emperor Chandragupta Maurya). Jainism became very popular there especially among mercantile community.

Royal patronage was also bestowed upon Jainism. The great Maurya Emperor, Chandragupta, was its devout patron. As noted above, he himself had joined Bhadrabahu's march to the South as his disciple. A cave is dedicated to him and the hill on which it exists is known as Chandragiri after him. During the second century B.C., King Kharvel of Kalinga (Orissa) professed Jainism and became its illustrious and renowned patron by setting up Jain images himself. In the Kushan period, Jainism flourished wen at Mathura and was dominant in Eastern India in the time of Harsha. During the early centuries of the Christian era, Mathura in the North and Sravana Belgola in the Deccan, were great centres of Jain activities as is evidenced by a large number of inscriptions, images and other monuments discovered at both the places. From the fifth century many royal dynasties of the South, such as, the Gangas, the Kadambas the Chalukyas and the Rashtrakutas, patronized Jainism.

Some of the Rashtrakuta kings of Manyakheta, from the

eighth to the tenth century, showed a special leaning towards Jainism. They were zealous patrons of it and gave a great encouragement to the development of Jain art and literature. Many celebrated Jain poets flourished under them. Jinasena and Gunabhadra composed their *Mahapurana* at the time of King Amoghavarsha, whose great work *Ratnamalika* became very popular with people of all sects. It is said that Amogba varsha became a Jain monk in the latter part of his life. According to epigraphical evidence one of his successors, Indra IV, died in the Jain form of renunciation, self- mortification' and asceticism. About the year 1100 A.D., Jainism gained ascendancy in Gujarat. There the Chalukya King Siddharaja (1094-1143 A.D.), the popular hero of the Gujarat legend and the ruler of Anhilwad, and his son Kumarapala were great patrons of the Jain sect. They openly professed Jainism and encouraged the literary and temple building activities of the Jains in Gujarat. At the court of Kumarapala Jived the famous Jain scholar Hemchandra who was the royal pandit and annalist.

During the Muslim period, Jainism continued to flourish without much molestation from the Muslim rulers of the country owing to the very peaceful ways and non-interference policy of the Jains. But their numbers began to decrease. They, however, received some patronage under the benign Mughal Emperor, Akbar. During the Muslim period, the Jains, particularly, increased in the states of Rajasthan, where they occupied many important offices of State including generalships and ministership. But the period that followed was of steady decline.

Causes of the Decline of Jainism : (1) A large number of unselfish workers, provided by the religious monastic order for preaching and proselytizing were no longer enthusiastic in those activities. (2) The days of liberal royal patronage had passed away. (3) The lay community became split up by the internal divisions that made it impossible for them to combine for any solid religious or social work. (4) Caste distinctions and divisions, that were once brushed aside, were reimposed and they became active with all their inflexible rigidity. This sapped the original vitality of the Jain community though it continued to survive in ever decreasing numbers. (5) In the meanwhile, counter reformation in favour of orthodox Hinduism set in and it had the effect of nearly exterminating Jainism.

The present day population of the Jains in India is nearly sixteen lakhs distributed all over the country, but they are predominantly found in Rajasthan, Gujarat, and some districts of Madhya Pradesh and the South. Mostly they are rich and prosperous traders and have founded and maintained many charitable institutions in the country, such as, dispensed, *dharmasalas* (rest houses) and houses for animal protection. Now they are paying more attention to the reform of their society, the spread of education, revival of their faith, construction and repairs of Jain temples and shrines and the publication of ancient Jain literature that has for centuries remained locked up in manuscript form in Jain temples all over the country.

Contribution to Indian Culture

Jain Literature and the Growth of Vernacular Languages : Though a mall community, the Jains have played a very important part in the development of the language of the country. Sanskrit and Pali have been the mediums of sacred writings and preachings of the Brahmanas and Buddhists respectively. But the Jains utilized the prevailing spoken languages of the different times at different places in the country for their religious propaganda and the preservation of the sacred knowledge. Their religious literature which is written in Prakrit is very vast. Thus, they exercised a healthy and predominant influence on the development of the Prakrit language. They even gave a literary shape to some vernaculars for the first time. Mahavir himself preached in the mixed dialect called *Ardha Magadhi* so that people speaking Magadhi or Sauraseni might understand him the roughly. His teachings, which were classified into twelve books called *Srutangas,* are written in Ardha Magadhi. Recently, a very rich literature produced by the Jains has come to light. It preserves the form of the language as it was current prior to the evolution of the present day vernaculars, especially Hindi, Gujarati and Marathi.

This literature is written in the language called *Apabhramsa.* It links the classical languages Sanskrit and Prakrit on the one hand and the modern vernaculars on the other; and, therefore, its study is very significant from the philological point of view. Jain thought and inspiration can be traced in the literature of the South. The earliest literature in Kannad is of Jain influence. The Jains have also written some of their scriptures in Sanskrit. In fact, they have produced a rich literature in Sanskrit, both narrative and philosophical, and works on grammar, prosody, lexicography, and mathematics are also not wanting.

Jain Architecture : The beauty of Jainism finds watermark during the eleventh and the twelfth centuries early centuries they erected *stupas,* like Buddhists, in honour its high In their of their saints, with their accessories of stone railings, decorated gateways, stone umbrellas, elaborate carved pillars and abundant statues. Some of these, that have been discovered at Mathura, in Bundelkhand and some parts of Northern Madhya Pradesh, are full of Jain statues. They belong to the eleventh and the twelfth centuries. The gigantic statues of *Bahubali* called Gommatesvara at Sravana Belgola and Karkal in Karnataka are examples of the wonders of architecture. The former statue, 21 metres high, carved out of a mass of granite, standing at the top of a hill was erected in 984 A.D by Chamundaraya, the minister of the Ganga King, Rachamalla. The colossal reliefs carved out of rock in Gwalior fort in Madhya Pradesh belong to the fifteenth century. The Jain caves with their relief works and statues at Udaigiri hills, near Bhilsa in Madhya Pradesh and Ellora in Maharashtra are examples of excellent architecture, sculpture of the period.

The Jains have also constructed cave temples cut in rocks, the earliest examples of which belonging to the second century B.C., and later, exist in Orissa and are called Hathingumpha caves. Other examples of different periods are still existing at Junagarh, Junnar, Osmanabad and other places. Many Jain places of pilgrimage, such as, the Parsvanath Hills, Pavapuri and Rajgiri in Bihar, and Gimar and Palitana in Kathiawar have temples and other architectural monuments of different ages. The Jain tower at Chittor in Rajasthan is one of the best specimens of Jain architecture. The Jain temple at Mount Abu in Rajasthan, belonging to the eleventh century, carries to its highest perfection the Indian genius for the invention of graceful patterns and their application to the decoration of masonry.

Conclusion : Traces of Jainism go far back into history and it is undoubtedly older than Buddhism if not Vedic religion. Though it neither became the dominant religion in India nor spread abroad, yet it has remained a powerful sect in the country. The orthodoxy of Jainism, its affinity to Brahmanism, its non-missionary spirit, and absence of hostility towards other rival faiths account for the fact that Jainism still flourishes in several parts of the country.

Buddhism

Life of Gautam Buddha : Buddhism was the movement that gave the greatest shock to Brahmanism. It was started by Gautam Buddha who was a notable contemporary of Mahavir. He was the son of Suddhodhana, the chief of the Sakya clan of Kapilavastu in the Nepal Tarai. His mother was Maya, a princess of neighbouring clan of the Koliyas. He was born about the year 566 B.C., in the village of Lumbini, a few kilometres from Kapilavastu. The site of his nativity is marked by the celebrated Rummindei Pillar of Ashoka Maurya, containing an inscription dated 249 B.C. As Maya died in childbirth, Siddhartha was brought up by his aunt and stepmother, *Prajapti Gautami.*

From his boyhood Siddhartha showed signs of contemplative turn of mind and a deep compassionate nature. The royal splendour failed to captivate the prince's heart even from his boyhood. Observing in his son a great indifference to worldliness, Suddhodhan married him to a beautiful and accomplished princess Yasodhara, daughter of a Sakya noble, and surrounded the married couple with the choicest material of luxury and pleasure. But the prince was not happy at heart. The sight of an old man, a sick man, a dead body and an ascetic intensified his deep hatred towards the world and made him realize the hollowness of worldly pleasures. He was perturbed by the eternal problems of life, its suffering, disease, death, and mortality, and he felt powerfully attracted by the calm serenity of the passionless recluse. After the birth of a son named Rahula, he left his home and kingdom in 537 B.C., at the age of twenty-nine, as a wandering ascetic in search of Truth. This is known as the Great Renunciation.

For six continuous years he lived as a homeless ascetic, seeking instruction under two Brahmana religious teachers and visiting many places including Rajgriha in the Patna district and Uruvila near Gaya. Finding no satisfaction there he practised the severest penances and the most rigid austerities, and made fruitless efforts to find the Truth. He then, gave up penance, took a bath in the stream of the river Niranjana (modern Lilajan) and sat under a *pipal* tree at Bodh Gaya. Here he attained supreme knowledge and insight. Revelation came to him that the Great Peace was within his own heart and he must seek it there. This is known as the Great Enlightenment and since then he became known as the Buddha or the Enlightened One or *Tathagat* (one who has attained the Truth). Then he proceeded to the Deer Park near Sarnath in the vicinity of Varanasi where he gave his first religious discourse, as a result of which five disciples joined him. For the next forty-five years, he roamed about as a wandering teacher and proclaimed his gospel to the princes and peasants alike in Oudh, Bihar and some adjoining districts. Kings like Present it of Kosala and Bimbisara and Ajatasatru of Magadha accepted his doctrines and became his disciples. He laid the foundation of the Buddhist Church or Order of Monks *(Sangha)*. Preaching and delivering sermons for salvation and making conversations, he at last died at the age of eighty in 486 B.C., at Kusinara, modern Kasia in the Gorakhpur district of Uttar Pradesh.

Teachings of Buddha : Gautam Buddha never endeavoured to establish a new religion or creed. Neither he talked of codes and conventions, *nor* of laws and rites. He indicated a new way of life the virtuous path by treading which one could attain deliverance from births and deaths. He advocated not a set of doctrines or dogmas but a rational scheme of spiritual development. Simple goodness of spirit, deed and conduct is the basis of his teachings. He rejected the infallibility of the Vedas, condemned animal sacrifices, protested against the complicated, elaborate and meaningless rituals, challenged the caste system and priestly supremacy and denied or doubted the existence of a supreme creative spirit.

It was, according to him, the individual exertion at self-improvement and virtuous life that mattered most. Self-culture is the key note of his teachings. The virtuous path as suggested by him is a code of practical ethics that has a rational outlook. Buddhism, therefore, was more a social than religious revolution. It taught the code of practical ethics and laid down the democratic principle of social equality.

Buddha preached his followers the four 'Noble Truths' concerning sorrow, the cause of sorrow, the remedy or destruction of sorrow, and the way that leads to the destruction of sorrow. In other words, he pointed out four certainties there is suffering in life, this suffering has a cause, this suffering could be removed by destroying its cause, the cause of the suffering is *trishna* or desire for material enjoyments and earthly things. And it is this desire that is responsible for the births and rebirths of man. When this selfish desire or craving for existence has ceased to act in man, be urged, it is only the possible for the individual soul to obtain *Nirvana* or deliverance front his unending cycle of births and deaths and the consequent suffering. How to annihilate this craving or remove this desire is, therefore, the real problem before a man. Self-mortification, he argued, could never overcome *trishna* and bring about an escape from rebirth and sub-sequent suffering. Mere repetition of prayers, or sacrifices or the chanting of the Vedic hymns was futile in cleansing the mind of gross desires. Desire, suggested Buddha, can only be removed by following the noble eight-fold path or the *Arya Ashtanga marga.* It consists of the following steps:

1. *Right Views or Faith the* knowledge of the four truths which Buddha enunciated in his first sermon;
2. *Right Aspiration that* requires us to renounce pleasures, to bear no malice and do no harm to others;
3. *Right Speech signifying* that we should abstain from lying, slander, abuse, harsh words and idle talk;
4. *Right Action meaning* that we should refrain from taking what is not given and abstain from carnal excesses;
5. *Right Livelihood requiring* us to abstain from any of the forbidden modes of living;
6. *Right Effort consisting* in suppressing the rising of evil conditions, in eradicating those that have arisen and in stimulating good states or conditions;
7. *Right Mindfulness requiring* us to look on the body and the spirit in such a way as to remain self possessed and careful, over coming both hankering and dejection; and
8. *Right Contemplation Meaning* to take the form of four meditations. It is the end and the crown of the eight fold path.

This *eight-fold path* lies between the two extremes, namely, gross sensualism or vile pleasure seeking, on the one hand, and the extreme asceticism or the severest self-mortification, on the other hand. It teaches men how to live a moral and religious life. It is this path that ultimately brings, according to Buddha, final bliss or *Nirvana. Nirvana* literally means 'blowing out' or extinction of craving or desire or *trishna* for existence in all its form and the consequent cessation of suffering. It is not mere disappearance or extinction, but cotranquil state to be realized by a person who from all craving or want is free.

It is deliverance or freedom from rebirth. This may lead one to conclude that Buddhism teaches the doctrine of inaction, that is, cessation of activity, desiring little or doing little. But Buddhism does not teach inaction. It teaches the non doing of evil deeds, the doing of various kinds of good things. Buddha rightly prescribed *moral precepts* for his followers. He laid stress on purity of conduct, truthfulness, love and benevolence, obedience to parents and respect for the elders, non-drinking, charity and kindness and mercy to all living beings. He did not like flattery and once he rebuked a man who indulged in his praise. He valued the observation of the true path and hated sin not the sinner. The fact that once he preferred a meal prepared by a dancing girl, Amrapali, to the sumptuous banquet of the nobles at Vaishali (Bihar) bears testimony to the overflowing mercy of his heart and his tender regard for the welfare and happiness of the common people.

Another doctrine on which Buddha laid great emphasis is the *Law of Karma* and its working, and the transmigration of souls. The condition of man in this life and the next, he argued, depends upon his own actions. Neither a sacrifice to gods can wash away sin, nor any prayer of any priest or any prayer of any man can do himself or any other man any good. A man reaps what he sows. As a man acts, so shall he be. Every individual is the maker of his own destiny and no God or gods could change it. We are for ever making our own moral world for good or ill. We can never escape the consequences of our deeds. We are born again and again to reap the fruits of our *Karma*:. This is the Law of *Karma*. If an individual sins no more, he dies no more; and when he dies no more, he is born no more; and, thus, he comes to live the life of Final Bliss.

Another prominent feature of his teachings is *Ahimsa*. According to him the spirit of love is more important than good deeds. Non-violence towards life is recognized as an integral principle of his practical morality. But it is not given so much exaggerated importance as in Jainism. Though Buddha enjoined love and non-violence for all living beings, he permitted his followers to take meat under certain conditions.

In his religious teachings Buddha may be called an agnostic, because he neither accepts nor rejects the existence of God. He refused to be drawn into any theoretical discussion about God or nature of the soul. Whenever he was questioned about them, he either maintained silence or remarked that God or gods were also under the eternal Law of *Karma*. It seems that he was merely concerned with the deliverance of man from suffering, other things being beyond his purpose.

Buddhist Councils and Scriptures : When Buddha was on the death bed, he said to his favourite disciple Ananda: "The truths and rules of the order which I have set forth and laid down for you all let them, after I am gone, be the teacher to you." Shortly after Buddha's death, therefore, the first Buddhist Council was held in 483 B. C. in Sattapanni cave near Rajgriha to compile the *Dhamma* (religious doctrines) and the *Vinaya* (monastic code). There the five hundred monks representing different local *sanghas* assembled, and adopted authoritative canonical texts by dividing the teachings of Buddha into two *Pitakas Vinaya* and *Dhamma*. A few centuries later, about 90 B.C., these were reduced to writing in Sri Lanka in the Pali language in which we have them now.

A century later a dispute arose regarding the code of discipline, as the monks of Vaisali wanted a relaxation of the rules in respect of the ten points. Opinion was divided particularly as to whether the monks should not accept gold or silver from the people when offered. A second Council, therefore, convened in or about 383 B.C., at Vaisali, which condemned the ten heresies. As the Vaisali monks stuck to their views no agreement was arrived at and the Council ended in a permanent split of the Buddhist Church into *Sthaviras* and *Mahasanghikas*. The former held the orthodox Vinaya and the latter were pro-changes.

The third General Council was held at Pataliputra during the reign of Asoka, 236 years after the death of Buddha, under the chairmanship of a learned monk Moggaliputta Tissa to revise the scriptures. "The Council accomplished two important results firstly, it made a new classification of Buddhist, canonical texts by the addition of a third Pitaka called the *Abhidhamma Pitaka* which contained the philosophical interpretations of the doctrines of the existing two Pitakas." As a result of this the sayings and discourses of the Buddha now came to be known as the *Tripitaka*. Secondly, the canonical literature was precisely, definitely and authoritatively settled so as to eliminate all disruptive tendencies, making all divisions within the church punishable.

The fourth Council was held during the reign of Kanishka in Kashmir under the leadership of the elder Vasumitra and the great scholar Asvaghosha. This Council was not a general assembly but probably a gathering of only the Hinayanists of Northern India. It decided certain controversial questions which arose out of some differences of opinion between the Sarvastivada teachers of Kashmir and Gandhara. The council also composed three large commentaries of the three Pitakas. They are known as *Vibhashas*.

The Buddhist scriptures known as *Pitakas* are divided into three sections, namely, the *Sutta*, the *Vinaya* and the *Abhidhamma*. The first, the *Sutta Pitaka*, consists of five collections of religious discourses and sayings of Buddha and is, therefore, the most important part of the scriptures. The second, the *Vinaya Pitaka*, contains the rules of monastic discipline, and the third, the *Abhidhamma Pitaka*, contains the philosophical development of the teachings of Buddha. Every sect of Buddhism had a *Tripitaka* of its own. The fifth collection of the *Suta Tripitaka* contains celebrated *Jatakas or* Buddhist birth tales. They were not so well known in the second as in the fifth century B.C. The *Jatakas* belong to a class of literature, which fore shadows the great epics of the Ramayan and the Mahabharat.

Buddhist Sangha

The Sangha : The Buddha had two kinds of disciples: monks *(bhikshus)* and lay worshippers *(upasikas).* The former were organized into the *Sangha* or the Religious Order, the number of which swelled with the spread of Buddhism. The membership of the Sangha was open to all persons, male or female, above fifteen years of age, and who were free from leprosy, consumption and other infectious diseases. Persons who were in the service of the king *or* an individual, or who were in debt or had been branded as robbers or criminals were refuse admission into the Sangha. But exceptions were made in the case of convicts, slaves or persons with physical deformities. There were no caste restrictions. Thus, the Buddhist Sangha or Church formed a community of persons who were physically and morally fit to perform the noble service required of them.

It was a systematic and thoroughly organized church which became a very powerful weapon for the spread of Buddhism. In due course, it became one of the greatest religious corporations ever known in the world. In fact, later on it became a model for church organization of other religions. One of the primary causes of the rapid progress of Buddhism was the devoted and selfless service of the Sangha. The lay Buddhists led the life of householders and financially contributed to the maintenance of the Sangha.

Monastery : Monasteries were constructed to give suitable accommodation to the monks and nuns for carrying on their studies and meditation. Gradually monasteries developed into academic centres for producing the right type of men, well grounded in religion and philosophy, to propagate the teachings of Buddhism. Large monasteries were usually provided with dwelling rooms, a service hall, storehouse, cloister, well, bathroom, and rooms for exercises. The monasteries were allowed to be furnished with certain articles of furniture. The ownership of the monastery vested in the Sangha.

Three garments *(chivara)* an upper robe, a lower one, and a sort of cloak worn over these two were allowed to the monks. These garments were made out of pieces of cloth, cut and dyed yellow. For food and alms, begging was the usual rule, but the monks were allowed to accept invitations to meals *or* offerings sent to the monasteries by the faithful. The monks accepted food and robes offered by the devotees of Buddhism. They took medicines prescribed by the physicians.

During the four months of the rains, beginning from the day next to the full moon day of *Ashadha*, the monks were required to take up a fixed abode and depend for their subsistence on the neighbouring householders. During this period of their stay in monasteries, they preached Buddhism to the people in the evening just like the *katha* system (narration of stories) of the present day. At the close of the re-treatment or *vasa*, the monks met together to confess their offences, if any, committed during their stay in the rainy reason. This ceremony was called *Pavarana*. At the end of the ceremony monks accepted gifts from the laity.

There was a special code of rules for the nuns. It contained certain extra-restrictions relating to movement, residence and general supervision of the nuns by monks.

Monks living within a definite boundary were to hold fortnightly assembly, were to elect their president *(Sanghathera or Sanghaparina yaka)* and to select two speakers, one on *Dhamma* and the other on *Vinaya*. In the assembly meetings, there were the systems of formal moving of resolutions *(Jnapti)*, ballot voting by means of wooden sticks *(Salaka)*, formation of sub committees, etc. For the different kinds of religious acts like giving punishment for an offence, admission or readmission of a monk into the Sangha, restoration of the privileges of a monk, the minimum number of members required to form the panels was fixed.

Admission into the Sangha and its Government : The ceremony of inctitation into the Sangha was simple and plain. Whenever a new person, a man or a woman, desired to join the order, he or she had to have his or her bead shaved, put on a yellow robe and before the President of the local Sangha take the following oaths of fidelity to the Buddha, the Dhamma and the Sangha:

1. I take refuge in the *Buddha*.
2. I take refuge in the *Dhamma*.
3. I take refuge in the *Sangha*.

Next, he was to repeat the ten commandments of Buddha. Then he was required to attach himself to a monk who would give him certain preliminary training after which he was to present him to an assembly of monks and make a formal proposal for admitting him to the Sangha. When the permission was given, he was to be ordained as a monk. Henceforth, he was required to observe the internal discipline of the Sangha and abide by its rules for leading a life of poverty, chastity, devotion, austerity, simplicity and celibacy.

The Sangha was governed on absolutely democratic lines and was empowered to enforce discipline amongst its members. It had also the power to punish the erring members. Whenever a meeting, of the Sangha was held, the members or monks took their seats according to their seniority. No assembly was valid unless at least ten monks were present, though in border countries the quorum could in exceptional cases be reduced to five. Novices and women were not entitled to vote or to constitute the quorum. Every question was decided by those present, and the questions to be decided at a Sangha had to be formally presented.

In every Sangha, office bearers were elected and unanimous

consent was required to carry on its various functions, such as, distribution of food and clothes, provision of beds, creation of monasteries, etc.

The absentees could send their opinion on different points included in the business of assembly, and the various questions put forth in the meeting were decided according to the teachings of Lord Buddha. The President was empowered to see that the Sangha did not go beyond its jurisdiction. The ultimate authority was vested in the hands of the General Council of the Sangha which was convoked whenever any occasion arose. The interpretation of the sacred law also rested with the General Council. With a view to maintaining a rigid observance of disciplinary rules, the monks in a *vihar* held, every fortnight, a meeting where the rules were read out by the senior member, and the breaches thereof, if any, were confessed by those present, and those confessing their guilt were made to undergo penitence, penance or punishment as the case might be.

Life of the Monks : The life of the monk and the nun was governed by the laws and the ten commandments, and there was no room for personal likes or dislikes. Property was held in common, and the possession of private property was strictly forbidden. The monks were forbidden the use of garlands, scents and other articles of personal decoration. They were not to indulge in liquor drinking, meat eating, dancing, or singing: they were required to sleep' on a hard and narrow bed and to beg their food from door to door. It was a hard, puritanic life of destitution and stem morality. The regulations for the nuns were stricter. It was feared that if equality was promised to them, it might lead to in discipline and immorality. Gautam Buddha was not in favour of ordaining women as nuns but he did so reluctantly at the repeated requests of his chief disciple Ananda.

The monks wandered for eight months in the year and preached in the neighbouring districts, but were required to retreat into the *vihars* during the four months of the rains.

Absence of Co-ordinating Authority : The grave defect of the Sangha was absence of a central co-ordinating authority. There was no central representative body of all the scattered Sanghas. This fostered the spirit of repeated schisms even on difference of minor points. This necessitated the frequent calling of the General Council where the points of difference were reviewed and settled. An account of such Councils has already been given in the preceding pages.

The Use of Vernacular : Another striking feature of Buddhism and its Sanghas was that they discarded Sanskrit as it was unintelligible to the common people and adopted the vernaculars of the people for their religious books and discourses. It was one of the important factors responsible for the rapid growth of Buddhism.

It has often been argued that Buddhism was not a new religion. It was a revolt against the commercial rituals of the Brahmanas and a strong protest against the caste system. It laid before the masses a practical code of ethics which was already known to them. In fact it was a reform movement aimed at purging Hinduism of various ills. It is, therefore, not astonishing if there are many points of resemblance between Hinduism and Buddhism. As regards their teachings, Hinduism believes in God, Matter and Soul as three self-existent entities and considers God the Creator of the Universe; while Buddhism has belief in Matter and Soul as two self-existent entities. God finds no room in the Buddhist thought of the world. It simply ignores the spirit of God as Creator. But the agnostic attitude taken up by Buddha was not the first departure from the theology of strict Hinduism. Kapil and Kanada, before Buddha, had taken up similar view.

Hinduism considers the Vedas as divine and the Vedic rituals as essential for salvation. It has deep faith in sacrifices. In fact, the Vedas form the bedrock of Hinduism. But Buddhism denied the authority of the Vedas and had no faith in the efficacy of the sacrifices or *yajnas* and other elaborate rites and sacraments enjoyed by them.

The Vedic rituals are not regarded as necessary for salvation. Buddhism, as a matter of fact, was a revolt against ceremonial rites and sacrifices.

The final goal of life in both the religions is the same to secure release from the cycle of births and deaths and to achieve salvation *Moksha* or *Nirvana.* Both faiths have strong belief in the doctrines of Transmigration of the Soul and the Law of *Karma.* Gautam Buddha's teachings, in fact, were largely based on the Brahmanic ideas of *Punarjanma, Karma* and *Moksha.* During his life Buddha counted many worthy Brahmanas among his disciples. He forbade any attack on Brahmanism and never encouraged any conflict or schism with it. The principles of Hinduism as described in the Vedas are very complicated and are, therefore, unintelligible to the common people. The teachings of Buddhism, on the contrary, were very simple and brief, and were within the comprehensive power of the masses. Hinduism is abstract and philosophical, while Buddhism was practical and ethical.

As regards 'the *practices* of the faiths, Hinduism believes in the performance of elaborate ceremonies, reciting hymns and daily prayers. It lays emphasis on moral and virtuous life as leading to salvation. The ceremonies of Hinduism are accompanied by oblations and sometimes slaughter of animals. Buddhism, on the contrary, advocated the principle of *Ahimsa* or non-injury to living beings. In fact. *Ahimsa* formed the most important part of the Buddhist ethical code.

There is no personal element in Hinduism, while Buddhism introduced it in the form of Buddha as the saviour to be worshipped later in the form of idols. Hinduism has been imparting spiritual and religious instructions through Sanskrit. It has been the language of their scriptures. But the Buddhists have been administering spiritual knowledge through the spoken language of the masses, and they composed their scriptures in the language of the people.

Though the practical code of morality taught by Buddhism is not at all different from the ideal of Hindu life, yet a Brahmana or a Hindu would discuss higher problems of life here and life hereafter. On the other hand, a Buddhist would lay emphasis only on the virtuous conduct in this life on this earth.

With regard to *social and religious organizations* of the two faiths, the Hindu society is organized on the fourfold division of the castes in which the Brahmanas enjoy supremacy. The caste system and the dominance of the Brahmanas are very striking features of Hinduism. Buddhism made no such distinction and treated all alike. It did not recognize the priestly class. The Buddhist society was democratic in which a low born had the same privileges as a high, born, provided his moral conduct justified this privilege.

Hinduism has no Church or regular religious order of monks and nuns. Buddhism instituted such order. It was congregational. Vihars and Sanghas played a very important part in Buddhism. Due to the missionary spirit of the Sanghas, Buddhism has been very dynamic and is, therefore, followed by one quarter of the human race. Hinduism, on the other hand, is never marked by a missionary spirit and it never sought converts. Hence, it has always been static.

In social outlook, Hinduism did not possess the spirit of adapt ability. But Buddhism has been very flexible and adapted itself to the needs of the countries to which it travelled.

Resemblance of Jainism and Buddhism : Jainism and Buddhism resemble each other in many respects. Both of them have been protestant religious movements against the corruptions of Hinduism. They were the products of the same religious ferment that prevailed in the sixth century B.C. They were the off shoots of Hinduism. In their search for truth they did not strike a new path but followed the old one of Hinduism.

The goal that they placed before them was the same as that which Hinduism strove to attain, namely, salvation or *moksha* from the cycle of births and deaths. Therefore, both of them accepted two famous doctrines of *Hinduism Karma* and transmigration of souls as the indispensable factors for attainment of salvation. They differed from the orthodox Hinduism in their belief in the automatic and relentless working of the Law of *Karma*. Jainism and Buddhism both held that the Law of *Karma* is above all creatures whether men or gods: and even God or gods cannot alter the course of this law.

Hence, the Brahmanic practice of pleasing tire gods by sacrifices and Vedic rites was of no avail in attaining *moksha* or salvation. *Moksha* could be attained by a person by his own virtuous deeds and not by the meditation of God or gods who are themselves subject to the Law of *Karma*. So, both Jainism and Buddhism denied the Brahmanic ceremonies, rejected the authority of the Vedas, abhorred and condemned the blood sacrifices, and ignored the belief in God as the Creator of the Universe.

Both Jainism and Buddhism advocated a virtuous and holy life and abstention from sinful thoughts, actions and injury by word or deed to any living being. Both laid emphasis on the doctrine of Ahimsa non-violence. In this matter the Jains went even a step further than the Buddhists.

Both Mahavir and Buddha' preached their religions in the common language of the people, denounced caste system and advocated equality of men and women. Unlike Hinduism, each had a well organized Sangha of devoted missionaries and each depended on the support of the monastic order free from worldly tangles.

As the founders of both Jainism and Buddhism were Kshatriya princes, drawing their inspiration from the teachings of the Upanishads much of their success was due to the patronage of the Kshatriya princes and kings.

But in many other respects both differed fundamentally from each other. The Jains gave laity a very prominent place in their order while the Buddhists relied mainly on their monastic order. The *Nirvana* of the Buddhists differed fundamentally from that of the Jains. The *Nirvana* of the former was escape from existence, whereas that of the latter was escape from body. The Jains believed in rigorous asceticism and approved self-mortification which was discarded and condemned by Buddhists strongly. The doctrine of *Ahimsa,* believed in by both, was carried by the Jains to a far greater extent than ever contemplated by the Buddhists. The Jains believed in the principle of life in the vegetable kingdom too. Buddhists emphasized the non-existence of the soul as a permanent entity, whereas Jains believe that not only animate but inanimate things also possess souls.

Jainism even today retains many Brahmanic practices and ceremonies and a modified form of caste system which was completely discarded and condemned by the Buddhists. Buddhism soon spread outside India and is still followed by one quarter of humanity; but Jainism never went beyond India and the number of its followers has been very limited.

Buddhism and Jainism, as mentioned above, have their roots in Hinduism. "They are mere offshoots of Hinduism, arising in protest against some of the corruptions of the latter, discarding its evils, but retaining its fundamental principles, like the Law of *Karma,* Rebirth, *Ahimsa,* etc. ; the popular mythology is not discarded by them." Brahma, Indra and other gods figure in both Buddhist and Jain stories. Many of the old doctrines are presented merely as new ways of attaining the goal of liberation. But Jainism, so to say, is a via media between Hinduism and Buddhism.

3

Exposure to Outside World

Traditional Trade Routes

For a period of about a thousand years from the invasion of Darius to the sack of Rome by the Goths—India was in more or less constant communication with the West. This naturally raises the question: Had this long intercourse of nearly ten centuries any influence upon the development of the art, literature or thought of either India or of the Greeco-Roman world?

From remote antiquity, India had cultural relations and commercial intercourse with western countries by land and sea. There is enough evidence for drawing conclusion that the Indus-valley people in the third millennium B.C., had trade relations with Sumer and other renowned centres of culture in Western Asia and probably Egypt and Crete. In the Old Testament we have references to trade between India and Syrian coast as far back as 1400 B.C. Archaeological evidence reveals to us that in the eighth century B.C., India carried on trade both by land and sea with Mesopotamia, Arabia, Phoenicia and Egypt. From the fourth century B.C., specially under the Mauryas, commercial and maritime activities made considerable progress and definite land and sea routes were opened for the purpose. "The overland route passed through Khyber to the upper Kabul valley, and thence across the Hindukush to Balkh, which stood on the great highway linking the East and the West. There were several routes from Balkh both towards Central Asia and China on the east and to the Mediterranean and Black Sea on the west. One of the western routes went down the Oxus river to the Caspian Sea and wares then were carried, partly by land and partly by river, to the Black Sea ports. The other skirted the Karmanian desert to the north and having passed through the 'Caspian Gates' reached Antioch by way of Ctesiphon and Hekatompylos."

The sea routes from the mouth of the river Indus lay along the coast to the mouth of the river Euphrates. Then ships either sailed up the Euphrates and reached the land route at the point where it crossed that river; or, they continued their coastal voyage along the shores of Arabia and sailing through the Red Sea reached its head near the Suez. From this point goods were carried by land to Egypt on the west and to famous ports like Tyre and Sidon on the north, and from thence to the Mediterranean seaports. Merchandise often changed hands at important commercial centres, towns and harbours. Whenever direct sea voyage was made, the sailors had to keep close to the coast to avoid the perils of the deep. Later on, the great discovery, made by Hippalus about 45 A.D., "of the existence of the monsoon winds, blowing regularly across the Indian Ocean," enabled the ships to sail straight across the Indian Ocean and thus reach the Indian ports soon. "From Okelis, the port at the mouth of the Red Sea, the monsoon winds would carry ship in forty days or even less to Muziris (modern Cannanore on the Malabar coast).

Thus, Alexandria was now less than three months journey from the Indian coast. Henceforth, the ships from southern India could easily avoid the long coastal voyage." The importance of this route lies in the fact that it linked India not only to the gold fields and fabulously wealthy incense country of southern Arabia and Somaliland, but to Egypt and Judea.

As a result of these trade routes there was a considerable sea borne trade between India and the western countries as far as the African coast before the Christian era, and articles of commerce bearing their Indian names reached the western world from time to time. Indian ivory became widely known in the Mediterranean at an early date and so rice was brought from the southern ports of India by Arab traders and Indian spices were carried on camels. We are told that there were Indian women, Indian hunting dogs, Indian cows etc., in the possession of Ptolemy Philadelphus (285-246 B.C.), the Greek ruler of Egypt. His yacht had a saloon lined with Indian stones.

Similarly, we have references to imported Greek girls, guard of Yavana (Greek) women and a bodyguard of dumb Mlechchhas in southern India. Greeks were, thus, employed in India as mercenaries. Whether India was affected in the prehistoric period by her contact with her nearer and more powerful neighbours, the Assyrians and Babylonians, is an interesting question. Prof. H. G. Rawlinson stated that the *Brahmi* script, the parent script of India, was borrowed from Semitic sources about the seventh century B.C.; the 'Fish Incarnation' of Vishnu is reminiscent of the Babylonian stories of flood; the conceptions of *Nakshatras* and the division of the week into seven days and naming them after the sun, the moon and five planets were borrowed from Chaldean astronomy, Alexandria:' and in architecture India borrowed details of ornamentation, such as, the bell capital and the lion pillar, indirectly from Assyria through Persia. These statements it seems, are biased and open to question.

Glorious Persian Period

In 538 B.C., the last of the great Semitic Empire of Western Asia came to an end and Cyrus of Persia founded the great Persian Empire. His successor, Darius, in 510 B.C., advanced upon India from Bactria and reaching the river Indus at the town of Kaspapyrus, a frontier city of Gandhara sent an expedition under a Greek mercenary named Skylax to explore the Indus down to its mouth. To Skylax belongs the double distinction of having been the first Greek to visit India to make the Red Sea voyage. As a result of this, Darius annexed the Indus valley and made it the twentieth province of the Persian Empire.

The new province paid to the Great King the enormous annual tribute of 360 talents of gold dust (£ 1,078,272) and supplied a light division to the Persian forces. With the gradual break up of the Persian Empire, the practical independence of Eastern Iran, and the war with Greece, the traffic between India and the West sank to practically nothing and the province of the Punjab, in due course, had shaken off its allegiance to the Persian King. But the Persian Empire made a profound impression upon the Indian mind. According to some scholars India's contact with Persia for nearly two centuries influenced Indian culture. The Kharosthi script, introduced by the Persians in their official documents, remained in use on the north-west Frontier till the fourth century A.D. The remains of Persian and Babylonian customs at Taxila as observed by the Greeks may point to this place as the capital of the Indian province under the Persian Empire.

The Maurya Emperors, as shown by Megasthenes, lived in Persian style. They, like the Persian monarch, lived in seclusion surrounded by guards and only appearing at rare intervals or religious festivals. Chandragupta Maurya adopted the Persian custom of "hair washing festival, *Tykta.*" The Buddhist architecture of Asoka, particularly the Asokan pillars and the style of their architecture, shows some traces of Persian influence. The lion capitals of the Asokan pillars are Persian in style with considerable modification. Persia suggested to Mauryan artists the use of stone instead of wood, brick and stucco. Asoka's plan of propagating the Dharma by means of inscriptions, upon the face of the rock, may have been borrowed for similar practices in vogue among the Persians, for instance, the Behistun inscriptions of Darius. Even the Royal Road running through the Mauryan domains finds its parallel in Persia. Some writers still go further and suggest that the Mauryas borrowed the idea of an empire from the Persians. Certainly this is going too far. Havell rightly points out that the resemblances between the Persian and the Indian cultures were due to common traditions and that none imitated the other.

Greek Era and Hellenic Trait

With the break-up of the Persian Empire and invasion of Alexander and the subsequent rule of the Greeks in the Punjab and the frontier provinces of India, a new epoch in the history of India's intercourse with the western world was ushered in. The Greeks, long before the annexation of the Punjab by Persia, appear to have heard, in a dim sort of way, of India. Herodotus, born in 485 B.C., was the first Greek who wrote a graphic, careful and accurate account of India.

The next Greek to write about India was Ktesias who was for twenty years in the Persian court which he left in 398 B.C. Statements and remarks of Ktesias did not possess sobriety, accuracy and truth like those of Herodotus and so Ktesias is responsible for most of the grotesque legends about India which fill the pages of classical and medieval writers to the days of Sir John Mandeville. Greece borrowed her first knowledge of India from the Persians who ruled over Indian frontier provinces and indirectly from Egypt with which India traded. To the Persians, thus, Greece owes her first knowledge of India. Then came Alexander's invasion in 326 B.C. Before this event the intercourse between India and Greece was through Persian and Phoenician caravans. Greece had no direct communication with India. Whatever she knew of India, she had learnt from Greek officials in Persian service like Skylax, Ktesias, etc. But Alexander's invasion established close contact between East and West—more precisely between India and

Greece. Besides considerable bodies of Greek settlers who remained behind Alexander in the Punjab, there was a great Greek colony at Bactria, once capital of Eastern Iran, on the high road to India. After the break-up of the Mauryan Empire, disturbances in Central Asia drove the Bactrian Greeks south of the Hindukush where they established a kingdom with its capital at Sagala, afterwards splitting up into a series of petty principalities. The Greek principalities, after enjoying considerable power for nearly two centuries, were succeeded by the Saka chief and finally by the Kushan tribe who quickly absorbed all petty Greek States of the Punjab and established a vast empire.

Now, the question is: How far these Greeks influenced the Indian culture and civilization? It is difficult to determine to what extent the Greek culture influenced Indian life and thought. The earlier view put too much stress on the effects of Alexander's invasion, and the western scholars held that Indian civilization owes a great debt to Greece. This appears to be a biased view. On the contrary, others have been minimizing the influence of Hellenism on Indian culture and civilization. Except for a few traces of Greek influence on Indian coins and Gandhara School of Sculpture, Indian culture remained uninfluenced. A critical examination of Hellenistic influence upon the various phases of Indian civilization and culture shows that Greek or Hellenic influence on Indian civilization was slight and superficial. On the other hand, Greek thought, particularly the domain of philosophy, owes much to India.

The invasions of Alexander, Seleucus and Antiochos were of little consequence as they left no permanent marks on the life and culture of the Indians. Megasthenes's description shows that Indian culture remained unadulterated. But embassies were exchanged with the Hellenic powers by the Mauryan Emperors of Magadha. Syrian and Mauryan monarchs continued for several generations to maintain close and friendly relations. Seleucus sent Magasthenes to Chandragupta, and

Deimachus to Bindusara, son and successor of Chandragupta, and Ptolemy Philadelphus sent Dionysius to the Mauryan court. Indian philosophers, traders and adventurers were to be found in the intellectual circles of Athens and in the markets of Alexandria. During the reign of Asoka, Alexandria possessed a colony of Indian merchants, while the Alexandrians had created their own settlement in south India on the Malabar coast.

The first of the Mauryas, Chandragupta, had entered into marriage contract with a Greek potentate and corresponded with the Syrian monarch. His son Bindusara asked the Greek King, Seleucus, for a sample of Greek wine, some raisins and the services of a Greek sophist. Seleucus wrote back saying that he sent the wine with much pleasure, but regretted that it was not a good form among the Greeks to trade in philosophers.' When Asoka was converted to Buddhism, he despatched missionaries to his friends, the Greek monarchs of Egypt, Syria and Macedonia so that they might share in the glad tiding of his new creed. Later on, Asoka entrusted the government of a wealthy province, Saurashtra, and the execution of important irrigation works there to a Yavana chief. In spite of all this, Indians did not ape the Greeks. Their art, architecture and literature bore no traces of Greek influence so far.

If any Greek influence affected Indian life, it was when Indo-Greek kingdoms were founded in the north-west of India. It was during this period that the two cultures came in close contact and affected each other. But still there is no evidence that the Greek culture affected the Indians appreciably. There might have been some influence of Hellenistic polytheism on the development of the Mahayana cult of Buddhism, but the Indians neither adopted Greek faiths nor worshipped Greek deities. "The tendency was for Indo-Greek and other foreign princes and people to become Hinduized rather than for Indian princes and people to become Hellenized." The Bactrian Greeks very largely adopted Hinduism, the religion of their neighbours. The conversion of Menander to Buddhism is as dramatic as that of Asoka. In the Nasik caves is a *lena* owned by "*Indragnidatta,* a Yonaka from Dattamitra (Demetra) in the north." In the Karle caves are several votive offerings from Greeks. Yavanas or Greeks bearing Indian titles were donating liberally for the Buddhist caves of Karle and Nasik. Then there is the Garuda pillar from Besnagar, Vidisha in Madhya Pradesh with an inscription that it is the work of "Heliodorus, son of Dion, a Greek envoy from Taxila, sent by Maharaja Antalkidas." These point out the Greeks in the Punjab and Western India rapidly embraced Hinduism and even took Hindu names.

Let us now take up the various aspects of Indian culture and see whether they bear any marks of Greek influence.

Art : Though Indian architecture was uninfluenced by Greek architecture, Indian sculpture in the frontier provinces during the rule of the Kushans was considerably influenced by Greek art.' The forms of Greek art were applied to Buddhist subjects with considerable artistic success in many cases. The images of Buddha appeared in the likeness of Apolo, and the Yaksha Kubera is posed in the fashion of the Phedian Zeus. Consequently, a new school known as the Gandhara School of Sculpture arose.

As regards the Gupta Art, Smith remarks: "The influence of Greek taste on the sculpture of the Gupta age, although necessarily less obvious, is not less certain." According to him, although the works are truly Indian in the Gupta period, they form a charming combination of East and West. Another scholar, however, says that whatever influence Hellenism had exercised on Indian art, was practically exhausted by 400 A.D. After that date the traces of Hellenistic ideas have been too trifling to be worth mentioning. Hellenic and Indian conceptions of art differed fundamentally and it was for this reason, as explained by Marshall, that Hellenistic art never took a real and lasting bold upon India.

Coinage : In the Mauryan period coinage continued to be purely Indian or at any rate Asiatic in character. Asoka did not care to imitate the beautiful Bactrian issues, and he was content to use the primitive rudely struck coins which formed the currency of India before his time. The Indian coins were usually punch marked. The idea of striking coins with two dies, obverse and reverse, one side bearing the effigy and title of the king and the other side having some other device, was gradually adopted by Indian princes in imitation of the issues minted by dynasties of foreign origin Greeks, Sakas, Parthians, Yuch-chi and the rest. Indian artists who attained brilliant success in other fields, never cared much about die cutting, and consequently, never produced really fine polished coins.

The coins of Kanishka do betray Greek influence. In fact, they exhibit a strange medley of Greek, Indian and Iranian deities. They bear traces of imitation of both Bactrian and Roman models, but they also show a great deal of artistic originality and power of realistic portraiture. Later on the Saka, Indo-Parthian and Kshaharata sovereigns issued coins which were more or less a compromise between Greaco-Roman and Oriental ideas: but the coins of Nahapana were a clever imitation of the Greek style applied to realistic portraiture.

In the Gupta period the best Indian coins were struck, according to some scholars, under the influence of western models. But they do not bear comparison with the magnificent dies of the earlier Bactrian kings. However, the Guptas introduced many coins of original artistic types, novel in conception and fine execution, bearing no traces of foreign influence; for example, the Tiger slayer type, the Lion slayer type and the Asvamedha type of coins.

Philosophy : In the realm of philosophy the Greeks owe a huge debt to India. The mystical philosophy of Orphic and Pythagorean Schools borrowed a good deal from the Indian beliefs. There are many points of resemblance between them. The Greek belief in reincarnation and the doctrine of *Karma* (appearing in the closing episode of Plato's *Republic)*, and Pythagorean 'taboos' on wine animal food, etc. have been taken from the Indian Philosophy. The Indian philosophy, according to Rawlinson, influenced the Greek philosophy through Egypt. The Greeks adopted the Indian doctrine of Yoga or meditation to free the soul from body, abstinence from flesh and the Indian ideas of asceticism. The Neoplatonic School of Alexandria and Gnosticism show traces of Hindu influence. Indian ideas of monasticism had considerably influenced both Paul of Alexandria and his disciple, St. Anthony, who expired in 356 A.D.

Language and Script : The influence of Hellenism on Indian language and script is insignificant. No inscription in the Greek language has as yet been discovered in India or Afghanistan. Probably a corrupt Greek language was spoken among those Greeks who had settled in the Punjab and were being rapidly absorbed by the surrounding population, and perhaps this corrupt Greek was the lingua franca of the Greeks, Indo-Parthians and Saka tribes for some time. But the Indians neither used the Greek names nor the Greek language. However, the Kushans used for their own legends the Khotanese language, which resembled much the Saka tongue, although they engraved it in Greek characters.

Drama : It is believed chiefly by Weber, Windisch and Schroder that the Indian drama was influenced by the Greek and we are indebted to Greek dramas for the idea of the screen, the parasite and the clown. The Indian drama, like the Greek, avoids the portrayal of violent or unseemingly action. But many arguments have been levelled against this view, specially by Sylvain Levi and Rapson. H.G. Rawlinson rightly observes that "the Indian drama, with its neglect of the unities, its mixture of prose and verse, comedy and tragedy, resembles the severe Greek tragedy as little as florid Indian temple resembles the Parthenon." The art of play writing in India, in fact, is absolutely native. "The resemblances are so few and superficial, and the differences so many and fundamental, that the theory has been generally discarded." However, in literature we may say that the Greeks borrowed their folklore from the Indians. The Greeks have taken many animal stories from the *Panchatantra*.

Astronomy, Mathematics and Medicine : The influence of Greek writers on Astronomy may be traced in the works of Indian authors who quote Yavanesvara or Yavanacharya with respect. The Indians learnt astronomy from the Greeks and this is openly admitted. "The Yavanas are barbarians. Yet the science of astronomy originated with them and for this reason they must be reverenced like gods." *(Gargi Samhita).* Greek names are used in Indian books on Astronomy. Greek influence can also be traced to some extent in Indian works on Mathematics. The *Charak Sastra,* the work on Indian Medicine, is supposed to betray Greek influence (the theory of three humours), but there is no strong evidence to support this contention.

The Hindus do not appear to have derived their knowledge of medicine from any of their neighbours, far less from the Greeks. About the elementary theories of Physiology, the Hindus and Greeks are in accord, although it is uncertain whether these common ideas were developed independently. On the whole, we can conclude that Greek rule in India was all through fighting for its existence and therefore could not have time or energy left for the development or art, science and literature, and as such could not be influenced considerably by India. On the other hand, though a few aspects of Indian culture betray Greek influence, the Hellenic institutions and culture were never allowed to triumph over indigenous institutions and culture.

India and Roman Empire

The establishment of the Roman Empire in Europe, in the first century before Christ, gave a great impetus to the Indian trade, The *Pax Romana* secured the trade routes, and the articles of luxury from India were in great demand in Rome. Fine muslins, jewels especially beryls and pearls, drugs, spices and condiments from India were in great demand. The volume of trade was, therefore, increased to an unprecedented extent. The sea borne trade between India and Rome received great impetus in the reign of Emperor Claudius by Hippalaus' discovery, in 45 A.D., of the existence of the monsoon winds, blowing regularly across the Indian Ocean. The epoch making change has already been referred to in the beginning of this chapter.

According to Pliny nearly £ 5,50,000 flowed every year from Rome to India to pay for the balance of trade.' This statement is borne out by the huge hoards of Roman coins unearthed in Indian soil in Tamil Nadu. Palmyra, Alexandria and later on Adule, the chief port of Ethiopia on the African coast, were the chief emporiums of active commerce between the Roman Empire and India. This trade between India and Rome continued to thrive steadily during the second and third centuries A.D., in spite of a temporary lull in the demand for luxuries after the extraordinary extravagance in the reign of Nero and some set backs caused by wars. Apart from this, the oriental expeditions of the Roman Emperors in the third century A.D., brought them into close and sometimes almost direct contact with India.

One of the results of the increased intercourse between India and Rome was the appearance of several books on India and Indian geography by western writers of the age. Pliny, Strabo, Ptolemy of Alexandria, Philostratus, Callistratus, and Dion Cassius deserve mention in this connection. They give a more accurate knowledge of India in the western literature. Another result of the commercial intercourse between the two countries, India and Rome, was the in creased political intercourse between the two. When Emperor Augustus finally came out triumphant from the civil war and established the Principate, one or more Indian sovereign states sent their embassies to him. Other Indian embassies also visited Rome during the first four centuries of the Christian era and no less than eight are expressly referred to as having been sent to Emperor Augustus (26 B. C.), Trajan (98-177 A.D.), Hadrian (117-138), Antoninus Pius (138-161), Heliogabalus (218-222), Aurelian (270-275), Constantine (323-353), and Julian (361-363). It seems, two more Indian embassies were sent to Justinian in 530 and 552 A.D.

The commercial and political intercourse between the Roman Empire and India must have brought an increasingly larger number, both of Indian and Roman subjects, to visit each other's country. Alexandrian and Syrian traders frequently visited India. The first Alexandrian to visit India was Scythianus, a contemporary of the Apostles. In due course, Romans had set up their colonies in southern India where they had acquired a greater intimacy with Indian customs than had been possible before. On the other hand, a large number of Indians visited Alexandria, which being in the central position, was the great meeting ground between the East and the West. Ptolemy and Dion Cassius mention Indians in Alexandria. An interesting evidence of such visit, even in Ptolemic days, is well preserved in an inscription on the temple of Dedesiya near the Nile river which contains 'Sophon', the name of an Indian.

Even as late as 470 A.D., some Brahmanas from India visited Alexandria and they were lodged in the house of Consul Severus. This had the effect of developing Indian shipping considerably. The subsequent expansion in trade and frequency of voyage is marked by the rules for merchandise, shipping and products found in the Code of Manu. Later on, an interesting treatise on shipping, *Yuktikalpataru* of Bhoj Narapati, was written.

In 364 A.D., the first fatal step in the downfall of the Roman Empire had been taken when it was divided. In 410 A.D came the Goths, and fifty years later the mightiest kingdom of Europe had ceased to exist. After this the Roman trade with India dwindled rapidly, though it struggled on feebly till the sixth century A.D.

The intimate, friendly and commercial intercourse between India and the western world naturally affected the culture of both. It is difficult to estimate the scope and nature of their influence upon each other, but some of its aspects can be broadly mentioned. There is no doubt that the art and coinage of India were profoundly affected by those of the West. The influence of Roman astronomy on the progress of science in India is also undeniable. *Romaka Siddhanta* is freely alluded to by Varahamihira and the *Paulisa Siddhanta* is based on the astronomical works of Paul of Alexandria (*c.* 378 A.D.). On the other hand, Indian medical science, astronomical terms and the system of numerals were adopted by western countries. Some Indian books like *Panchatantra* were also very popular there and were translated in many languages. Many Indian legends have found their way into Europe and may be found in the *Gasta Romanorum* and the *Decameron* and other medieval collections.

The same reciprocal influence is observed in the realm of religion and philosophy. It is generally agreed that Indian philosophy exercised a great influence on the development of Neoplatonism. As noted above, its doctrines abstinence from meat, subjection of the body to asceticism, meditation to free soul from the body to attain union with the Supreme (the *Yoga* doctrine of Patanjali) and so on are derived from Indian sources. Plotinus, the Neoplatonist and Bardesanes and Basilidas the Gnostic writers, all came to the East for instruction in philosophy.

The rise of Christianity affected Indian religion which had still some hold in the West. The Syrian writer Zenob gives us interesting information about the iconoclastic zeal of Christian missionaries which led to the destruction of two Hindu temples in the Canton of Taron (upper Euphrates, west of Lake Van). The temples were constructed by an Indian colony settled in that region in the second century B.C. About 304 A.D., St. Gregory attacked these temples and, in spite of the heroic defence by the Indians, broke, like Mahmud of Ghazni, two images of gods which were 12 and 15 cubits high. T.S.I. Gregory must have been instrumental in wiping out to a large extent the trace of Indian religion in the West. But the fact remains that Indian religion, both Brahmanical and Buddhist, was still a living force in the region where Christianity arose and had its early field of activity.

There is no wonder, then, if Indian religion had its effect upon Christianity. The resemblance of the interior of the Christian Church to a Buddhist Chaitya, the extreme and extravagant forms of asceticism in early Christian sects, such as, the Thebaid monasticism, metempsychosis, relic worship and the use of the rosary might all have been borrowed by Christianity from Indian religious ideas of Buddhism and Brahmanism. They are the eastern survivals. "The crozier, the mitre, the chasuble, the cardinal's robe, the double choir at the Divine Office, the chants, exorcism, the censor with five chains, the blessing imparted by extending the right hand over the heads of the faithful, the rosary, the celibacy of the clergy, their separation from the world, the worship of saints, the fasts, processions, litanies and holy water of Christianity are the results of contact with Indian Buddhists." It is also certain that several religious leaders of the West took the name of Buddha. Buddha was worshipped by the Christians under the name of Josaphat. The Jews practised monasticism Buddhist ideas.

In view of the above facts, there is no shadow of doubt about the general influence of Indian ideas upon Christianity; but it is more difficult to estimate the effect of Christianity on India. How ever, it may easily be accepted that Christian missionaries visited India from an early period and small Christian communities were established here. "We have reference to the progress of Christian Church in South India, in the 'Nations of India,' a pamphlet included in the *Romance History of Alexander* of the Pseudo Kallisthenes (fifth century) and in the *Christian Topography* of Cosmas Indiko-pleustes, a Christian monk who visited India in the first half of the sixth century A.D."

Conclusion : Hindu culture reached its high watermark under the Guptas. Hindu religion then attained the form that is bequeathed to us even today. The Gupta administration, which perfected the imperial traditions, served as the ideal for contemporary and later states. Peace and prosperity, secured by the Gupta government, led to a rich and remarkable development of art, literature, philosophy and science. Hindu culture continued to be evolved independently.

The establishment of Hindu colonies abroad spread Hindu culture and civilization, and considerably influenced the life and thought of other peoples. India did not lead an isolated life evolving its own culture in a stagnant pool but kept close contact not only with the East but with the civilizations of the West through trade and commerce. Such relations with the West began much earlier, and continued to be fairly constant and active till the sixth century. But, in spite of this, western life and thought failed to impress Indian culture and civilization deeply. Though some aspects of Indian culture do betray a few traces of the Greeco-Roman culture's influence, yet Indian culture continued to evolve so independently and effectively that whatever influence the Greeco-Roman culture exercised, had completely dwindled and disappeared by the fourth century A.D. On the other hand, the influence of Indian culture continued on western philosophy for centuries together, and Christianity even today exhibits some traces of this influence.

4

Expansion of Hinduism

Culture's Significance

The culture of India has been one of the great civilizing and humanizing factors evolved by man." For centuries together, the general spiritual life of the larger part of the continent of Asia "meant mainly its response to the call of the eternal ideas discovered, systematized and humanized by the sages and saints of ancient India." In other words, culture in Asia has been a complex fabric of life, woven by several different strands, of which Indian is the most prominent.

Undoubtedly, India was a civilizing force in many backward countries of Asia. "India was the civilizer" from after the synthesis of Hindu culture about the beginning of the first millennium B.C., down to the closing centuries of the first millennium A.D. Because it was during this long period that there was the cultural unification of India, and it went on simultaneously with the cultural expansion of India into overseas countries like Lanka, Burma, Siam, Indo-China, Malaya, Indonesia and to a large extent into the countries of north-west like Afghanistan, Baluchistan and Turkistan in Central Asia.

The transformation of the eastern countries like China. Korea and Japan was achieved through their close contact with the spiritual forces from India. Thus, in moulding the Asian culture, Indian share has been very significant. But India or more precisely the Hindu culture of India was not merely a civilizing force. It brought to them intellectual awakening, social consciousness and material prosperity.

With many backward races of Asia, the sense of social order and organization, arts and crafts seems to have dawned for the first time with the advent of the merchants and the Brahmana and Buddhist missionaries from India. It not only brought material uplift to these backward peoples, but their dormant intellectual and other powers and talents were quickened to life, and they were enabled to attain the fulfilment of those powers without any difficulty or hindrance. Hindu culture thus helped other peoples to make their own contributions to world civilization, while it absorbed them and participated in the deeper and wider life. Hindu culture brought to other nations its own spiritual ideas and values.

"In the case of ancient and highly cultured people like the Chinese, contact with Indian thought gave the finishing touch in the formation and in the highest expression of their culture. Buddhism which was carried to China by the Indians brought home to the Chinese the necessity of going into the fundamental questions of existence and endeavour." Java and Siam, China and Japan enjoyed richness of life and witnessed the astonishing efflorescence of their minds and spirits manifesting itself in literature, fine arts and religious ritual which contact with Indian culture brought about. Assimilation and unfoldment and not hindrance and suppression was the key note of Hindu cultural expansion. Indian philosophy and culture went abroad not to destroy and ruin but to awaken and fulfil. It went there like the refreshing showers and life giving rain and not like the burning wind or the killing blight. Hence its achievement unlike that of the western culture, is more than that of a mere force of material civilization or civilized organization.

Wherever the Indians went and settled, they spread their own culture but at the same time were absorbing the native cultural trends. Consequently, they evolved a new culture the key note of which was Indian. Thus, they created culture in other Asiatic countries the values of which were "awareness of the unity of life and a love for the ultimate and the universal in preference to the immediate and the particular."

Factors behind Cultural Expansion

It is true that cultures have been spreading in the wake of conquest and commerce. Undoubtedly, the spread of Hindu culture in the Far East began through commercial relations between India and the countries of the Far East. Lucrative commerce and economic gains encouraged Indians to sail across the Indian Ocean, go to distant lands and suffer innumerable difficulties and dangers. Being situated in the Indian Ocean, India occupied central position and in ancient times was on the sea routes to cultured and civilized countries of the world. Her geographical position enabled India to form a link between the East and the West. Consequently, Indians under took innumerable voyages for commerće. In ancient India eastern countries like Java, Sumatra, Malaya were regarded as the veritable El Dorado which constantly allured enterprising traders by promising immense riches to them. This view is reflected in the name *Suvarnadvipa* or *Suvarnabhumi* (Land of Gold) which was applied to this vast region of the eastern countries.

1. The desire to acquire immense gold provided a potent stimulus to the Indians to sail to these countries. The uncivilized wild races came in close contact with these Indian merchants from whom they learnt the first lessons of culture.
2. Besides the enterprising merchants, the Buddhist missionaries and the Brahmana teachers, the torchbearers of the Hindu culture, accompanied the Indian merchants' community to the distant lands. They

carried abroad Indian thought and culture. But they did not go there as members of an alien ruling race with natural advantage by virtue of their superior position. Having no political power and administrative rights, Indian missionaries used to mix amongst the wild and uncultured alien races and in face of overwhelming hindrances and great dangers used to deliver sermons to them and indirectly made them more cultured and civilized. Some times Indian saints and sages set up their hermitages in foreign lands which, in due course, became the significant centres of Indian culture and spread the Indian cultural trends like a radio station. Kaundinya and Agastya had such hermitages and *Ashramas*. Kaundinya's name is revered in inscription as the founder of the Hindu royal families in greater India.

3. Besides these two agencies Indian merchants and missionaries many Indians who settled in foreign lands contributed substantially towards Hindu cultural expansion. They had established their own colonies. Naturally, their cultural influence on the foreign peoples was very deep and far reaching.
4. Sometimes adventurous young Kshatriya princes sailed to the distant regions to seek their fortune and carve out new kingdoms for themselves. The history of Indo-China provides many examples of such Indian Kshatriya princes and persons of royal blood. Consequently, Indians had established a large number of kingdoms in the eastern countries. They had offered their own valuable contribution towards the formation of Greater India. Thus, the principal agencies for cultural expansion were merchants, missionaries, emigrants and Kshatriya princes and persons of royal families.

However, it should be noted that the Hindu culture did not spread in the wake of a world conquering king who carried at the head of his legions fire and sword, savage barbarities and innumerable sufferings. India neither enforced her culture aggressively nor made herself manifest to the outside world in the person of a world shaker and conqueror like Alexandar, Caesar, Mahmud of Ghazni, Chengiz Khan, Timur and Nadirshah. "Her *digvijaya or* world conquest was the conquest of truth and law the *dharma vijaya*." Those who disseminated Hindu culture abroad were impelled by inner spiritual urge and conscious will to carry the message of ideal spiritual life into distant lands. Their yearning for the general welfare and salvation of all persons inspired them to settle down in inaccessible lands, and sacrifice themselves for the realization of the highest good and the conquest of piety. Herein lies the eternal glory of the Hindu culture.

It built a unique empire "an empire sharing not in a political life under a suzerain, but in a common cultural and spiritual life in a commonwealth of free peoples. The empire that India built overseas and overland was conquered by the piety and the spiritual energy." The guiding principle of the empire was *dharma* or religious *culture* and righteousness. Indian colonial empire differed fundamentally from those of the western nations. Though Indians had established their colonies in the south-east Asia, they did not think it right to settle down their growing population there, nor did they regard these colonies as a profitable market for expanding their industries and increasing commerce.

These colonies were never exploited anyway by the Indian emigrants or conquerors. Moreover, there is nothing to show that Indian States derived any political advantage or economic gain from this extensive empire. It is even doubtful whether the colonial powers maintained any regular contact with the political powers in India, though the claims of Samudragupta that he exercised suzerainty over all the islands of South-east Asia might have reference to some of them. But the most outstanding effect of the establishment of this overseas Hindu Empire was the spread of Hindu culture and civilization in the distant regions. Let us now explain the political and cultural extension of this empire.

Imperialism and Culture

From time immemorial the people of India had been maintaining free and intimate intercourse with the outside world. Even in the prehistoric age, the Neolithic people had relations with countries of the Far East, and they emigrated in large numbers both by land and sea, and settled in Indo-China and the Indian Archipelago. In succeeding ages, while a rich and prosperous civilization of high degree flourished in the Indus valley, there was undoubtedly friendly and familiar intercourse with the countries of western and central Asia or the two important races that moulded to a great extent Indian culture and civilization, the Aryans and Dravidians, entered into India from outside, and necessary relations were established and maintained by them, atleast for a few centuries, with the countries where they had lived before the occupation of India. From the very ancient times India had commercial relations both with the hinds of the East and the West. The stories of the *Mahabharat*, the *Jatakas* and the *Katha Sarit Sagar* have reference to Indian merchants sailing to the countries beyond the seas in search of gain. A Jatak story informs us how Indian merchants sailed to the land of Baveru (Babylon) with a varied cargo that included an Indian peacock. Other stories relate how Indian traders sailed to the regions stretching from Burma to Indonesia called *Suvarnabhumi* (the land of gold). Thus, India had trade relations with Babylonia, Syria and Egypt in the most ancient periods.

In the centuries immediately preceding the Christian era, India had commercial and cultural relations with the countries of Central Asia in the north, Greek kingdoms of the west and the islands of the Pacific in the east. In the Mauryan period such relations became more definite compared to the past. The account of the *Periplus* and Pliny informs us that Indian merchants and missionaries sailed from such harbours as Barbarika, Barygaza, Muziris, Nelcynda, Bakari, Korkai and Puhar. Later on, for the commercial purpose, Indians settled in some islands of the Arabian Sea and the island of Sacotra, and the port of Alexandria had colonies of Indian merchants. When the Roman Empire came into existence, Indians maintained political and commercial relations with the Romans. In the seventh century when the Arabs controlled land and sea routes, India carried on active trade with the Arabs. Thus, India's commercial relations with Babylonia, Syria, Egypt, Greece, Rome and Arabia left traces of Indian culture on the Egyptian, Greek, Roman and Arabian cultures, because culture and civilization follow in the wake of trade and commerce.

As noted above, the Indian merchants, Buddhist and Brahmana missionaries, adventurous Kshatriya princes and enterprising emigrants sailed from India and settled down in the countries and islands of south-east Asia. There they introduced Indian customs, manners, philosophy, religion, rituals, literature and fine arts. In due course, they intermarried with the local people and Indianized them. "Indianized kingdoms soon came into being either as a result of an Indian imposing himself on the native population, or else through a native chief adopting foreign civilization (Indian)." This process of Indianization commenced in the third century B.C., and continued till the thirteenth century A.D. It would, therefore, be not unreasonable to conclude that India had never led lonely and isolated life completely cut off from the rest of the world.

The view that ancient Indians 'were a stay at home people, isolated from the rest of mankind by mountains and ocean barriers and leading a peaceful, quiet and unadventurous life within the boundaries of their own land, has been shattered now by the recent discoveries. Many remains of Indian culture in various parts of Asia have been brought to light. These indicate that Indians went beyond the seas and the mountains that gird India, and established their colonies. Indian art and literature reared its head abroad, and Indian culture penetrated into some of the obscure corners of the world. An account of the process of Hindu cultural expansion is given below.

Sri Lanka (Ceylon) : According to Indian traditions Rama was the first to carry the message of Indian culture to Lanka. It seems that the Aryans were the first people to migrate from Northern India and settle down in Lanka and not the Dravids from Tamil land of the southern India. But historically India's relations with Lanka can be traced back to the sixth century B.C. Lankan chronicles narrate how King Vijay of Bengal conquered and colonized Lanka approximately 500 years before Christ. He married a local princess and became the progenitor of the Sinhalese race and gave the island of Lanka the name of Simhala. Some historians do not agree with this view. However, since then streams of immigrants from Bengal, Orissa, Gujarat and Kathiawar flowed into Lanka, and Buddhism and Hinduism remained dominant there.

The Aryans from the north and the Dravids from the south intermingled there. They brought with them social customs, religion, arts and crafts. In the second century B.C., during the reign of Asoka, his son Mahendra and daughter Sanghamitra went to Lanka as the Buddhist missionary. There they succeeded in making *Devanampriya Tissa*, the ruler of the island, a convert to Buddhism. Since then the people of Lanka have continued to follow the Buddhist religion and remained under the cultural influence of India for a pretty long time. In due course, Lankan Buddhist *Samghas* or orders of monks and nuns were set up and Buddhism became the official religion there. Old Buddhist relics from India found their way to Lanka, a large number of the Buddhist stupas were erected, rock edicts in Asokan style were inscribed and a branch of the Bodhi tree was transplanted in a Vihar at Anuradhapur. In the history of Buddhism, Lanka has special significance as the *Tripitaka* of the oldest Buddhist sect *Sthavir*, written in the Pali, was available only there.

It is said that Lanka has retained the Buddhist religion and practices in their purest form in the Pali language and script. Buddhism in Lanka brought into being great creative forces which manifested themselves through literature and fine arts.

It is Buddhism which gave to Lanka the Brahmi script, Pali language, Indian architecture, sculpture and painting, and introducing cultural unity among the diverse rival races, organized them in sound social order. Later on other waves of Hindu cultural influence penetrated Lanka and "the antiquities of Isurmuniya, Anuradhapur and Polonnaruwa reveal the Gupta influences, and the frescoes of Sigiria are clearly an extension of the Ajanta School." Thus, Lanka is immensely indebted to India for religion, literature, philosophy and fine arts.

Central Asia : In Central Asia, India's cultural conquest completely overshadowed her trade relations. The expansion of the Mauryan Empire towards the north-west, the missionary activities of Asoka and the domination of Kushan Kings over parts of Central Asia brought India into intimate contact with Central Asia. Here partly by the Buddhist missionary propaganda and partly by the political influence of the Kushans, the torch of Indian culture and civilization was carried beyond the Pamirs into Turkistan and Mongolian regions of the nomadic peoples that settled in the vast region extending between the shores of the Caspian Sea and the Wall of China. Colonist Indians from Kashmir and north-western India also settled in large numbers in the region round modern Khotan. It was in Khotan that there existed the great Buddhist establishment of Gomati which was a centre of learning. Kashmir, Yarkand, Khotan and Kuchi were significant centres of Buddhism. Flourishing Indian colonies once dotted the area which now lies buried under the sands of the desert of Gobi.

According to the account of Chinese pilgrim, Fa-Hien, Indians were living in this region in the early centuries of the Christian era, and by the fifth century A.D the whole of Central Asia was completely Indianized. He informs us that the tribes living in the west of the Lake Lobnar had embraced Indian religions and used Indian languages. We have enough evidence to conclude that in the thirteenth century A.D., Prakrit was the state language and Kharoshti was the official script in Khotan and other southern colonies. The rulers of Kuchi and other countries were Buddhists and had adopted Indian names, Haripuspa, Suvarnpuspa, etc.

The archaeological explorations of Sir Aurel Stein in Central Asian region carried on in 1908 have laid bare the ruins of several cities peopled by the Indians 2,000 years ago. Numerous Buddhist stupas, shrines and monasteries, images of Buddha, Ganesa, Kubera and other Brahmanical gods, coins with Indian legends, and many Buddhist canonical works and manuscripts and shorter records and documents written in Indian languages and Indian alphabets have been unearthed. These show the wide prevalence of Buddhism and Hinduism the use of Sanskrit language; the extension of Gandhara School of Art, the fresco painting of the Buddhist grottoes and the influence of the classical Indian art in sculpture.

All this indicates the complete Indianization of these out of the way colonies and tells the tale of Indian adventures beyond the 'Roof of the World'. Even as late as the seventh century A.D., when Hiuen Tsang passed through Central Asia on his way to and back from India; he noted the dominance of Buddhism and Indian culture over that wide area. Central Asia was the meeting place of the two great cultural traditions of India and China, and it was this region which was responsible for receiving and spreading Indian religion, philosophy, literature and fine arts over a large area. Thus, before the rise of Islam in Central Asia, Indian culture and civilization predominated there, and it is said that the Mongol leader Chengiz Khan was a Buddhist.

China, Korea and Japan : From Central Asia Indian culture spread to China, Korea and Japan. In China, Indian culture was carried by Buddhism which travelled from Khotan to China in the first century A.D., and it remains a living faith even today among millions of Chinese. Credit goes to the first two Indian missionaries, Dharmaratna and Kasyapa Matanga, for taking Buddhism with its sacred texts and relics to China. The Chinese Emperor, Ming-ti of the Han dynasty (56-76 A.D.) constructed the 'White Horse' monastery for the residence of these two missionaries.

It was the first Buddhist Vihar in China. Till 265 A.D., Buddhism spread slowly in China but it progressed with wonderful rapidity between the third century and the six century. The reign of T'ang dynasty (618-907 A.D.) is the glorious and golden age of Buddhism in China. It is difficult to determine precisely the influence which Buddhism and Indian culture exerted upon the ancient civilization of China. She showed the proverbial zeal of a new convert. Streams of Chinese pilgrims visited India and bands of Chinese monks undertook the perilous journey to India to study at first hand the religious beliefs and practices of Indian Buddhism and to collect Buddhist manuscripts, relics and statues. Hundreds and thousands of Buddhist books and manuscripts were carried from India to China and then translated into the Chinese language.

For this not only did the Chinese themselves learn Sanskrit and Pali, but they also invited many Indian scholars to go to China. Hundreds of Indian scholars and monks visited China, settled there and dedicated their lives to the sacred task. The most notable among them are Kumarjiva, Gunavarman, Bodhi Dharma and Parmartha. Buddhism as interpreted by Indian scholars like Jingupta, Jinayasa, Dharmagupta, Jnanabhadra and Bodhiruchi, quickly became "a force to be reckoned within the intellectual and cultural life of China." In short, "Buddhism built up the philosophical and metaphysical framework of Chinese thought" and was responsible to a great extent for such qualities of Chinese culture as spirituality, tenderness, compassion, philosophical serenity, delicacy of feeling, etc. A large number of Chinese Buddhist pilgrims Fa-Hien, Hiuen Tsang, Sung Yun, I-tsing and others came to India from time to time.

The result was that many important works of Indian literature and philosophy were translated into the Chinese language, and 'it is singular to observe that there are Chinese translations of Buddhist texts whose originals can no longer be traced in India. Indian Buddhist art of which many specimens were transported to China also profoundly: influenced art at China. The stone sculptures and bas-relief of the Han period and its music and sciences betray Indian influence, Like Indian stupas Chinese constructed the pagodas.

The renowned artist Nandlal Bose revealed to us that the figures engraved in the famous pagoda in Ki-Fong are those of the Bengalis. Inscriptions written in Bengali letters have been discovered in a temple in Peking. The art of Tunhuang, where one thousand Buddhist caves are situated, bears testimony to the influence of Indian art. The rock cut images in the Yun Kang gorge at Tatung fu in Shansi and at Lung Men in Honan show clearly the influence of their Gupta and Gandhara prototypes. The Chinese pagodas seem to have been a development of the celebrated relic tower of Kanishka at Peshawar so greatly admired by the Chinese Buddhist pilgrims.

Similarly, the music and sciences of China have traces of Indian influence. China has encouraged the study of Indian mathematics and astronomy. Many Indian medicinal drugs were also utilized there. Dr. Gokhale remarks that "Sanskrit language and literature exerted great beneficial influences on the growth of the Chinese language as can be seen from the *Tonal-Samadhi* in the Chinese and the large number of philosophical works in the language inspired by Buddhist devotion." In addition to this, close contact established by religion, political and commercial relations between India and China and the existence of a fairly regular traffic by way of the sea are also to be noted.

From China Buddhism spread to Korea and from Korea to Japan in the sixth century. There it is still a living force and has moulded their civilization during the last fifteen hundred years. In fact, Japan was the farthest outpost of Indian culture in the East. In the thirteenth century, the Mongol emperors embraced Buddhism in Mongolia and Siberia.

Afghanistan : Afghanistan used to be a part of India in early times. It was included in Mauryan and Kushan empires. Being situated on the borders of India the ancient Indian culture extended there far and wide. Consequently, there had developed famous centres of Indian culture like Bamiyan and Rudda. Bamiyan possesses, within the folds of its hills, innumerable remains of once extensive Buddhist art. There existed many Buddhist monasteries in Afghanistan. They were centres of Indian learning and culture exercising beneficial influences on the lives of millions of people. It is not surprising therefore, to find such remains of Indian culture as stupas, vihars, images, etc., in Afghanistan. The period in which Fa-Hien and Hiuen Tsang visited India, Afghanistan enjoyed the blessings of Buddhism and before the invasion of Subuktagin during the medieval period Hinduism was predominating in the valley of Kabul. According to Alberuni, Buddhism was prevailing in Iran, Khurasan, Syria and Iraq before the rise of Islam.

Nepal : It is a kingdom along the southern slopes of the Himalayas extending for about 800 kilometres from Almora district on the west to Darjeeling hills on the east. In the middle of the third century B.C. Asoka exercised suzerainty over it and it is said that he had gone there with his daughter Charumati and son in law Devapal Khattiya (Kshatriya) and there he constructed many stupas and vihars. Probably Buddhism entered Nepal in the reign of Asoka. Emperor Samudragupta exercised his sway over Nepal which paid regular tribute to him. In the closing years of the sixth century the Lichchhavi dynasty established its rule there. In the medieval ages owing to the incessant invasions of the Muslims many Brahmanas and Rajputs fled to Nepal and sought shelter there.

They had taken with them to Nepal, Indian religion, philosophy, literature and art. When the Gurkhas had established their power in Nepal in 1768 they introduced Hinduism there. Before this Hinayan, Mahayan and Tantric Buddhism prevailed there. But in course of ages degeneration had set in and Buddhism was gradually strangulated by Hinduism. Consequently, Hinduism dominates today in Nepal. Like religion, Nepal's literature, language, art, customs and traditions, betray deep influence of Indian culture. There are many stupas hundreds of temples and many different places of pilgrimage. The most famous and principal temple is that of Pasupatinath where lord Siva is worshipped. The architecture and sculpture of Nepal's temples bear resemblance to those of India.

There are magnificent stone temples having very high *sikhars* (massive towers). Besides these, there are pagoda like wooden temples, the roofs of which are made of copper. In the medieval period, the Pala art of Bengal entered Nepal and influenced its art. The social structure of Nepal reveals the influence of Hindu caste system. Although Hindu culture over shadows life in Nepal, yet the influence of China and Tibet is also visible on cultural life of Nepal.

Tibet : Buddhism with Indian culture penetrated into Tibet in the reign of the famous Strong-tstan Gampu, the founder of Lhasa, in 639 A.D. He married a Nepalese and a Chinese princess. They were ardent Buddhists and their influence converted him to the new faith, and consequently, he introduced Buddhism in Tibet. Along with the new religion he with the zeal of a new convert introduced Indian alphabets which were in use in Khotan and formed Tibetan grammar and thus was paved the way for a new culture and civilization in Tibet. The first group of the Buddhist missionaries went to Tibet in 651 A.D. Later on, a Kashmiri scholar Padma Sambhava went to Tibet in 747 A.D., and introduced there Tantric Mahayan Buddhism and afterwards it was transformed into Lamaism. Shant Rakshita, a Nalanda scholar, paid a visit to

Tibet in the ninth century at the invitation of king Ti song De-tsen who constructed a vihar for him. He was the first to initiate Tibetans into the Buddhist Samgha and translated many Buddhist scriptures in the Tibetan language.

In the eleventh century, Atisha, a leading scholar of Vikramasila University, visited Tibet. He became the patron saint of Tibet. Tibetan Buddhists came to India in large number and the proximity of India enabled them to come into close and intimate contact with the home of Buddhism. In the eleventh century, the Pala emperors of Bengal helped towards the reforms of Buddhism in Tibet and there was a lively intercourse between Tibet and the Pala kingdoms. Tibetan monks studied at the monasteries of Nalanda, Oddantapuri, Vikramasila and Jagaddala, and many Indian Buddhist monks visited Tibet. In 1028, Bengal's scholar Dipankarshrijnan toured Tibet and preached Vajrayan Buddhism. Hundreds of the sacred texts of Buddhism were translated into Tibetan language of which two famous collections *Tanjur* and *Kanjur* still exist. The art of Tibet resembles Indian art and has excelled in the productions of copper gilt statues of the numerous Mahayan gods and goddesses inlaid with turquoise and other precious stones.

Thus, Tibet absorbed through Buddhism many Indian cultural trends in the realm of religion, philosophy, literature and art. Tibetan religion, methods of worship, ceremonies, rituals, language, script, grammar, literature, arts, social customs and traditions show Indian origin. In its turn Tibet rendered great cultural service to India. Several Buddhist works that were lost in India after the Muslim invasions and destruction of Nalanda, Vikramasila and other Buddhist universities and monasteries, were preserved in their Tibetan translations in Tibetan monasteries. They throw a flood of light on the evolution of Buddhist religion, philosophy and traditions.

Kashmir : The state of Kashmir was also culturally important because it lay on the route between India and China.

It formed the part of the Mauryan and Kushan empires and was afterwards for a time subject to China. Many Kashmiri monks visited China and colonists went there in large numbers. It helped in the spread of Indian culture abroad.

Imperialistic Expansion

The colonizing activities of the Hindus and their maritime adventures found their full scope in south-east Asia. Across the Bay of Bengal lay Indo-China and the islands of Java, Sumatra, Borneo and Bali, and they were inhabited by primitive, uncultured, wild races and had almost a monopoly of the world's spice trade. These extensive fertile regions were also rich in minerals, and consequently, they soon drew the attention of the Indians. The eastern coast of India, from the mouth of the river Ganges to the Cape Comorin, was studded with many harbours.

It was from these ports that Indians had sailed and developed important commercial relations with the Far East in the second century A.D. Indian literature including Buddhist texts has faithfully preserved the common traditions of the ancient times of such perilous voyages to unknown distant lands beyond the sea. As pointed out in the beginning of the Chapter, the tales in the *Jatakas*, the *Katha Sarit Sagar* and other similar collections frequently refer to traders' voyages to *Suvarnabhumi* (the land of gold), which was a general designation of several lands in the Far East. Enterprising merchants and adventurers returned from these lands with immense riches. On the other hand, many, met with ship wrecks and there were also dangers, sufferings and miseries of various other kinds.

Some stories relate how persons of royal blood and young Kshatriya princes, dispossessed of their hereditary kingdoms, sailed to *Suvarnabhumi* to carve out their own destiny. We have reason to believe that to some such Kshatriya enterprises we owe the foundation of Indian political power in these far off regions of south-east Asia. Indian princes, merchants and adventurers founded settlements and established their political power and social and cultural institutions there. From the second century A.D onward, there are references to kingdoms and principalities ruled by persons with Indian names. Their religions, languages, social customs and manners all were Indian. They may, therefore, be safely regarded as Indian colonial kingdoms. Indian religious thought and culture spread in these kingdoms and attained glorious heights. Between the second and the fifth centuries A. D., such kingdoms were successfully set up in Malaya Peninsula, Combodia, Annam and the islands of Sumatra, Java, Bali and Borneo.

The Brahmanical religion, mainly Saivism, flourished in these kingdoms, though Buddhism, specially the Mahayan form, was also followed by the people. The aborigines adopted the civilization and culture of their masters (Indians) and there was a gradual fusion of the two distinct races. Hindu institutions, customs and manners were modified to some extent by close contact with these peoples, "but still for nearly one thousand years the essential features of the Hindu civilization and culture were the dominant characteristic of society in these kingdoms." This affected complete cultural conquest. Some of the splendid monuments of Indian' art and culture which still remain there are undying testimony to the early Indian colonizing enterprises. At first Indians tried to establish colonies in the countries near home. Thus, Burma, Siam, Lanka and Indo-China were the earliest fields of their colonizing activities. An account of these is given below.

Burma : The history of the relations between India and Burma in the early period is obscure. Some of the South Indian Tamil kingdoms had trade relations with Burma across the Bay of Bengal. The people from Kalinga, both merchants and missionaries, established contact with the people of Burma and also made a few settlements near the coast. The rise and growth of Buddhism in Burma was due to two of Asoka's missionaries, Sona and Uttara; but actually the apostle was Buddhaghosha the famous Sinhalese scholar, who went to

Burma from Lanka in 450 A.D., and established there the Hinayan form of Buddhism. Later on, in the eleventh century, the Chola king, Rajendra I, sailed over to Burma and conquered and annexed it.

In the thirteenth century, Lankan Buddhism and Pali scriptures were introduced in Burma. During all these centuries of close contact, Indian thought and art influenced Burmese life. There is no wonder, therefore, if Buddhist and Hindu remains of the Gupta period are found at Thatun, Pegu and Prome. Ruins of some stupas together with other objects were discovered in Prome, lower Burma. One of these ruined stupas was "a majestic structure rising from the super imposed terraces." A manuscript written in a script bearing resemblance to the Kannada Telugu script was also discovered in lower Burma.

The kings of these regions were Indianized and they adopted Indian titles of Vikram and Varman. In the eleventh century, the ruler of upper Burma had carried to his kingdom Buddhist religious ideas, monks and scriptures from lower Burma. White bell shaped massive pagodas temples, bells and gongs, charming Buddha images, carved works illustrating Buddhist legends, yellow robed monks all these reveal to us that Indian culture had penetrated deep in Burmese life through Buddhism. Even today a large number of Burmese are Buddhists and their language, script and religious rites and ceremonies have deep impression of Indian culture.

Siam : In the second or the third century A.D., in the central region of Siam there arose an Indian kingdom named Dwaravati founded by the Mons. It became a flourishing Indian colony. In course of time the whole of Siam was completely Indianized. Later on, the Mahayan form of Buddhism from the neighbouring Hindu colony, Combodia, made its way into Siam and it became the official religion. Hinayan form of Buddhism was carried there by the Lankan Buddhist Sangh. The Hindu and Buddhist religious literature and art considerably influenced the Siamese language, literature, art and social institutions. The Siamese language which borrowed its script from India was deeply influenced by Pali. Many of the technical terms describing social and political ideals were absorbed bodily from Pali in the Siamese language. Bronze Buddha images of Amaravati style, Gupta figures from the Ganges valley, remains of stupas, monasteries and the Buddhist doctrines written in Pallaya script have been discovered in Siam. "The influence of Indian teremonial in Siamese court life is very extensive, and even today the coronation of a Siamese prince can be performed only by a Brahmana priest." (Dr. B. G. Gokhale).

Many of the Hindu rites and *samskaras,* fashions and festivals have become a part and parcel of Siamese customs and rituals. Even today they perform *Chudakarma samskara* and observe *Dashahara* festival commemorating Rama's triumph over Ravana. Many of the episodes and elements of the two famous Hindu epics, the *Ramayan* and the *Mahabharat,* have been freely taken over in Siamese literature. In the realm of art, the Siamese borrowed the conception of the Buddhist temples and Buddhist images from India. They evolved the famous Siamese Buddha "a slender figure with flame crowned oval face wearing a strange all pervasive smile and distinctive pagoda style often made of broken bit of Chinese porcelain.", The names and the titles of the kings, people and towns of Siam even today reveal traces of Hindu influence. They remained under the cultural influence of Indians till the sixteenth century A.D.

Colonies in Indo-China Region

Champa : On the main land of Indo-China, Hindus established two powerful colonial kingdoms Champa and Kambuja. The former colony included south Annam and Cochin with Amaravati as its capital, and was founded probably in the second century A.D. This colony continued to flourish for a period of thirteen hundred years (150-1450) and served as an all important half way house between the Indian and Chinese commercial and cultural relations. Among the early rulers of Champa, Dharma, Maharaj Sri Bhadra varma (387-413) and his successor Changaraj are famous. Being a devotee of Siva, Bhadravarma constructed a Siva temple at Myson. It became a national sanctuary.

The Siva Lingam in the temple was named *Bhadreswara* or *Bhadreswora* Swami. Another king of Champa abdicated his throne and undertook a pilgrimage to India. Indravarma III (911-972) was another famous ruler of Champa. He was well renowned for his mastery and deep study of six systems of Hindu philosophy, Buddhist philosophy, Panini's grammar and doctrines of Saivism. From the tenth century A.D onwards the Aunamites and the Mongols began to attack Champa. Some of its rulers, such as, Jaya Parmesvaravarmadeva Isvarmurti (1050-1060), Rudravarma (1060-1069), Harivarman (1070-1081), Maharajadhiraja Sri Jaya Indravarman (1163-1180), and Jays Simhavarman (1257-1287) were great heroes and warriors. They fought bravely and defended their country successfully against the attacks of their western neighbours, the Kambujas, and the great Mongol Chief, the famous Kublai Khan. They had diplomatic relations with the Chinese.

After a glorious existence of more than thirteen centuries, the power of this Hindu colony was broken by the repeated attacks of their neighbours, the Annamese, who gradually conquered the whole of Champa and in sixteenth century it was over run by Mongolian hordes. There were many flourishing cities in the colony of Champa and the whole country was adorned with beautiful and highly original temples both Hindu and Buddhist. Two temple cities, Misong and Dong-Duong in Champa, are famous even today. The native people were completely Hinduized. They worshipped Hindu gods and goddesses among whom Siva, his *Sakti* or power, his two sons, *Ganesa* and *Skanda,* were occupying predominant position. The object of Siva worship was the *Linga.* One of the oldest of the *Lingas,* placed in the Bhadreswara temple in

Myson, was held to be the national deity. Besides Siva, Vishnu, Krishna, Buddha and other gods were also worshipped. As regards art, the people of Champa followed closely the Gupta art not only in subject matter but in technique also. The complicated stone foliation, celestial dancer poised on one toe, intent on pleasing the gods, and a bronze statue of Buddha discovered amongst the ruins of Champa reveal unmistakable influence of Indian art on the Champa art. A large number of temples were constructed in the whole country.

In fact, the Champa art had attained a high level of excellence in abundance of decoration and gorgeous ornamentations in temples, *toranas* or main entrances and pillars. Sanskrit inscriptions and documents, discovered there indicate that Indian language, Sanskrit, must have been very popular. Probably, it was the official language. There was considerable literary activity. A Hindu society modelled on the orthodox Indian type developed in Champa. The Brahmanas occupied a high place, but the rank of the Kshatriyas was hardly inferior to theirs. Though Brahmanism dominated, Buddhism also enjoyed the patronage of several rulers. However, Brahmanism and Brahmanic culture flourished, and saturated life in Champa.

Kingdom of Kambuja or Funan : Another Hindu kingdom, named Kambuja, was established in the south of Champa by the Hindus who made their way up Mekong river there before the Christian era. The Chinese named Kambuja as Funan. Ancient Kambuja roughly corresponded to modern Combodia and Cochin China. The natives called Khmers believed that in Indian *rishi* or sage was their ancestor, hence, their country was called Kambuja or Combodia. The origin of this kingdom is shrouded in mystery. While discussing its origin, Dr. R. C. Majumdar explains that according to an old legend Kaundinya, probably a Brahmana landed there and he married Soma, a Naga princess, and founded the royal dynasty of Kambuja. It is said that he planted a spear which he obtained from Drona's son Asvatthama. Another version of the legend makes him a son of Adityavarma, king of Indraprastha. In any case, he seems to be a Hindu and one can trace the earliest Hindu kingdom in Kambuja to the first or second century A.D. The royal dynasty so established accepted Hindu rites and codes and became in fact Hindu.

The natural resources of the country, its mineral wealth, its rich and fertile soil and its river systems were fully and freely developed by the hardy and industrious Indian colonists during the following three hundred years and in the eighth century the kingdom of Kambuja reached a stage of high cultural development, and exercised suzerainty over several vassal states. In the ninth century, Jayavarma II became the famous king of Kambuja. He shifted his capital to the Angkor region which, later on, acquired international fame for its architectural monuments. He also instituted the Tantric cult of *Devaraja* worshipped in a temple on a mountain. It was a kind of Saivism. Indravarma (877-889), the grandson of Jayavarma II, claimed that rulers of China and Champa obeyed his commands.

His successor Yasovarman (889-908) was one of the most remarkable kings of Kambuja. He was the founder of a new capital city Yashodharpur (later on known as Angkor Thom). He was not only a great conqueror but a versatile scholar and great builder. It is said that he acquired proficiency in the art of music, dancing, architecture and script, and mastered many *Sastras* and *Kavyas* and composed a commentary on Patanjali's *Mahabhasya*. Yasovarman established the institution of *ashramas* (monastic establishments), homes of pious devotees, who consecrated their lives to study and meditation. Adequate endowments were provided for their maintenance. Detailed and definite regulations were issued by the king for the maintenance and conduct of these *ashramas*, modelled on the lines of Hindu hermitages or *tapovanas*.

Another famous and mighty monarch was Suryavarman II (1113-1145), who earned undying fame by erecting the famous Angkor Vat, veritable wonder of the world, But the kingdom of Kambuja reached its greatest extent during the reign of Jayavarman VII who ascended the throne in 1181. He conquered Champa and a part of lower Burma, founded a new splendid capital city known as Angkor Thom, and established and maintained many religious institutions and several works of public utility. The kings of Kambuja sent ambassadors to both India and China.

In the fifteenth century, the Annamites from the east and the Thais (who had conquered and occupied Siam) from the west attacked Kambuja continuously, and soon reduced this powerful kingdom to a petty principality. At last Ang Duong, the last king of Kambuja, placed himself under French protection in 1854. Since then Kambuja became a French protectorate. But the people of Kambuja being awakened to their political rights, endeavoured to shake off this protectorate and regained their independence.

The kingdom of Kambuja which exercised its sway over distant and extensive countries for centuries rose to far greater power than Champa. Numerous Sanskrit inscriptions give us the detailed history of its kings and wonderful temples like Angkor Vat, and those of Angkor Thom, and a hundred others still tell the tale of their grandeur and magnificence.

Angkor Vat, a wonder of the world, is a shrine dedicated to Siva built by King Suryavarman. It is the largest temple ever built by man. A ditch runs close to the boundary walls of the temple and surrounds it. The total length of the ditch is four kilometres. The temple stands on the top of a massive and extensive terraced structure and has several spires and towers. There are three terraces standing one above the other, the first is 246 metres long and 207'50 metres broad with a total running length of nearly 923 metres. The second and the third measure less compared to the first. These galleries or terraces are linked together by stairs and intervening open terraces. The innermost terrace is dominated by five tall domes, the central one rises to a height of more than 65 metres above the ground level. The Ankgor Vat is a pyramid temple. The general plan of the temple, as noted above, consists of a wide ditch, "the two external enclosures, the approaches, the three concentric galleries, the central mass, the large tower in the centre, the smaller towers on the corners of the two inner galleries and three still smaller ones on the west entrance of the outer enclosure twelve in all." Thus, the temple combines magnitude and magnificence. The gorgeous decorative sculptures invest the temple with a peculiar magnificence.

The decoration is treated as embroidery work and the ornament is everywhere, even at the most invisible corners. The temple walls and galleries are adorned with birds, flowers, dancing maidens and scenes from *Ramayan,* the *Mahabharat* and the *Puranas.* Angkor Vat is an excellent example of the oldest art, both architectural and sculptural as it was developed in these foreign countries by master Indian builders. It brilliantly and most effectively reflects the religious devotion and artistic urge as it was felt by the Indianized people of Kambuja. Another famous temple of Kambuja was To Prahm. It was dedicated to the Buddhist divinity *Prajnaparamita* of the Mahayan sect.

Angkor Thom is the modern name of the capital city of Yasodharapura, founded by King Yasovarman. The city was enclosed by a wall which was surrounded by a ditch. It was square in shape, each side measuring more than three kilometres, with the grand temple of Bayon in the centre, containing fifty towers. This temple is second in size to Angkor Vat. Everything in the city was conceived on a truly noble scale; "the city of Yasodharapura was one of the grandest cities in the whole world in that age." It was a city full of grandeur and glory.

In Kambuja empire, Hinduism specially Saivism was the predominant religion. It had almost become national religion, though Vaishnavism and Buddhism occasionally enjoyed royal patronage. Sanskrit became the official language. Several

Sanskrit inscriptions, discovered there, were composed in beautiful *Kavya* style. Indian religious texts, the *Ramayana*, the *Mahabharat* and the *Puranas*, were studied with keen interest. Indian books of medicine and Indian methods of treatment were very popular.

It is said that a Kambuja king Rudra Varman, had appointed two Indian physicians in his court. There were several *ashramas* founded and maintained by royal charity and private munificence. They formed a salient feature of the religious and social life in Kambuja and served there as radiating centres of Hindu culture and religion. In short the people of Kambuja had embraced Hindu religion, culture and civilization and accepted the political and social ideas and customs of the Hindus. They had given to the world the biggest temple of Angkor Vat which is the brightest testimony and the greatest monument of India's cultural conquest.

Colonies of Malaya Archipelago

Hindu colonies also flourished in Java, Sumatra, Bali and Borneo (Malaya Archipelago) where the remains of Hindu culture have also been discovered in abundance. This region, called *Suvarnadvipa* saw the rise and fall of two big Hindu empires. The first one was formed by the Sailendra dynasty in the fourth century A.D. It comprised the Malaya Peninsula and the whole of the archipelago including the islands of Sumatra, Java. Bali and Borneo.

The Arab merchants who traded in these parts described in rapturous terms the power wealth and magnificence of the grand monarchs who exercised supreme sway there had each styled himself as *Maharaja*. The daily income of these Sailendras was supposed to be two hundred mounds of gold. The available evidences justify the assumption that there were many Hindu colonies in the Malaya Peninsula during the early centuries of the Christian era and the "region around the Bay of Bandon was a cradle of further eastern culture inspired by waves of Indian influence."

Sailendra's Srivijaya Empire : Probably the Sailendras (Lords of the Mountains) sailed off from Kalinga on the eastern coast of India. First they conquered south Burma and north Malaya and, later on they established their sway over nearly the whole of *Suvarna dvipa,* comprising Malaya peninsula, Sumatra, Java, Bali, Borneo and other islands of the East Indies. The Sailendras founded a town called *Srivijaya* in Sumatra. They made it their capital and hence their kingdom was called Srivijaya Empire. It was founded about the fourth century A.D. and reached the height of its glory in the eighth century..

The Sailendras ruled in glory and magnificence till the eleventh century when Rajendra Chola I a famous king of southern India, who possessed a splendid fleet invaded the dominions of the Sailendras several times. Though he conquered a large part of the Sailendra Empire it was a very difficult task to maintain control over such distant overseas provinces. The Chola conquest was more spectacular than substantial and, therefore after nearly a century the Sailendras succeeded in shaking off the Chola suzerainty. However, the Sailendras were considerably weakened and in the fourteenth century a new Hindu kingdom of Java eclipsed the Sailendra Empire and the Sailendras practically disappeared from the scene.

The Sailendra kings not only gave political unity to a large part of Indonesia, but their liberal patronage and munificence developed its culture and gave it a new shape. The Sailendras were followers of Mahayan Buddhism which received a new vigour under them. They derived their religious inspiration from Bengal which was then the principal flourishing centre of Mahayan Buddhism in India. Kumaraghosha who was a Buddhist monk of Bengal became the *guru* or preceptor of the Sailendras. About the middle of the ninth century, a Sailendra king Balaputradeva built a monastery at Nalanda and a Pala king, named Devapala, granted five villages for its upkeep. Another Sailendra king Sri Maravijayattunga Varman built a Buddhist Vihar at Nagapatnam for the maintenance of which the Chola king granted a village in the first quarter of the eleventh century. It was due to Sailendras' patronage that art developed so highly that it produced such splendid monuments as Chandi Kalasan and Borobudur in Java. In fact the Sailendras were great builders and the famous stupas of Borobudur stand even today as the living monument of their splendour. It was constructed during 750-850 A.D on a hill in central Java. The whole edifice of Borobudur consists of nine successive stone terraces, each of rising height and diminishing size.

The centre of the topmost terrace is crowned by a simple bell-shaped stupa. Six of the nine terraces are square while the upper three are circular. The five lower terraces have balustrades and galleries. Each balustrade consists of a row of arched niches having images of *Dhyani* Buddha within. There are more than 32 of such images in the whole building. The upper terraces have a circle of stupas each of which contains a Buddha image set in a perforated framework. A staircase, with a gateway in the middle of each side of the gallery; leads to the next higher one. These galleries have eleven series of 1,500 sculptured panels showing scenes from the lives of the Buddha in his various past incarnations and other stories from the *Avadanas* and the *Lalitavistar*.

These images and sculptures are the finest 'examples of Indo-Javanese art and display the highest skill and workmanship of master artists. Fine model ling, masterly planning refined elegance of features, excellent grace, attractive pose, close fitting, smooth robes, and a noble divine spiritual expression on face are the salient characteristics of the images of Borobudur. They resemble the Gupta figures and therefore it is certain that the Javanese art was derived from the art of the Gupta age in India. Though Borobudur resembles more a pyramid rather than a stupa, yet it is Indian both in conception and architectural form. To sum up, Borobudur is the finest manifestation of Indo-Javanese art.

Java : Hindu colonies were established in Java. According to the traditions and legends of Java colonization in the country was attributed to Indian sages like Parasar, Vyas, Panduete etc. But Java appears to have been colonized in the first century of the Christian era and the first wave of colonists went from Kalinga. Javanese chronicles record that 20,000 Indian families migrated there in the second century A.D. By the beginning of the second century, a Hindu kingdom was established there and its king, Devavarman, sent an embassy to China in 132 A.D. Fa Hien, the great Chinese pilgrim who was in India during 399 to 414 A.D., returned to China by the sea route and stayed in Java for five months. He described the country as a stronghold of Brahmanical religion. Four Sanskrit inscriptions, discovered there record that a king named Purnavarman ruled in the region of the western Java about the fifth century A.D.

These inscriptions exhibit that Hindu culture was predominant in Java. Two or three centuries later Sanjaya founded a powerful Indianized kingdom in central Java. As its capital was a Mataram it was styled as the kingdom of Mataram. But it soon came under the sway of the Sailendras. Java formed a part of the Sailendra empire till the ninth century, when it recovered its independence. Now the central political authority and gravity shifted to eastern Java. Several powerful kingdoms rose to power in eastern Java.

The most important among them were the kingdoms of Kadiri and Singhasari. In the eleventh century, Airalangga became the most celebrated king of this region. Towards the close of the thirteenth century a new royal dynasty was founded by King Vijay with Majapahit as its capital. The kingdom of Majapahit was conquered by surrounding islands, and by 1365 the empire of Majapahit included nearly the whole of the Malaya Peninsula and the Malaya Archipelago. Its most important and renowned king was Rajasanagara (1350-89). Early in the fifteenth century, a fugitive Hindu chief of Java founded the kingdom of Malacca which soon rose to be a great political power and an important commercial centre. But the conversion of its second king to Islam with some members of his royal family made Java a stronghold of Islam gradually. The aggressive attitude of Islam forced the last Hindu ruler of Java to take refuge with his followers in the neighbouring island of Bali.

Indian art and literature flourished in Java to an extent unknown elsewhere. There are still hundreds of ruined temples of both Buddhists and Hindus. There is the famous Hindu temple of Lara Jongrang in central Java. It consists of eight principal temples, three in each line with two between them. They are surrounded by a wall. There are three rows of smaller temples round the wall. All these temples number *156*. The biggest and the most famous temple is in the centre of the western row of the three chief temples. An image of Siva is installed there.

Another main temple on the north contains Vishnu's image while that to the south Brahma's image. There are series of relief sculptures in these temples. They depict the episodes from the lives of Rama and Krishna. These sculptures are the Brahmanical counterparts of the Buddhist reliefs on arabudur. The sculptures of Lara Jongrang are dramatic dynamic and vital, while those of Borobudur passive, static and less naturalistic; the former represent the romantic phases of the Indo-Javanese art whereas the latter the classic phases.

An extensive literature in manuscripts based on Sanskrit is discovered there. The epics of the Ramayan and the Mahabharat were the most popular in that island, and even today provide the theme of their popular shadow play, Wayang, and theatrical performance Javanese dances, dramas and puppet plays are modelled on the Indian themes and epic material.

The poetry and prose works of the Javanese language were immensely influenced by the rules of prosody and literary traditions of India. In fact, India exercised its many sided influence in Java. The king of Malaya Peninsula and Indonesia bore Indian names. Their court customs and manners reflect

Indian patterns. Their law codes were modelled on the Indian legal system. Saivism, Vaishnavism, Mahayan Buddhism and Tantricism gained popular favour and royal patronage. The Indo-Javanese art makes "an extensive use of Indian motif the *Kalamakara a* lion's head and a crocodile in decoration." With the decline of Majapahit, artistic activities came to an end in Java.

Bali : The neighbouring island of Bali is the only surviving Hindu colony in the Far East. In the fourth century A.D., a Hindu kingdom was established in Bali. In the sixth century A.D., a rich and prosperous Hindu kingdom flourished there under the Kaundirya Kshatriyas. According to the Chinese traveller, I-tsing, *Mul-Sa-vaptivadi* sect of Buddhism prevailed there under the patronage of the Kaundinyas in the later half of the seventh century. One of the Kaundinya kings sent an envoy to China in 518 A.D. In the tenth century Ugrasen, Kesary and other kings bearing Indian names ruled there. In the later half of the tenth century, Bali came under the Javanese sway and for several centuries together formed a part of the kingdom of the Javanese rulers.

In 1839, the Dutch established their supremacy over Bali and 1911 witnessed the end of the reign of the last Hindu king of Bali. But it was the aggression of Islam in Java that forced its Hindu king to go to Bali. Henceforth, the island of Bali became the seat of flourishing Indo-Javanese culture. Consequently, even today Hinduism with all its old traditions and practices flourishes there. Thus, while Hinduized Java succumbed to the raids of Islam, Bali retains its old and indigenous culture even to the present day. It is the last refuge of Brahmanical religion and Hindu culture in the Far East.

Borneo : It is a very big island to the east of Sumatra. There the Hindus established their colony as early as the first century of the Christian era. The oldest inscription and antiquities, pointing to the Hindu cultural influence in Borneo, were discovered at Muara Kaman on the Mahakam river. In the twelfth century, Borneo was under the Javanese sway. Recently, the ruins of a wooden temple and the stone images of Buddha and Siva have been unearthed there. One of the kings of Borneo, Mulavarman, son of Asvavarman and grandson of King Kundunga (Kaundinya), performed the great sacrifice called *Bahu Suvarnakam* (large quantity of gold) and created *Yupas* (sacrificial pillars) with Sanskrit inscriptions to commemorate it. The inscriptions are dated about 400 A.D., and record. Mulavarman's rich donations and gifts of 20,000 cows to the Brahmanas in the holy field of Vaprakesvara. In eastern Borneo, many antiquities have been discovered at many places especially in the cave of Kombeng. Twelve stone images of the Brahmanical gods, Siva, Ganesa.

Agastya, Brahma, Mahakal, Nandisvar, etc., have been found in the cave. Though indigenous elements are visible in the architectural art of Borneo, yet it is evolved on the Indian patterns of art. Hindu culture still flourishes there.

Philippines : Modern researches have proved that the people of South India had established their colonies in Philippines and they had considerably influenced all aspects of daily life. Handicrafts, coins folk songs, traditions and many religious customs exhibit the Hindu influence there. The scripts of the people of Philippines bear striking resemblance with those of South India. In the realm of religious rites rituals and assigning names, the natives of Philippines followed Indians closely. The names of the places situated on the Luzon coast and the shores of the Manila Bay indicate their Sanskrit origin. The discovery of a Ganesa statue proves that people followed Brahmanism. The hill tribes of Luzon worship early Vedic *gods* even to this day.

Beyond the Philippines several islands are situated in the Pacific Ocean. Scholars have to reveal to us the deep cultural influence of India over these islands. The people of these islands have physical appearance similar to that of the Indo-Aryans. Their languages bear resemblance with those of the pre-Aryan Indians like Santhals. Their religious and social customs and beliefs betray traces of Hindu cultural influences. The Huladance of Hawaii Islands and Siva dance of Samoa are similar to the folk dances of Bengal. Their use of conch shells nose flute, musical bones, staple food stuffs and animals reveals Indian origin. "Many of their decorative designs, crafts, traditions, ideas of phallic symbolism and images are examples of old Polynesian cultural traits derived from the Brahmanical civilization."

Hindu Culture in the Colonies

For nearly fifteen hundred years and even down to the period when the Hindus lost their political independence in India, Hindu sovereigns were ruling over Indo-China and several islands of the Malaya Archipelago, from Sumatra to New Guinea and Philippines in the Pacific Ocean. Indian religion, literature and social institutions moulded the lives of the primitive races and made a thorough conquest of these far off lands. The people of the Far East felt the impact of Indian civilization and culture. The aborigines imbibed a more elevated moral spirit, noble sense of spirituality and higher intellectual taste through the religion, art and literature of India. In fact, they were raised to a higher plane of culture and civilization. A greater India was established by a gentle fusion of races, by richly endowing the original inhabitants with the spiritual heritage of India.

Religion : The inscriptions and images discovered in these colonies prove that besides the Brahmanical religion, Buddhism had also made its influence felt in these regions. Both often mixed together and flourished amicably. However, Buddhism was dominant in Burma and Siam, whereas Brahmanism was firmly established in other remaining colonies. Brahma, Vishnu and Siva were worshipped together with their satellite gods and goddesses. Magnificent temples were constructed for them and images of all the known Hindu gods and goddesses were made. Hindu religion is still prevalent in Bali. There the statues of Indra, Vishnu, and Krishna are installed and Lord Siva and Durga are worshipped, and all those things which are used in India for worship are used even to this day in Bali. The Ramayan, the Mahabharat and the Puranas are recited in the temples there. Hinayan and Mahayan forms of Buddhism and the most debased tantric cults also flourished in these colonies. Java became an important renowned centre of Buddhism and attracted great scholars like I-tsing, Dharmapal of Nalanda and Dipankara Srijnana of Vikramasila University for study.

Language and Literature : The Sanskrit language and literature were highly cultivated and most of the records were written in good and almost flawless Sanskrit. Several Sanskrit inscriptions of very high literary merit have been discovered in these colonies. There seems to have been dominance of Indian literary style. This indicates that the writers of these regions had an intimate knowledge of Sanskrit literature, grammar, rhetoric, prosody. Indian epics, Puranas. Kavyas, Vedas, Vedanta, Smritis, works of Manu. Susruta, Panini and Kalidas. Epics and religious texts of Buddhism and Jainism were studied. Kings, ministers and high officials were scholars and they took a leading part in literary activities. Indo-Javanese literature flourished under the considerable influence of Sanskrit.

It borrowed subject matter from Indian literature. Its important monumental works are the old Javanese Ramayan, the prose translation of the Mahabharat and numerous Kavyas and other works written on the stories of the Puranas. Indo-Javanese literature is the most remarkable product of the Indian colonization. In Burma and Sri Lanka, the study of the Buddhist texts in Pali led to the development of a new classical literature adopted everywhere.

Development of Arts

All the architectural and sculptural monuments of the colonies were religious structures. They were most remarkable for their massive grandeur and artistic excellence. The buildings, shrines temples and images show the thorough going influence of Indian art. "The colonial art, in fact, forms a type by itself. Although it went from India and the skilled and unskilled workmen imbibed traditions of their mother country (India), yet in their new environments, the Indian engineers and artisans assimilated new ideas and produced works which were different and in some respects assuredly 'superior to their original standard in India. The massive temples at Angkor Vat in Combodia, the greatest colossal Buddhist shrine of Borobudur in Java the temples of the Lara Jongrang group and the Anand temple at Pagan in Burma are the most renowned monuments of Indian colonial art. They far exceed in grandeur of conception, of design and skill of execution, finish and ornamentation that we know of in India itself."

Political Institutions and Administration : In addition to religion the influence of Hindu civilization is also clearly marked in the political ideas and the system of administration. About the government of the colonies the Chinese annals inform us that the king had eight great ministers, called the "Eight Seats" all chosen from among the Brahmanas. The king rubbed his body with perfumes, wore a very high hat and necklace of different kinds of jewels, was clothed in muslin, rode in carriages and mounted elephants. In war, people blew conches and beat drums. It was the result of Hindu cultural influence.

Society : The social life of Hindu colonies was based on the Indian pattern. The caste system of the Hindus was introduced early enough in the colonies. Although the colonial society was divided into four broad divisions, Brahmanas, Kshatriyas, Vaisyas and Sudras, yet the caste system had not attained that rigidity which is seen in India. Marriage among different castes was not prohibited. The marriage ceremony with all its details and the conjugal relations bears resemblances to those of India. Castes were not tied to specific professions or crafts. The

Brahmanas were divided into two groups designated after the deity which they worshipped, Siva or Vishnu. The kings assumed Kshatriyahood and took the name of 'Varman' meaning protector. Though untouchability was not known there, the Sudras formed a distinct caste. Women generally held high honourable position in society. If some ascended the throne, others held high posts in administration. Though the women practised the sati system, they did not observe *parda*. They had full liberty to choose their life partners. As in India, the people of the colonies enjoyed gambling, cock fight, music, dancing, theatrical performances and shadow play, *Wayang*.

The diet, dress and ornaments resembled those in India. The Indians, according to certain statements, who went there, intermarried, and gradually the colonial society was transformed into a nominal Hindu structure. The colonial customs of Kala referred to by the Chinese are Indian in origin. "When they marry they give no other presents than arecanuts, sometimes as many as two hundred trays. The wife enters the family of her husband. Their musical instruments are a kind of guitar, a transversal flute, copper cymbals, and iron drums. Their dead are burned, the ashes put into a golden jar and sunk into the sea. Hindu culture in the colonies continued to be a vital dynamic force so long as Hinduism was in full vigour in India.

The subsequent downfall of the Hindus in their own country, India, led to the decay of their colonial supremacy in the Far East. The fountain head having dried up, the streams fed by it were also gradually choked, leading to their ultimate disappearance, and from the eleventh century onward in the Hindu colonies of the south-east Asia, the indigenous elements began gradually to assert themselves freely till Islam, taken there by the Indian Muslims, was firmly planted there in the fifteenth and sixteenth centuries. "The history of the colonies demonstrates the unsoundness of the popular belief that Hinduism cannot be adopted by foreigners but is meant only for those who are born within its fold.

It shows the great vigour with which it could absorb and vitalize foreign culture and could elevate even the most primitive races to higher sphere of culture and civilization. If we remember that Indian culture and civilization played a similar role, though perhaps in a lesser degree, in western, central and eastern Asia, we can realize an aspect of the true greatness of India, not always sufficiently emphasized. The colonial and cultural expansion of India is one of the most brilliant, but forgotten, episodes of Indian History, of which any Indian may justly feel proud."

5

Impact of Islam

In the preceding chapter it was explained how several different elements have hindered the smooth flow of Indian cultural trends before the advent of Islam in India; the predominant tendency of the age was segregation, disruption and disintegration. Consequently, the cultural evolution of India was obstructed, the assimilative power of the Hindu society had disappeared and the creative powers of Indian culture had become dormant. In the medieval age Hindu culture had to face the opposite trends of foreign culture. The age witnessed the close contact of two different and distinct cultures the Hindu and the Muslim or Islamic. Hence, the Hindu and the Muslim cultural ingredients coalesced to form a new cultural life. Let us endeavour to understand it.

The new Islamic or Muslim culture was introduced in India by the Arabs. The expansion and propagation of Islamic culture was attempted by means of peace as well as force. The former was followed by the Arab traders and Muslim saints or *durvishes.* The latter was adopted by the Arab, Turkish and Mughal invaders. It has been already explained in that the Greeks, Romans and Persians participated in the external trade of India. Later on, the Arabs took a very active part in India's commerce with East as well as West. The Arabs, therefore, entered India as traders and sailors. Before the advent of Islam the Arab Settlements had gradually grown up on the western coast of India. The rise of Islam in the beginning of the seventh century and the integration of the Arab tribes under a sovereign centralized state provided a tremendous impetus to the movements of expansion of Islam. Soon the Muslim armies began to hover on the frontiers of India and the Arab fleet appeared in Indian waters in 636 A.D., when an Arab army was sent across the ocean to Thana in western Maharashtra.

In the meanwhile, commerce by sea continued and the Arabs made their settlements in some towns along the South Indian coast. Rowlandson and Francis Day both remark that the Muslim Arabs first settled on the Malabar coast about the end of the seventh century. In the eighth century, the Arab fleets attacked Broach and other harbours on the Kathiawar coast. Their trade began to flourish and settlements continued to multiply. Henceforth, they were welcomed as traders and all facilities were provided to them to settle peacefully, acquire landed property and openly and freely follow their religion.

Before the ninth century was far advanced the Arabs had spread over the whole of the western coast of India. In Gujarat, they erected their mosques and received liberal protection from the Hindu kings. The Zamorin rulers of Calicut patronized the Arab merchants considerably. All along the Malabar coast there were houses of the Muslim Arabs and they had their own *Qazis* and *Muftis* and mosques. Several *Sufis,* or Islamic saints, visited India and delivered sermons; the earliest of them was Al-Hujwiri who expired in 1072. In the tenth century followers of Islam made their advent on the eastern coast of India. Within comparatively short time they acquired influence both in politics and society. "On the one side, their leaders became ministers, admirals, ambassadors and farmers of revenue, and on the other, they made many converts, propagated their religious ideas, established mosques and erected tombs which became centres of the activities of their saints and missionaries." All this could not but influence the cultural trends in South India. But before we attempt to discuss the impact of Islam in the south, let us survey the advent of the Muslims in northern India.

Muslim Invasion

Within a century after the death of Muhammad, the prophet (570-632), the Arabs conquered extensive territories and in 711 the empire of Islam extended from the frontiers of China to the shores of Atlantic. In the middle of the seventh century the Arabs made an attempt to enter India but failed miserably. However, it was in 711-713 that Sind and Multan were conquered for the Arabs by Muhammad bin Kasim, nephew of Al-Hajjaj, the Arab Governor of Basra. The Arabs had to fight contested battles with the forces of Sind's ruler Raja Dahirat Debal, Rewar and Brahmanabad. Though the Arab conquest was confined to Sind and Multan, they failed to retain their political power in that region for long. The Arabs being unskilled in the art of government left the administration of the conquered country in the hands of the natives. The death of their leader Muhammad bin Kasim meant the end of the first Muslim occupation of Sind. Though Arab conquest of Sind was politically insignificant, yet it had far reaching effect on Muslim culture. It was India and not Europe that taught Islam in the impressionable years of its youth. The Arabs learnt from the Hindus, philosophy, astronomy, mathematics, medicine, chemistry and the art of administration, and carried these to the West.

Next followed the Muslim conquest of the Punjab by the Turks of Ghazni Subuktgin and his son and successor Mahmud (995-1030). The Punjab at this time was ruled by the Shahi dynasty of the Hindus whose sway extended as far as Kabul in the west. Subuktgin defeated and deprived Shahi ruler Jaipal of his trans Indus territory and his son Mahmud gradually wrested the rest of the kingdom. Acquisition of the fabulous wealth of India and the propagation of Islam at the point of sword were the two motives that inspired him to invade India almost annually. He attacked northern India, except Bengal and Bihar, seventeen times. But the treasures which he had carried away were replenished and the temples that he desecrated were rebuilt and repaired, and his expeditions were altogether barren of permanent political results. However, he was a pioneer who after exposing the political and military weakness of India to the Muslim world, opened the way for the conquest of the land of infidels by later generations of his co-religionists.

Foundation of Empire

In spite of the previous repeated attacks of the Muslim powers, foundations of the Muslim Empire in India were laid by Shahab-ud-din Ghori (1175-1206). The struggle between the rulers of Ghazni and their feudatories of Ghor that went on for about a quarter of a century enabled Shahab-ud-Din and his elder brother Ghiyas-ud-din to seize the throne of Ghazni in 1173 and drive out Bahram Shah, the degenerate descendent of Mahmud of Ghazni. Shahab-ud-din then turned his attention towards the fertile plains of India and in the following ten years he easily conquered and quickly annexed Multan, Uchh (Sind) and Lahore.

The Ghori invader, Shahab-ud- din, then confronted the Rajput rulers. He defeated Prithviraj of Delhi, the Rajput leader, in the second battle of Tarain in 1192. This was followed by the conquest of Ajmer, Kannauj and Varanasi. On his retiring from India, Shahab-ud-din's lieutenant Qutub-ud-din Aibak and Muhammad Bakhtiyar Khilji continued his work of conquest. They conquered Gwalior, Kalinjar, Gujarat, Bengal and Bihar. Within thirty years, the entire region between the Indus and the Brahmaputra permanently passed over to the hands of the Muslims. The foundation of the Muslim rule in India was now laid rather permanently.

Establishment of Delhi Sultanate

The Slave Dynasty (1206-1290). After the death of Shahab-ud-din Ghori, his viceroy Qutub-ud-din Aibak, who founded the Slave Dynasty, ruled India from 1206 1210. He greatly extended the conquests made by Ghori and with the assistance of Muhammad Bakhtiyar Khilji he brought the whole of northern India under his sway. Other famous rulers of the dynasty were Iltutmish and Balban. The former saved the infant Muslim Empire from ruin and dismemberment by putting down the resistance offered to the authority of the Sultan of Delhi by Kubacha, Yalduz and the Khilji governors of Bengal and Bihar. He extended the dominion by conquering Malwa and Sind. Later on, Balban, as a minister, crushed the rebellious Hindu kings and the Muslim governors and repelled the attacks of the Mongols. As a king, he reorganized the administration, strengthened the north-western frontiers of the empire and protected it from the raids of the Mongols, raised the royal dignity and struck deep the roots of Muslim power into the fertile soil of India. The last ruler of the dynasty was murdered and Jalal-ud-din Khilji became the Sultan of Delhi.

Delhi Sultanate Expansion and Consolidation : The Khilji Dynasty (1290-1320). The Khiljis retained the throne of Delhi for nearly thirty years. The most important and successful ruler of this dynasty was Allauddin Khilji (1296-1316). He made Muslim power more stable in India. By 1312, the kingdom of Delhi reached its zenith. Nearly the whole of India was under Allauddin Khilji. His empire extended from Lahore in the north to Dwara samudra in the south and from Gujarat in the west to Lakhnauti in the east. It was the first Muslim Empire that covered the whole of India. But this Empire lacked the elements of permanence, as its very vastness was the cause of its decay and decline. On account of continuous wars Allauddin Khilji did not get any time to unite the different parts of his empire into one organic whole, and consequently, the last years of his empire witnessed the unwieldly fabric crumb ling. However, the reign of Allauddin Khilji is significant for the following reasons:

Firstly, if he himself conquered and subjugated the Rajput kingdoms of Mewar, Ranthambhor, Gujarat, etc., his commander Malik Kafur conquered and annexed the Deccan kingdoms of Devagiri, Warangal and Madura. This ushered in an era of aggressive imperialism in the history of the Sultanate. *Secondly,* his abolition of the feudal system of administration led to the centralization of all kinds of authority in the hands of the Sultan of Delhi. *Thirdly,* his military government and reforms led to general prosperity and internal peace and security from external invasions. In view of his reforms, he may be said to deserve the title of a 'political economist'. *Fourthly,* he expounded the theory that the king was responsible for the good government of the country and as such he should not be bound by the verdict of the Muslim Ulamas." This was the commencement of the process of secularization of the state in India. The Khilji rule is, therefore significant in the medieval history of India, both for the territorial expansion and for the beginning of a new noble ideology in the realm of administrative doctrines. The last ruler of the Khilji dynasty was assassinated and Ghazi Malik ascended the throne as Ghiyas-ud-din Tughlaq.

Dynasty of Tughlaq (1320-1412) : Ghiyas-ud-din Tughlaq founded Tughlaq Dynasty. The Tughlaq Sultans rose into power as the great champions of the Muslim cause that was being seriously endangered at the time by converted Hindus like Malik Kafur and Malik Khusrau. The imperial policy of the Tughlaqs was different from that of the Khiljis. Allauddin was contented with the acknowledgment of his suzerainty by the Hindu monarchs of the South, whereas Ghias-ud-din and Muhammad Tughlaq both believed in the policy of conquest, subjugation and direct annexation. The Deccan kingdoms of Devagiri, Warangal and Dwarasamudra were all conquered and annexed. The empire of Delhi, thus, reached its widest territorial limits covering nearly the whole of India under the Tughlaq Sultans. It was divided into 23 provinces and included Punjab, U. P., Bihar, Bengal, Tirhut, Sind, Malwa, Gujarat and the Deccan. But its integrity and solidarity could not be maintained for long by the Tughlaqs.

The period of Muhammad Tughlaq's rule (1325-1351) is both interesting and instructive. The remarks that he was a "mixture of opposites" and a "compound of contradictions" do not appear to be true. He was a distinguished scholar and a man of ideas who introduced several schemes, such as, the transfer of capital, token currency and ambitious schemes of conquests. These schemes have been described as visionary and their failure is assigned to their impracticable character. This is far from the truth. His schemes which had nothing wrong in them show that he was capable of ingenious schemes and possessed a marvellous breadth of vision. Dr. Ishwari Prasad rightly remarks that his mistake lay in their execution rather than in their originality. However the civil administration that he organized, bears the stamp of his individuality, spirit of toleration and justice. The closing years of his reign witnessed widespread discontent and rebellion, and the seeds of the disintegration of the Delhi Empire then were sown. Bengal and Gujarat had become independent and the Bahamani Kingdom and Vijayanagar Empire were established in the Deccan.

Muhammad Tughlaq was succeeded by his cousin Firuz Tughlaq. During his rule (1351-1388) India enjoyed a remarkable spell of peace. He called bait to the policy of territorial extension and annexation. He let slip the provinces of Bengal and Sind and made little effort to recover Deccan. Though he could not shake off his bigotry and treated the Hindus and the Shias unjustly and harshly, he deserves our admiration for his administration. "He was the first Muslim king of India who had accepted the principle that the duties of a sovereign are not limited only to the protection of the person and property of his subjects but that the State must also adopt measures which contribute to their happiness and general welfare." He revised the entire penal code of the age and abolished some of the very brutal and inhuman punishments of the period. He made extensive arrangements for irrigating agricultural lands, reduced the taxes on land, revised the revenue regulations and abolished many other vexatious duties on small trades and professions. Education was encouraged and several schools and colleges were maintained by the State. Free education was provided to the people there. He was exceedingly fond of building new towns, palaces and mosques and planning gardens. He revived the Jagir and Slave systems that proved rather detrimental to the State.

Unfortunately, all the beneficent activities of Firuz Tughlaq could not stay the hand of disintegration and the Empire of the Tughlaqs was quickly broken down to pieces after his death. To make the situation worse, there appeared two Sultans of Delhi, within a short distance, at one and the same time and the Imperial Crown was tossed to and fro like a shuttlecock between the contending factions. It was at this time that Timur invaded India and attacked Delhi and converted it into shambles. His invasion struck a fatal blow on the tottering Tughlaq Empire.

Delhi Sultanate on Collapse

The Dynasty of Sayyid (1414-1451) : After the Tughlaqs, Sayyid Khizra Khan ascended the throne of Delhi and founded the Sayyid Dynasty. There were four rulers of the dynasty. V. A. Smith considers that Sayyid rulers never assumed the royal style or struck coins in their own names and their rule was confined to the walls of Delhi. During their reign rebellions broke out frequently in the whole of the empire. "The history of this dynasty is nothing but a record of marchings and counter marchings to get the allegiance of rebellious nobles and to collect the revenues of the State." The last ruler of this dynasty abdicated in 1451 in favour of Bahlol Lodi, who was the Governor of the Punjab.

The Dynasty of Lodi (1451-1526) : Bahlol Lodi founded the Lodi dynasty. When he became the Sultan, he suppressed all the disorder, and conquered Jaunpur which considerably strengthened his position. By his conquests of Kalpi, Dholpur, Bari, and Alapur, he partly recovered the former glory of Delhi Sultanate. He was succeeded by his son Nizam Khan who assumed the title of Sikandar Lodi. He was the most notable sovereign among the Lodis, but he was a staunch Muslim and persecuted the Hindus. However, he was a patron of learning. His death in 1517 was a signal for the disruption of the Delhi Empire. His successor Ibrahim Lodi was defeated by Babar on the historic plain of Panipat in 1526. It brought the Sultanate of Delhi to an end.

The forces of disintegration gained considerable speed during the period of the successors of the Tughlaqs. In course of time, the provincial governors established petty independent kingdoms on the ruins of the mighty Delhi Empire. The decline and disintegration of the Delhi Empire did not affect the political ascendancy of the Muslims; on the other hand, the rise of new Muslim kingdoms meant further consolidation of Muslim power.

During the early part of the sixteenth century before the advent of Babar, the whole of India was divided into four zones of independent kingdoms the northern belt of Muslim kingdoms comprised Sind, Multan, Delhi, Jaunpur and Bengal; the middle belt consisted of Gujarat, Malwa, Khandesh and Bahamani kingdoms. Wedged in between these two groups of Muhammedan powers were Hindu Rajput States of Marwar, Mewar, Bundelkhand, Gondwana and Orissa. In the south of the Muslim kingdom of Bahamani was the Hindu kingdom of Vijayanagar. The Mughals later on conquered these petty kingdoms and annexed them one after the other.

Significant Features

The Muslim conquest of India tells a different tale. The first salient feature is that the history of the Mohammedan rule in India is more a chronicle of kings, courts and conquests than of an organic or a national growth. It is the kings and their doings that fill page after page of Mohammedan history. The people and their culture do not very much matter and, therefore, are given a secondary place. Second characteristic of the. Muslim rule in India is that the early dynasties were short lived. Dynasty after dynasty tumbled down after ruling for a very short period. Their history is of unceasing round of valour, greatness, discord, degeneracy and decay. The third salient feature is that the Mohammedans were the first invaders of India who were not absorbed into the elastic and ever expanding Hindu fold. Many invaders before them the Greeks, Scythians, Mongolians, Parthians, etc. had been completely Hinduized in name, speech, manner, religion, dress and ideas a few generations after their settlement in India. In fact, they had lost themselves in the ocean of the Hindu community. But the Mohammedans ever remained a separate community in India. Islam, being a fiercely monotheistic religion, could not allow any compromise with polytheism or admit a plurality of deities.

The fact is that the assimilative power of the Hindu religion, which absorbed the ingredients of different and distinct sects making them its own parts, had disappeared by the time the Muslims entered India. Those very Hindus whose ancestors embraced foreigners, and offered them an honourables status in their society, now considered mere touch of a foreigner a grave sin. Therefore, there is no wonder if the Hindus and Muslims had to live in the same land without being able to mix together freely. Nothing has enabled them to bridge the gulf between them.

Though Pandit Nehru in his book, *Discovery of India*, has stated that the Muslim invaders were absorbed in India, their royal dynasties were completely Indianized and they considered India as their motherland, yet Sir Jadunath Sarkar's view about the Muslims in India deserves mention. He remarks that the Indian Muslims, throughout the succeeding centuries, turned towards a spot in Mecca, had their own law code, their own administrative system, their own language literature, shrines and saints. They never restricted themselves to India as is the case with the Hindus. They always looked to the countries outside India and sought models from Arabia Syria, Iran and Egypt. Moreover, they were frequently engaged in oppressing and persecuting the majority of the country with which they had cast their lot. The Hindus, on the contrary, in their zeal to absorb the Muslims, went so far as to make an *avatar* of the Emperor Akbar in the Allopanishad. But the Muslims neither yielded on the cardinal points of their faith nor accepted the few conventions needed to enter Hindu society. Moreover, of all the invaders in India, the Muslims were the only people, who led militant religious crusade upon India. They were full of religious zeal and had come to India with the definite idea of converting others to their own religion and not to be absorbed by others. In fact they were religion conscious.

The fourth feature is that, from 1200 to 1580 the Muslim State and society in India retained its original military and nomadic character, the ruling race lived merely like an armed camp in the land. As a matter of fact, "the Muslim settlers in India used to be in the land but not of it." They always preserved their exclusive identity in India, and in the twentieth century, India had to pay a very high price for it the partitioning of the country.

However, the great interaction of the different cultures Hindu and Muslim that took place in India has its own significance in history. The contact, fusion and synthesis of two different and dissimilar cultures is, according to John Marshall, not only remarkable and peculiarly instructive in the history of India but that of mankind also. The following causes contributed to the interaction between the Hindu and Muslim cultures.

Synthesis of Two Cultures

During the three hundred years of the rule of the Sultans of Delhi, the interaction between Hindu and Islamic cultures was mostly confined to the prosperous cities and well to do upper classes, but the Mughal period witnessed a remarkable Hindu Muslim synthesis. The following factors led to it.

Hindu Support for Peace, Law and Order : With all their limited resources the Muslim rulers in India found it difficult to establish a stable and efficient government in a vast foreign country like India. Though they had gained political sovereignty, they could not deprive the Hindus of their economic supremacy. Therefore, they had to seek the cooperation of the Hindus and depend considerably on their goodwill and support for a stable government, peace, law and order in the country.

The Muslim sovereigns had neither seasoned diplomats, nor experienced administrators, nor far sighted statesmen in their ranks. Their followers were neither farmers nor businessmen. In fact, the Muslim invaders did not bring with them merchants, agriculturists, artisans and clerks. The Hindus dominated the economic life of the country. Agriculture and business was controlled and managed by them. Clerks and accountants in government offices and revenue collectors in the villages were Hindus. Architecture was done by the Hindu artisans. Hindu Pandits offered advice to the Muslim judges in administering justice. The employment of the Hindus in civil administration and economic pursuits was a necessity of Muslim Government. Therefore the goodwill and support of the Hindus was indispensable for the Muslim monarchs.

Policy of Peace : The Muslim rulers could not afford to be always in a warlike mood for the establishment and, expansion of their kingdom in a foreign country like India. Psychologically the Muslim sovereigns could not constantly follow the policy of bitter animosity and persecution. After bloodshed and unmitigated tyranny, they had to act necessarily in the interest of their subjects for peace, prosperity and safety. Necessity compelled them to revert to the pursuit of acts of peaceful life.

Hindu Support Sought by Muslim Sovereigns for War Against Muslims : In the absence of a strong central power several independent Muslim kingdoms rose in prominence in distant provinces. Frequent wars were waged between the Sultans of Delhi and these independent provincial kingdoms. Thus, the Muslim rulers fought stubbornly the Muslims more than they fought the Hindus. The support and cooperation of the Hindus was sought by both sides. The needs of the time compelled the Muslim monarchs to favour the Hindus. Thus, various factors compelled even the most zealous and fanatical Muslim sovereigns to be favourably inclined towards the Hindus and their culture.

New Converts to Islam : Hindus converted to Islam, retained Hindu customs and manners in their new Muslim society. They, thus, indirectly endeavoured to diffuse Hindu cultural influence in the Islamic society.

Compromising Attitude of the Hindus : The Hindus realized the futility of waging wars with their Muslim masters. They surrendered to the political supremacy of the Muslim rulers, abandoned hostile attitude and began to lead a peaceful life. Besides this, they expressed a keen desire to compromise ,with and accommodate the Muslims in their country.

Rule of Hindu Muslim Intelligentsia : The intelligent and broad minded Hindus and Muslims realized the futility of war and persecution. Muslim scholars and saints began to study Hindu scriptures and mix freely with their Hindu brothers. Hindus also did not lag behind in the study of Muslim philosophy and the Quran. They were trying to understand each other and also to study the best elements of the culture of each other.

Religious Tolerarence Policy : With the exception of a few, the Muslim sovereigns adopted the policy of religious toleration. They patronized fine arts and encouraged literature of the Hindus as well as of the Muslims. Some of them went to the extent of adopting Hindu religious practices and undertaking pilgrimage to Hindu shrines.

Spirit of Mutual Harmony, Toleration and Cooperation : With the lapse of time a spirit of harmony, toleration, compromise and cooperation appeared gradually between the Hindus and the Muslims. This smoothed the path for the growth of amity between the two communities. Thus, various factors brought about the fusion of the Hindu and Muslim cultures.

Historians differ about the synthesis of these two cultures. Some scholars hold the opinion that the Hindu religion and society were influenced to the core by the forces of Islamic culture. Contrary to this is the opinion that the Hindu culture, instead of being influenced by Islam, had deeply impressed Islam and its followers. Dr. Tarachand in his book, *The Influence of Islam on Indian Culture,* has enthusiastically supported the former view. He remarks that the mutual intercourse led to mutual understanding. "Not only did Hindu religion, Hindu art, Hindu literature and Hindu science absorb Muslim elements, but the very spirit of Hindu culture and the very stuff of the Hindu mind were also altered." The latter view is advocated by scholars like E. B. Havell, Titus, Prof. S. R. Sharma and Dr. A. L. Srivastava. Titus in his book, *Indian Islam,* states that, "when all is said there seems to be little doubt that Hinduism has wrought a far greater change in Islam than Islam has wrought in Hinduism which still continues to pursue the even tenure of its way with a complacency and confidence that are amazing."

In spite of the political subjugation in the medieval age, India was culturally so much alive that it was like a tree which gives shade even to that person who cuts off its branches. E. B. Havell remarks, "Islam seized her political capitals, controlled her military forces and appropriated her revenues, but India retained what she cherished most, her intellectual empire, and her soul was never subdued." In matters of production and industrial organization, Islam did not compare favourably with what was achieved in India. Indian traditions, faiths and beliefs were still strong to resist the influence of Islam and its followers.

The political triumph of Islam did not lead to intellectual, moral or religious conquest. Whatever India lost in the battle fields was regained by her spiritual forces. The Hindus, even with the living example of brotherhood and equality in the Muslim community before their own eyes, did not relax in the least their social rigidity and inequality of men exemplified in the caste system and untouchability. The reciprocal influences of the Hindus and Muslims were too superficial in character to affect materially the fundamental differences between the two communities.

However, the truth lies between the two views. The interaction or fusion of the two cultures was never rendered complete. 'The Islamic culture could never transform entirely the Hindu culture. Whatever their mutual influence was exercised or synthesis achieved, was mostly confined to external phases of life, especially the urban life. The spirit of India and the character of her culture could never be altered completely by Islam. An account of the synthesis of Hindu Muslim cultures will be given in the succeeding paragraphs.

Nature of State and Government

General Features : The Muslim rulers of India were poor administrators and they lacked constructive genius. They failed to establish in the country an efficient system of administration. As noted above, the character of the administration was devised only to meet the requirements of the daily routine of administration. There were neither large administrative units like the Subahs or well organised assessment of land or the collection of revenues as was under the Mughals. On the contrary, the administrative methods were rude and oppressive. The whole empire was in fact a congeries of nearly independent states. The control of the king over the distant provinces was not based on any uniform principle of cohesion; but it varied from nominal allegiance to complete subjection and dependence on the personality of the Sultan. "As the country was held in military occupation, the length of the King's sword was the limit of his sway." The ambitious and powerful governors often looked upon the throne of Delhi as the ultimate goal of their ambition.

As there was no definite rigid law of succession, the death of the Sultan generally meant a signal for civil war. Jalal-ud-din Khilji, Ghiyas-ud-din Tughlaq and Bahlol Lodi all became

Sultans by driving the legal heirs away. Such absence of the law of succession often meant anarchy and it introduced the law of survival of the fittest; and the fittest was the one who could kill at once all other claimants to the throne. This, therefore, made the lives of those who participated in politics, nasty, brutish and short. However, one can say that the succession to the throne was elective. It frequently rested on the choice of the feudal lords and nobles, and it was often seen that the person who was elected was not necessarily a relative of his predecessor.

Monarchy at the Centre : The Muslim State in medieval India was a strong military theocracy. The Sultan was Caesar and Pope combined in one. He exercised the powers of an absolute autocrat. His will was absolute. But his authority was supposed to be limited by the Holy Quran. The hostility of the Hindu States and the Hindu fighting communities, absence of hereditary Muslim aristocracy and popular assemblies and want of strong public opinion made the Sultan a strong autocrat who favoured a powerful centralized monarchy. The Sultan was regarded as the representative of God upon earth and he governed in accordance with the wishes of the priestly class, the Ulamas, who naturally possessed an enormous influence in such a State. Allauddin Khilji and Muhammad Tughlaq were exceptions to this rule.

The Muslim Kings of India were sovereigns in their own persons. Instead of acknowledging the Khalifa's power, they struck their own coins and caused the 'khutbah' to be read in their own names and thus declared their independent sovereign authority. Some of them like Muhammad Tughlaq took the title of Sultan Zilab Ullah or Sultan, the Shadow of God.

Much of the success or failure of the kingdom depended upon the personality of' the Sultan. A strong ruler like Allauddin Khilji could bring under his control the powerful nobles and Ulamas. But under a weak ruler the nobles and provincial governors attempted to establish their independent kingdoms. As there was no law of succession, no Sultan felt safe on the throne of Delhi. Even during the reign of a powerful Sultan like Allauddin several attempts were made to put him to death and seize the throne of Delhi.

The mainstay of the Muslim State was the military class composed of the Muslims alone. The State being essentially military in character, the Sultan was the chief commander of forces, the chief law giver and the final court of appeal. For the control of the vast empire, curbing of the power of the feudal lords, suppression of provincial and inter provincial revolts and opposition of the external invasions, the Sultan maintained a huge standing army. Besides the standing army, the feudal lords and nobles supplied the Sultan with a large number of soldiers whenever he needed them.

Relation with Non-Muslims : The Muslims were the favoured children of the State and were always given preferential treatment. They monopolized all the high offices of the State, whereas the Hindus were not even recruited in the army, in spite of their having such a desire. They suffered many disabilities and had to pay frequently a special tax known as the *Jizya* or the poll tax for the protection of their lives and properties. The payment of *Jizya* was associated with humiliation and degradation. It was also collected very rigidly. Sometimes they were forcibly converted to Islam. Most of the Sultans could not rise above their narrow bigotry and religious fanaticism. They neither sought the cooperation of their Hindu subjects, nor allowed them to worship in their own way publicly. On the contrary, they tried to crush them in every possible way.

The Muslim occupation of India was, therefore, clearly marked by a spirit of intolerance and narrow mindedness which was responsible for the instability of the Muslim kingdoms. "Toleration under Muslim domination in India in the early medieval ages was not the rule but the exception." The Muslim rulers at best were like an armed camp in the land. They, together with the Muslim divines aimed at reducing the Hindus to the position of mere hewers of wood and drawers of water. However, there was no continuous planned suppression and no systematic attempt for the extermination of the Hindus.

Expansion of Islam : The progress of Islam in India was due vary largely to the fact that it was the religion of the dominant power which sometimes enforced it at the point of the sword among the subject races. The number of the followers of Islam multiplied rapidly during the first three hundred years of the Muslim rule. Various factors contributed towards this increase. Motives of personal gain, such as the desire to obtain high office in the State, sometimes led men to abandon their own faith. Daily contact with the Muslims, who naturally wielded great influence and power and controlled the wealth, must have induced some to accept Islam. The degrading position assigned to some in the Hindu social system, which made invidious distinctions between man and man, must have forced them to embrace Islam and be exempted from the payment of *Jizya.* Voluntary conversions to Islam, grounded on the appreciation of its tenets, were few and far between. Many times forcible conversions were ordered by the Muslim State authorities leading to the spread of Islam rapidly.

The Administration

Central Government : There was a regular hierarchy of officers in charge of various departments who carried out their respective duties according to the Sultan's order who was, generally, the pivot of the whole administrative machinery. The Sultan carried on the administration with the help of his ministers. The *Wazir* was the chief minister whose powers were not defined. These depended on his own abilities as well as the character of the Sultan. Generally, he was in charge of the finance department and exercised supervision over all the other civil departments of the government.

There were five main departments Revenue, War, Local and Provincial Governments, Markets and Agriculture, and Justice. The *Diwan-i-Wazarat* or Revenue Minister dealt mainly with finance. He controlled and supervised the work of the

Amirs or tax collectors, and determined the share of the State in the produce. The *Ariz-i-Mamalik or* the Minister in charge of the department of war looked after the recruitment of the army and feudal contingents and organized the transport and commissariat. The *Diwan-i-Insha or* the minister in charge of the provincial government was to be in touch with governors of the districts and provinces. He was to receive their communications, put them before the Sultan and take his orders thereon.

The minister in charge of the markets etc. issued licences to traders. He got octroi duties collected, and dealt with famine and other cognate questions of the kingdom. The minister of Justice or Chief Sadar supervised the work of the *Qazis* who administered justice and other officers associated with the Department of Justice. He also looked after the Department called *Diwan-i-Rasalat* which dealt with religious matters and endowments.

The Royal Household : There were many important officers of the royal household. The chief official was called the *Wakil-i-Dar.* He controlled the entire royal household, including the royal kitchen, the stables and the *sharabkhana.* Another important officer was the *Amir-i-Hajib,* who was the master of ceremonies at the court.

Source of Revenue : Land revenue, irrigation cess, one fifth of the spoils of war, import duties and other taxes like the house tax, grazing tax, water tax and poll lax or *Jizya* formed the important sources of revenue. The demand for land revenue was one fifth of the produce but later on raised to one half.

Police and Judicial System : Justice was administered by the *Qazi-ul-Quzat* or the Lord Chief Justice, aided by *Muftis. Qazis* dispensed justice in cities and provinces. The *Muhtasib,* an officer of the municipal police, kept a strict watch on the moral conduct of the people. The *Kotwal,* in charge of the police department, was the custodian of peace and order. The Penal Law was excessively severe, the penalties of mutilation and death being usually inflicted on the culprits.

The Army : It consisted of the royal bodyguard, and the troops of the capital reinforced by the levies sent by the provincial viceroys and the contingents of Hindus troops. The main branches of the army were the infantry including archers, the cavalry, and the elephants. There was nothing like artillery which came to be used in later times. But the cavalry formed the back bone of the army.

Court : The Delhi Sultans maintained a court. But it was not so splendid as that of the great Mughals. Culture of a rather limited type was patronized in these courts.

Administration in Provinces : Each province was a 'replica of the empire', and was placed in charge of a great noble who exercised absolute power within his jurisdiction. Provincial governorship practically amounted to vice royalties which tended to be hereditary. The provincial governors were required to defend the frontiers and to manage their internal affairs. The relation with that Sultan consisted mainly in paying the tribute regularly and tendering homage respectfully. Occasionally, they had to provide military aid. When these services were performed regularly and properly, the governors were left undisturbed in their provinces and there was nothing to limit their powers.

The constant intrigues of the nobles, and lack of healthy cooperation among the officers generally hampered the good working of the provincial government, and consequently, peace and order were not perfectly maintained. The control of the Sultan over the provincial governments was lax and ill defined, and the absolute power with which the governors were entrusted very often induced them to defy the central imperial authority. Each province was divided into *shiqqs* which, in their turn, were divided into *parganas,* collections of villages.

Local Administration : There is, however, one redeeming feature in the administration of Muslim kings and that is, they did not disturb the ancient local institutions of the people of the land. The village with its self governing institutions remained untouched. The officers of the State never interfered in the normal working of the rural administration, nor was it affected in any way by the political revolutions and civil wars at Delhi. The village republics were left undisturbed and independent in the management of their own affairs. Local administration was left discretely to the village panchayats.

The Nobility of Muslim Class : The Muslim nobility wielded "a predominant influence in the State as generals, administrators and sometimes as king makers. But it was not a hereditary homogeneous and well organized body." Though the turks formed the majority in the nobility, there were in it also men of other foreign nationalities, like Arabs, Afghans, Abyssinians, Egyptians etc. Some Indian nobles also held high positions. Such a heterogeneous class could never be expected to work with common aim or principle and provide a healthy or sound check to absolutism of the Sultans. "The nobility was nothing but a mere agglomeration of disintegrating atoms which failed to evolve a workable constitution of the country."

Criticism : The Turko-Afghan machinery of administration, as outlined briefly above, lacked the general will of the nation, and the habitual obedience of the people, derived from tradition. Its theocratic, military and feudal character was opposed to the traditional ancient government of the land. By the nature of its growth, it could seldom be established on the goodwill and support of the people. In fact, a tie of mutual attachment between the rulers and the masses was in many cases absent. There was a wide gulf between the ruler and the ruled.

The state grew on military strength, its rulers were mainly concerned to adopt measures to safeguard and strengthen their own authority and its aristocracy, having no consistent policy, pursued selfish interest and in course of time grew more ambitious and turbulent. Such a state could not but collapse.

The Economy

The State did not pursue any comprehensive sound economic policy which aimed at the improvement of the general condition of the people. Though the Khiljis and the Tughlaqs made a few experiments, they did not produce permanent results. "On the whole, any big improvement in the method of production, a more equitable distribution of the economic wealth or a better adjustment of the economic position of the various social classes, was outside the policy of the State." Most of the Sultans did not consider it their duty to devote their energy and attention or utilize State resources for the economic prosperity and general benefit of the people. However, the Sultans of Delhi and the minor provincial rulers and governors encouraged industries and trade not for general economic prosperity but for their own political and administrative needs. But, there were no factories or big manufacturing concerns or large scale industrial organizations as India has today.

Though agriculture formed the occupations of the bulk of the people of the land, there were some important industries in the urban as well as rural areas of the country. There were the textile industries (manufacture of cotton, woollen and silk cloth), metal, stone and brick works, and the industries of paper, dyeing and sugar. There were minor industries making cups, shoes, and arms. Manufacture of scents, spirits and liquors, etc., was also very popular.

The volume of India's internal trade was large except when thwarted by the monopoly of the State or rigid administrative control. As regards her external trade she had commercial relations with the distant regions of Europe, the Malaya Islands and China, and other countries of the east or the Pacific Ocean. Through her ancient land routes, India had her commercial intercourse with Central Asia, Afghanistan, Persia, Tibet and Bhutan. The chief imports were articles of luxury, horses and mules; and the main exports consisted of varieties of agricultural goods and textile manufactures. Opium and indigo were exported in large quantities. Some countries situated round the Persian Gulf in the west were entirely dependent on India for their food supply. Indian goods were exported chiefly from the harbours of Gujarat and Bengal.

As regards the standard of living of the different classes, the difference between that of the wealthier classes and of the peasants in the country was "almost antipodal". The nobility and the ruling and official classes enjoyed high standard of living. They rolled in opulence and luxury, but the peasants had a very low standard of living. Probably the incidence of taxation weighed heavily on them and their condition became miserable in times of famine or scarcity caused by drought or heavy rains. Farmers of medieval India do not seem to have been much better off than their descendants of modern times. But, judged by modern standards, they had fewer needs.

As the village was economically self-sufficient, the simple requirements of the rural population were supplied locally to their satisfaction. Again, in spite of political revolutions and conspiracies at the metropolis, the villagers followed their ordinary usual occupation of life in utter disregard and indifference to the political upheavals. Court politics seldom disturbed the even tenor of village life.

Cultural Assimilation

As noted above, so immense was the assimilative potentiality of the old Hindu culture and civilization that the earlier invaders of India like the Greeks, the Sakyas, the Huns, etc., were easily absorbed within the fold of her population, and in due course they completely lost their identity. But it did not happen so with the Turko-Afghan invaders of the country. In the wake of Muslim invasions new, different and definite social and religious ideas were brought into India and it was not possible to achieve a perfect absorption of these conceptions. Simple, clear cut, and aggressive Islam had nothing in common with the elaborate, ritualistic and absorptive Hinduism. Its well defined social system, philosophy, laws, and a strong monotheistic outlook made its absorption in Hinduism impossible. But it is a fact of history that whenever two different types of civilization and culture come into close contact with each other and remain associated for centuries, both are bound to be influenced mutually.

Thus, long association, the growth of the converted Indo-Muslim community and its mixing freely with the Hindu community, the demand for peace, justice, security, and proper government, the spirit of tolerance, the desire to admire and assimilate each other's customs, broader and tolerating outlook of the Hindu and Muslim saints and their attempts to unify the two communities, the Muslim rulers' liberal patronage to fine arts and letters, and the influence of several liberal movements in medieval India, led the Hindu and the Muslim communities to imbibe each other's thoughts, traditions and customs, and consequently many important social changes took place.

Political Subjection and Social Degradation of the Hindus, but their Predominating Influence Continued : The Hindus, under Muslim domination, fretted and chaffed at the loss of their political power. Their political subjection was followed by social degradation. They were looked upon as the worst enemies of the alien government that had been established in their midst. They were over taxed, were excluded, with rare exceptions, from high offices, were treated with severity, and reduced to a state of abject misery, and had to live like helots within the empire. Allauddin's aim was to reduce the Hindus to such a condition that they should not be able to ride on horseback, wear fine clothes, carry arms and enjoy luxury. They had to groan under heavy religious disabilities, had to suffer active persecution frequently and were usually required to pay a special *tax* called *Jizya.* Some of the Hindus embraced Islam to escape this tax. Under such circumstances, the Hindu talent naturally became stunted and dwarfed, and got little or no opportunity of developing to its fullest extent in the sphere of politics.

In spite of all this, the structure of economic life in the country was dominated by the Hindus. It was the Muslim army that occupied Delhi and destroyed the Hindu monarchies. The Muslim invaders did not bring with them cultivators, and though the lands were given in *jagir* to the Amirs, the cultivating class remained Hindu. Nor was conversion on such an elaborate scale as to displace the Hindu zamindar and the Hindu cultivator. The land system in fact did not change and, therefore, the Hindus in general in the country led fairly the same life as they had led before in spite of the Muslim domination.

Again, commerce and trade did not change hands to any considerable extent. The Muslim invaders were military adventurers who despised trade and failed to understand the elaborate Hindu credit system on which the business of the whole country was based. The commercial classes were undoubtedly mulcted heavily under the Muslim rule, but the Hindu *Baniya* or merchant remained, as now, a necessary element in the structure of the society in medieval age. He advanced money to artisans farmers, and others to obtain the merchandise required for internal consumption or foreign export.

The *Baniyas* of Gujarat used to do business all over the coast of India and even had commercial dealings in Persia and Arabia. Among them were many rich merchants, for instance, Virji Vora (1619-1670) controlled the entire trade of Surat and a large portion of the coastal trade of Malabar. He had his establishments in Agra, Burhanpur, Golconda and traded with the Persian Gulf and the Indian Archipelago. According to There not, the French traveller, who visited India in the seventeenth century, Virji Vora was considered to be the richest man in the world. The Muslims, however intolerant had to treat the Hindu mercantile community with consideration, though it was inspired by self-interest and often grudgingly. Allauddin Khilji, when organizing his economic reforms, had to depend upon the Hindu nayaks for grain and the Hindu merchants of Multan for cloth. Barni refers to the economic influence of the Hindus. Thus, while a certain section of the Muslim community dominated the administrative mechinery, the Hindus had monopolistic control of the economic life of the country.

Besides this, the lower ranks of the bureaucracy had of necessity to be Hindus during the Muslim rule. The Muslims being the favoured children of the State were accorded a preferential treatment. They monopolized the higher offices, but being unskilled administrators the lower rungs of officialdom had of necessity to be Hindus. The patwaris, the accountants, the treasurers and others in the districts were invariably Hindus, while the governors, police officials, judges and district officials were all Muslims. In spite of the Muslim delineation the employment of the Hindu bureaucracy continued. Moreover, the despotism and wrath of the Delhi Sultans used to fall mainly on the courtries, nobles, and provincial governors. This led to feudal disputes, atrocities and continuous revolts of the governors. Consequently, the Sultans had to carry on constant campaigns against the Muslim nobles, governors and their armies. This rendered the Central Government weak, but it hardly affected the Hindus. They were left a great deal more to themselves in the rural areas.

As regards religion, one is surprised to note that in face of Islam's conquest of north India the Hindu religion was strong enough to maintain its hold on the minds of the people. Everything was open to a Hindu who embraced Islam. He could get the highest office of the State if he deserved so. Some of the highest officers including Malik Kafur, Khusrau, etc. were Hindus converted to Islam. With the short cut to prosperity and power so clearly marked out for the converts, it is surprising that Muslims today in Uttar Pradesh which was continuously under the rule of the Muslim sovereigns for six hundred years, number only fourteen per cent. Hindu religion withstood the shock of Islam.

It continued to survive. Even more than this, under the

most bigoted Sultans like Allauddin and Firuz Tughlaq, the Hindu religious leaders and saints received royal honour and recognition. Jain sources enable us to know that Sultan Allauddin Khilji held religious discourses with Acharya Mahasena who was brought from Karnataka for the purpose. It is also reported that the Digambara Jain saint Purna Chandra of Delhi and the Swetambara ascetic Ramchandra Suri were in favour with the same Sultan. Ghiyas-ud-din Tughlaq had two Jain officers who exercised great influence over him, while Firuz held in high honour the poet Ratnasekhara.

Though the plight of the Hindus was miserable, their depression did not last very long. Resistance to Muslim invasions during the days of conquest was organized by the Rajputs and kept up with continuous heroism for a period of four hundred years. After the fall of the Chauhans of Delhi at the hands of Muhammad Ghori, the Hindu leadership was claimed by the Sisodia Dynasty of Mewar.

Its famous ruler Kumbha (1443-1468) and his successors were the champions of Hindu revival which apart from saving large areas from Muslim conquest put heart into the Hindu people of other areas in northern India. Beyond Rajasthan, Hindu influence also began to assert itself and by the fourteenth century even in the Gangetic Valley the great Hindu landlords or zamindars had come to have enough influence, power and authority to rebel against the Imperial Government when it became weak; and we have evidence to prove that the Sultan had to put down with a strong hand the revolts of zamindars.

Impact of Hindus Culture on Muslim Society

In the early centuries of the Muslim rule, Mohammedans lived in India as a garrison in a hostile country, holding little or no intercourse with their Hindu subjects. But it was inevitable that with the lapse of time the barriers between the two should be relaxed if not broken down entirely. Consequently, the mutual intercourse between the two communities influenced the culture of both. The following paragraphs will reveal how the Muslim society was influenced by the Hindus and their religion. Being the subjects of Muslim State, the Muslims were the favoured children of the State, while the Hindus suffered many disabilities. Most of the high offices of the State were reserved for the Mohammedans. However, the easy acquisition of the enormous wealth and the participation in the festivities of the court led to great vices among the Muslims and made the ruling class lead a life of luxury and pleasure. This sapped the manliness and vigour of the Muslim community.

Many Muslim conquerors married Hindu women, queens and princesses. Allauddin married the Hindu princess Kamla Devi, wife of Karna Deva, the Raja of Gujarat, and later on her daughter by the first marriage was wedded to his eldest son Khizr Khan. The Hindu women introduced their social customs and rites to their new homes. The influence of the Hindu women in Mohammedan harems was one of the factors which brought reconciliation between Islam and Hinduism. Havell observes: "The traditional devotion and the tenderness of Indian motherhood helped greatly to soften the ferocity of the Turki and Mughal Domads." Some scholars are of the opinion that Muslim morality was highly influenced by Hindu thoughts and customs. "Muslims became practically monogamous by a curious process which made divorce impossible. Remarriage of widows became rare under Hindu influence."

Apart from this, contact with Hindu society brought about the rise of class distinctions and differences among the Muslims. Some of the Sultans of Delhi appointed only men of noble birth to high offices. Balban, the famous slave Sultan, never countenanced upstarts. The conception of caste was gradually developed among the Muslims. Mutual contact developed new castes and sub castes. Various classes of the Muslims began to reside separately in different localities even in the same town, for example, Shaikhs and Sayyids. In the days of Delhi Sultans, a Turk, a Pathan, a Sayyid, or even a Shaikh would not think of matrimonial relations with a person of a lower rank, that is, one outside these four *dhats* or *quams*, or even outside his own particular denomination.

The lower functional groups were organized on the model of the Hindu caste system with their *panchayats* or caste councils and officers to enforce the observance of caste rules by the time honoured sanction of boycotting. Mutual jealousies among the foreign and Indian Muslim nobles and Amirs of the Sultan developed caste like groups in the higher and aristocratic Muslim society. The conception of untouchability evolved in due course in the Muslim society. The lower caste persons of the Hindu society were converted to Islam in large numbers due to the tyranny of the caste system, the prospects of escape from the poll tax and other social advantages. These new converts were treated like untouchables in the Muslim society.

They were given neither any share in the administration nor any place in the Muslim aristocracy. They were neither treated on a footing of equality with other Muslims nor could enjoy power with higher Muslims. These newly converted Muslims were not admitted into the aristocracy of the Turkish or Afghan conquerors. They were not given a share in their social and economic privileges. They constituted a separate and distinct class in the general Muslim population. Many of them followed handicrafts and were employed by the conquerors as artisans. Many of them were weavers, washermen, barbers, carpenters, black smiths, tailors, wood cutters, water carriers, engravers, painters, illuminators, physicians, etc. In course of time they developed their own class distinctions, like those of the Hindu caste system. They retained their Hindu mode of life to a great extent and avoided the eating of beef and widow remarriage, and continued to express reverence to local gods in subdued tone. Even today Muslim villagers consult the Hindu astrologer and propitiate the local gods in times of troubles.

It has been said that many features in the princely life and court ceremonies were borrowed by the Muslim rulers from the Hindus. They were probably adopted on account of the presence of the Hindu nobles and officials of the higher services in the Muslim courts. The gorgeous paraphernalia of the courts of the Rajput princes was borrowed by the Muslim rulers. The royal custom of *nyochhawar*, passing over of the gold and silver coins thrice over the head of the ruler and offering them to the menials and poor persons, was a Hindu court etiquette followed by the Muslims.

The adoption of a new court etiquette led to the growth of particular seating arrangements in the court for different classes of orders. They were classified into *Ahl-i-daulat*, the ruling class proper, *Ahl-i-saadat, the intelligentsia*, and *Ahl-i-murad* or the pleasure seeking class. As wealth Increased in the Muslim court and society, the hold of religion became somewhat weaker and, consequently, superstition, ignorance and evil practices began to gain ground. Sultan Firuzshah in his *Fatuhat-i-Firuzshahi* refers to several heretical sects which he suppres sed with a high hand and the leaders of which he caused to be imprisoned or put to death. Muslim festivals were celebrated with pomp and display like Hindu festivals.

The festival of *Shab-i-Barat* was celebrated like *Sivaratri* of the Hindus, with a night long vigil, bustle and noise. The ceremonies of *Aqiqa* and *Bismillah* were observed in the same way as the Hindu *Mundan* and *Vidyarambh sanskar*. Hindu marriage ceremonies influenced the marriage cere monies of the Muslims, especially the decoration and dowry of the bride. The *haft-o-nuh* is only another name of the *solah sringar* of a Hindu bride ibn Batuta refers to some of the Indian marriage customs while describing the marriage of a sister of Muhammad Tughlaq with an Arab named Saif-ud-din. The Hindu superstition of the evil eye *(nazar)*, *'the uttara'* and the ceremony of *arti*, which was termed by the Muslims *nisar*, had taken deep root in the Muslim society. The ceremony of *nisar* was performed by taking platefuls of gold and silver coins or precious jewels and passing them repeatedly (not less than seven times) over the head of the sovereign and then they were scattered or distributed among the poor persons, beggars, or any other assemblage of servants.

Muslim intellectuals and religious leaders' were profoundly impressed by the Vedantic and Yogic systems of Hindus. The mysticism of Islam in its Indian environment was not quite the same as the Sufis of the Islamic lands. The Muslim mystics under the influence of mysticism helped to shorten the distance between those who emphasized the ethical or metaphysical aspects of their faiths. The Hindus had cultivated the institution of hereditary *moths* with their *Gurus* and *Chelas.* The Muslims adopted it for their saints and evolved the office of the *Pit* or *Shaikh* and his descendants. Like the Hindus, the Muslims began to keep faith in vows *(manatas* or *minnats)* and they approached Hindu *Yogis* and *Sadhus* or hermits for the fulfilment of their long cherished desires.

Muslim sovereigns like Muhammad Tughlaq went with gifts to Hindu saints and sages to get their innermost desire fulfilled. Offerings were made to some *PITS* like *Manik Pit, Ghora Pit, Kumbhira Pit,* and *Maddari PIT,* for the fulfilment of one's desires. Milk and fruits were offered to *Manik PITS* and clay horses were offered to *Ghora Pit* so that the lame babies might get cured on account of the blessings of the *PIT.* Some eatables and meat were given to *Kumbhira Pit* (crocodiles).

As regards idol worship, Indian Muslims have been nearer to the Hindus of India, as compared to the Muslims of foreign countries. The reverence for and worship of tombs of *PITS* or saints is seen among Indian Muslims. Worship of the *Pit* is another form of Hindu practice of *Guru Puja.* The Muslims perform rites at the tombs of the *PITS* or saints who are believed to have the power of averting disease or disaster or any other evil. Muslims paid visits to the tombs of the saints and tied strings or ribbons on their mausoleum for attaining their desires. This is an age old practice of the Hindus.

There are references to the Rajput *Jauhar* custom adopted by the Muslims.Kamaluddin, the Governor of Bhatnair and his followers advanced to fight Timur after burning their women folk and their property. The Muslims adopted many Hindu customs of daily routine life. The Hindu turban became very popular among the Muslims. The Muslim rulers and nobles had to modify their dress to suit Indian environment and climate. The Hindu habit of daily bath and personal hygiene before performing any religious ceremony was followed by the Mohammedans. Many salient features of Hindu festivals and ceremonies were assimilated in the Muslim society. According to Ashraf, *Shab-e-Barizt,* the 'Guy Fawkes Day of Islam', is copied from the Hindu festival of *Sivaratri* as noted above. It was readily spread far and wide. It has been said that the Muslims in India admired and assimilated Hindu customs and traditions to such an extent that the pious Muslim invader Timur made it an excuse for attacking the territory of the Muslim kingdom of Delhi. In the realm of administration, the Muslim rulers retained infect many of the Hindu institutions of government specially in the departments of revenue and finance.

They followed the Hindu practice of using war elephants in open battles. In view of the above stated facts Titus has rightly remarked in his book, *Indian Islam,* that "Hinduism has wrought a far greater change in Islam than Islam has wrought in Hinduism." Though the political subjugation and humiliation of the Hindus could not break their belief in their cultural and racial superiority and they looked down on their foreign conquerors with deep contempt and treated them as *mlechhas* or untouchables, they assimilated some features of the culture of the new conquerors.

Islamic Impact on Hindu Society

In fact the Hindu society could not remain unaffected by social customs and religion of its new rulers. The Muslim occupation of India accelerated certain undesirable tendencies that had already manifested themselves in the Hindu society on the eve of the Muslim conquest. The following examples will bear testimony to this statement. The birth of a girl was looked upon as an inauspicious event. Consequently, infanticide spread widely among the Hindus. It was a measure adopted by the Hindus so that their virgins might not run the risk of losing their chastity at the hands of the Muslims. Many Hindu chiefs and well to do persons were compelled to offer their daughters in marriage to the. Turkish Sultans, their nobles and followers.

The *purda* system, seclusion of women, unknown in early days of Hindu rule, was introduced elaborately into the Hindu society and women generally lived in seclusion in the sphere of their homes. They now moved outside their houses in palanquins covered with curtains. In the royal harems of the Hindu rulers and princes, the *purdah* system was rigidly enforced. We have references to the queens of Raja Rudra Pratap of Puri who used to visit Chaitanya in covered palanquins. Child marriage was introduced in the society and it was said that the proper age of marriage for girls was seven, and that a marriage after the age of eleven or twelve was sinful. Early marriage of the Hindu girls to avoid their kidnapping by the Muslims became the fashion of the day.

The missionary zeal of Islam which aimed at converting the Hindus, compelled the Hindus to be orthodox in outlook and practice to save their religion and culture from the onslaught of Islam. So attempts were made to make caste rules more rigorous and daily rules of conduct more rigid. The numerous social taboos and restrictions regarding caste, marriage, eating and drinking had become all the more stringent among the Hindus. It is true that such a social structure was incapable of any progress; its very rigidity and stiffness served as a strong cordon which protected the Hindus from being submerged entirely in the new Islamic culture.

The condition of the Hindu women deteriorated considerably. Dependence of women on their husbands or other male relatives became a prominent feature of the Hindu society. Though they enjoyed a position of respect, they could not command equal rights with men and were not allowed to participate in the social functions and ceremonies. Women were expected to observe strict fidelity in their conjugal life. To safeguard their honour and chastity against the Muslims the customs of *Jauhar* and *Sati* both were widely prevalent throughout the country among the Hindus. But, according to Ibn Batuta, a sort of permit had to be obtained from the Sultan of Delhi before the burning of a wife on the pyre of her husband.

An unhealthy feature of social life that crept into the Hindu society due to the Muslims was slavery. Slavery was common in the Muslim society and to keep slaves was a recognized fashion of the time. It was a well known common practice with the Delhi Sultans, their nobles and Amirs to maintain slaves both male as well as female. The number of royal slaves was generally large. It is reported that Allauddin had 84,000 slaves and their number rose to 2,00,000 under Sultan Firuz Tughlaq. Besides a pretty large number of Indian slaves, many male and female slaves were imported from foreign countries, like Persia, China, and Turkistan, and all these were maintained by the Sultans at the cost of the State. Hindu leaders and feudal lords adopted the institution of slavery. The royal harems and palaces in Rajasthan even in twentieth century practised the system of slavery. Women slaves were offered in dowry among the Rajput royal families. The institution of slavery might have served certain useful purpose of service and pecuniary gains for the kings and amirs, but it produced some baneful social results. In fact, it was a stamp of unprogressiveness, inhuman feature and unhealthy element in the society.

Another result of the contact with the Muslims was that Mohammedan dress, etiquette and ceremonial came into fashion in the Hindu society. *Achakan* and *salwar*, popular dress in northern India, was introduced in Hindu society under Mohammedan influence. Muslim nobles, feudal lords and aristocrats generally leading a more luxurious life than Hindus set new fashions which were copied by the rich Hindu classes. Sumptuous dinners were the fashion of the day among rich communities. Gambling and wine drinking, which were the common vices of the Muslim society of the age, were followed by the Hindus. Recreational life and activity were influenced by Islamic contact. Hunting, hawking, and many other games became Mohammedanized. Hindu rulers adopted the Muslim etiquette and seating arrangement for various classes as practised in the Delhi court. The art of warfare was also influenced and developed as a result of Islamic contact. The introduction of artillery and a new mode of warfare, revolutionized the system of defence which the Hindu Rajput rulers were now able to put up in their strong forts of Rajasthan and other inaccessible regions.

Another social result of the introduction of Islam and Muslim rule in India as pointed out by K. M. Panikkar was the division of society on a vertical basis. Before the thirteenth century, Hindu society was divided horizontally. Neither Buddhism nor Jainism could effect this division but both were easily assimilated. On the contrary, Islam split Indian society into two distinct divisions from top to bottom Hindus and Muslims. In due course, these two sections evolved as two separate nations in the same country. Seeds were sown in the medieval age for the two nation theory. Two parallel societies were vertically established on the same soil. At an stages they were different in all walks of life. Besides this, the prose stytizing zeal of Islam strengthened bonds of conservatism in the ortho dox circles of the Hindu society.

The Hindus became more orthodox in their outlook and practice than what they were in the past. To fortify their position against the propagation and spread of Islam, the Hindus increased to a great extent the stringency of many social taboos and caste rules. New rigid rules of conduct, diet, marriage and religious rites and ceremonies were prescribed. They formulated a large number of rules in the *Smriti* works to strengthen the Hindu social body.

The increased rigidity of the caste system and new regulations produced far reaching consequences in the Hindu society. First, it was possible to safeguard Hindu culture against the alien Islamic culture. Secondly, initiative and continuous progress disappeared from the life of the Hindus. Their social structure was rendered incapable of any growth. Thirdly, lower castes found their lot more miserable. They were being crushed between the milestones of social and religious tyranny of the higher classes and the politico-religious tyranny of the Muslim fanatics.

Therefore conversion to Islam was an easy escape from such suffocating and soul crushing atmosphere. Some liberal Hindu leaders and reformers were opposed to the Decreased conservatism of the Hindu society and rigidity of the caste system. They favoured concessions to the higher classes who were reclaimed to the Hindu society. They borrowed some democratic principle of Islam and advocated equality of castes. They declared that caste was not a bar to salvation and, thus, promoted the growth of a popular and liberal religion especially the *Bhakti* cult.

Hindu society was confronted at this time with the problem of social adjustment. The Islamic invasions necessitated the Hindu social reconstruction. Defensively the Hindu society was to be strengthened and the *Smritis* to be recast to make apostasy difficult, and at the same time to make provision for taking those back into society who were forcibly removed from it. Consequently, for defensive purposes society became more rigid in its rules and regulations, more violent in its reactions towards non-conformity; in fact, it became reactionary. On the other hand, it attempted to find a solution for problems which the original law givers could not have dreamt of. It is not surprising, therefore, if we find voluminous commentaries on the *Smritis* and *Nibandhas* (digests) by the Hindus during the period between 1200-1500. To put it plainly, this period was the heyday of writers on *Smritis,* as the adjustment of social relationships had become an important problem. Deval who flourished in Sind and Medhadhiti, who himself had witnessed the Muslim raids, had to deal with the problem of social adjustment in their writings. Deval endeavoured to solve the problem of conversion of the persons of higher castes who were enslaved by the Muslims.

According to some historians, Vijnaneswara, the author of great *Mitakshara Smriti*, cannot flourish earlier than the twelfth century. Kalluka, a famous Bengali commentator of *Manu Smriti*, lived in the fourteenth century. Chandeswara who wrote many digests of *Smritis* was a contemporary of Allauddin Khilji in the early fourteenth century. Madhva of Vijayanagar, the commentator of *Parasara Smriti*, and Visveswara; the author of a *Smriti* called *Madanparijata*, and Raghunandan of Bengal who was a contemporary of Chaitanya flourished in this period. Dr. A L. Srivastava holds the opinion that the character, conduct and dignity of the Hindus were adversely affected by the rule of the Delhi Sultans. When higher and middle class Hindus came into close contact with their alien rulers, they were compelled to conceal their sentiments of time honoured customs, culture and religion, and in due course they developed servility of character to get on in the world. They abandoned honesty and sincerity, straightforwardness and integrity of character and imbibed vices like selfish cleverness and skill in deceit or evasion.

An important result of the advent of Islam was the restoration of India's contact with the outside world. In ancient times, India had very close and intimate cultural and commercial relations with the countries of South-east Asia, China, Rome, Egypt, Greece, Central Asia, etc. The collapse of the imperial powers of the Guptas and Harshavardhan, and the rise of the smaller states created vacuum in which India was isolated from other countries. The Arabs helped to restore these early contacts with their trade on the Indian coasts. With the establishment of the Islamic powers in India, hundreds of traders from Bukhara, Samarkand, Balkh, Khurasan, Khwarizm, and Iran, and many travellers from Europe poured into India. It is said that no less than 14,000 camel loads of merchandise passed every year from India to Kandhar through Bolan Pass early in the seventeenth century. The ports of

Tattab, Broach, Surat, Rajapur, Goa, and Karwar were Indian doors to Arabia, Persia, Turkey, Egypt, Abyssinia, Zanzibar, etc. Ships sailed from Indian harbours for Lanka, Sumatra, Java, Siam, and even China. This resulted not only in commercial contacts but also in an exchange of ideas, customs and traditions. It also led to the city economy which was based on commercial capitalism of the variety in vogue in Central Asian countries and in the Mediterranean world.

Growth of the Spirit of Mutual Harmony, Cooperation and Toleration, and the Synthesis of Hindu Muslim Cultures : In spite of the fundamental difference and bitter strife between Hindus and Muslims, beneath the ruffled surface of storm and stress, there began to flow a genial current of mutual harmony, cooperation and toleration in different spheres of life in course of time. Both the Hindus and the Muslims realized, with the lapse of time, the futility of war and persecution. Gradually spirit of harmony, fellow feeling and cooperation was appearing between the two communities. They endeavoured to understand each other. Consequently, not only Hindu art, Hindu religion, Hindu literature and science assimilated certain Muslim elements, but the very spirit of Hindu culture was transformed to some extent.

In the same way the Muslims also attempted to absorb keenly many elements of Hindu culture. They willingly offered themselves for mutual exchange of ideas. Many religious sects arose in this period which attempted to harmonize Islam and Hinduism, and to find a common meeting ground for the devout of both creeds in which differences of rituals, dogmas, and external works of their faiths were ignored. Ramanand, Kabir, Nanak, Dadu, Chaitanya, etc. were some of such devotees and forerunners. If the Hindu religious leaders and saints endeavoured to synthesize Hindu Muslim thoughts, the Sufi sects of the Muslims, their writers and poets adopted Hindu doctrines and followed many of their traditions. Famous Muslim scholars and saints began to labour for the dissemination of the ideas of Islamic philosophy and mysticism in India, and it has been proved that one of the sources of Muslim mysticism was Indian.

The healthy spirit of mutual toleration found expression in the growing veneration of the Hindus for the Muslim saints, particularly of the mystic school, and a corresponding Mohammedan practice of venerating Hindu saints, and ultimately, it led to the common worship of *Satya Pirt* (the true saint). The Hindus offered sweets with great pleasure on the tombs of Muslim *Pirs* or saints, and listened with reverence to the recitations of the *Quran*. They began to believe in the infallibility of the Quran, consult it as an oracle and keep a copy of it in their houses to ward off the evils in life. To express their sentiments of brotherhood and charity, they commenced feeding the *Muslim fakirs* and *shaikhs,* and began to observe Muslim festivals and fairs. They took pride in becoming the disciples of Muslim saints. We have references to the Brahmana disciples of Abdul Kadir Jilani in Rawalpindi (now in Pakistan) and the Hindu devotees of Sayyid Masud in Bahraich.

Similarly, a large number of Hindus were included among the devotees of Shaikh Muinuddin Chisti of Ajmer. His tomb at Ajmer, known as the *Dargah* of Khwajah Sahib, is the centre of attraction of thousands of Muslims and hundreds of Hindus. When the death anniversary of Muinuddin is celebrated in a festival form, called *Urs,* both Hindus and Muslims visit the tomb in thousands even today. Similarly, the tomb of Shah Badrud-din-Qitab-ul-Madar at Makanpur, in Kanpur district, is visited by thousands of Hindus and Muslims. To respond to the Hindu sentiments the Muslims were also favourably inclined towards Hinduism. Though they were opposed bitterly to the idol worship, yet in Bengal they followed the practice of worshipping the Hindu gods and goddesses, *Sita, Kali, Dharmaraj, Vaidyanath,* etc. Muslims in U.P worship Kalka Sahja Mai, the Mirasis of Amritsar worship Durga Bhawani, while the Turk Nawabs of Bengal, Laxmi Devi. New gods like Khwaja Khijra and Jindagaji were created by the Muslims.

It is said that Hussain Shah, the Muslim ruler of Gaud, instituted the common worship of a new god *Satya Pir*. Muslim kings in the provinces liberally granted endowments to the Hindu temples and their shrines. The nucleus of the zamindari of the Mahant of Bodh Gaya was a grant made by Muhammad Shah. In Kashmir, Sultan Zain-ul-Abidin frequently visited the famous Hindu shrine of Amarnath and Sharda Devi's temple and had erected rest houses to provide comforts to the pilgrims there. Being influenced by the mythology of the Hindu Puranas and the Epics, the Muslims invented myths and legends which the pristine Islam lacked. They could now sing of the glorious deeds of Hanif, a legendary brother of Hassan and Hussain Ali. He was raised to the status of mythical hero combining the roles of Bhim and Arjun, renowned heroes of the Mahabharat. They also invented the character of Amir Ummiya to serve as the counterpart of Hanuman, a great hero of the Ramayan and devotee of Sri Ram.

The spirit of harmony, toleration and cooperation also found expression in the growing attempts of some Muslim aristocrats to assimilate Hindu customs, religious beliefs and observances while living in Hindu environment. Many sections of the Muslims even today retain several Hindu practices. The Memons of Saurashtra live like Hindus. They neither eat fish nor practise circumcision. They worship Hindu Brahma, Vishnu and Siva and regard Imam Shah as the incarnation of Brahma. Similarly, the Shamis in the Punjab worship Agha Khan as an incarnation of Hindu trinity. Many Muslims have retained the joint family system of Hindus. The Moplas are governed in Malabar by the Hindu laws. Several social functions of the Hindus at the time of birth, marriage and death have been adopted by the Muslims. They practise them even today; for example, the custom of singing of songs at the time of birth of a male child, the pomp, procession, ceremonies, festivities and even jokes of the Hindus in marriage, and the use of certain Hindu ornaments. Dr. Rajendra Prasad in his book *India Divided* gives numerous instances to prove that

Muslims assimilated many of the Hindu practices. A large number of intermarriages between the ruling members of the two communities, though tainted with compulsion as a condition of conquest, helped a good deal for the spirit of assimilation, harmony and toleration to grow and "did much to soften the acrimonious differences between the two communities and assist the transplanting of the customs of the one to the fold of the other."

The feeling of friendliness and the desire for mutual understanding induced Muslims to study, translate or summarize Hindu Sanskrit literature in the Muslim courts like those of Hussain Shah and Nasir Shah of Bengal and Zain-ul-Abdin of Kashmir. Some Muslim courts, Muslim scholars, preachers, and saints began to study Hindu philosophy like *Yoga* and *Vedanta*. Many were attracted to the study of Hindu sciences of medicine and astrology. Similarly, the Hindu astronomers "borrowed from the Muslims technical terms, the Muslim calculation of latitudes and longitudes, some items of the calendar *(Zich)* and a branch of horoscopy, called *Tajik*, and in medicine the knowledge of metallic acids and some processes in Iatrochemistry."

As a result of the Hindu Muslim contact there gradually emerged a linguistic synthesis, and Urdu is the outcome of the mingling of Persian, Arabic, and Turkish words and ideas with languages and concepts of Sanskritic origin. In course of time Urdu became the lingua franca of the people. Hindu and Muslim writers and poets of the age exchanged ideas mutually and expressed their thoughts in the vernaculars, Urdu and the Persian languages. Muslim scholars like Amir Khusrau, Malik Muhammad Jayasi, Kutuban etc., wrote on Hindu life, culture and religion in Hindi. Hindu writers like Rai Bhanamal wrote in Persian on Muslim ideas and literary traditions. The advent of the Muslims and the spirit of harmony and toleration had profound effect on the growth of the Indian vernacular literature. Dinesh Chandra Sen in his book on 'the evolution of Bengali literature' remarks that, "This elevation of Bengali to a literary status was brought about by several influences, of which the Mohammedan conquest was undoubtedly one of the foremost." Through the efforts of the Muslim rulers of Bengal, Bengali came into its own. The Hindi language also could not escape the Muslim influence which is distinct in its vocabulary, grammar, metres, similes and styles. Many good works were composed and written in Hindi, Bengali, Gujarati, Marathi, etc. Many Arabicized Persian words found their way into the local languages. Many chronicles and autobiographies were produced and they are authentic sources of history.

The spirit of assimilation and synthesis between the Hindu and Islamic culture led to the evolution of new styles of architecture and music, "in which the basic elements remained the old Hindu, but the finish and outward form became Persian, and the purpose served was that of Muslim courts." The Saracenic emphasis on splendour and form was blended with the Indian emphasis on splendour and decoration. A synthesis was produced where the severity of the Muslim architecture was mellowed down and the plastic exuberance of the Hindu art curtailed. According to Dr. Tarachand, "The craftsmanship, ornamental richness and general design remained largely Hindu, the arcuated form, plain domes, smooth faced walls, and spacious interiors were Muslim superimpositions." This synthesis of style was followed not only in the monumental art of India, but also in the utilitarian works houses, streets, bathing ghats, and even in religious places of worship.

In music, Indian *veena* was combined with the Iranian *tambura*, and *sitar* was produced. It is a popular Indian musical instrument. The *tabla* is also a Muslim modification of the Hindu musical instrument *mridang*. A fusion of Hindu and Iranian systems of music led to the evolution of light songs, like *qawwalis*, instead of only classical strains. New arts and crafts were introduced in the country; for example, paper making, enamelling, inlay works of stones, metals and jewels, etc. Numerous *karkhanas* or workshops were set up for gold and silver articles and embroidery.

The spirit of harmony and cooperation was also visible in the political field. Besides retaining intact the existing Hindu machinery of local administration, the Muslim rulers sometimes employed a large number of Hindus. They distinguished themselves in different branches of administration and became prominent and popular, for example, Medini Rai of Chanderi and his friends. They occupied very high positions at Mandu in Malwa. Husain Shah in Bengal employed such prominent Hindu men as Purandar Khan, Rup and Sanatan. In the Deccan, the Sultans of Golkonda had Hindu ministers who rendered meritorious service to the Golkonda State. Distinguished Hindus were entrusted with offices of responsibility by Sultan Yusuf Adil Shah of Bijapur. Another Sultan of Bijapur, Ibrahim Adil Shah, liberally patronized the Hindus. Moreover, the records of the State were ordinarily kept in Marathi, the language of the masses in the State.

Some of the Muslim Sultans freely granted endowments to Hindu shrines. Examples of Hindu toleration and Rajput chivalry towards the Muslims are equally abundant. Rana Kumbha, the renowned Rajput hero and ruler of Chittor, respected the independence of his vanquished for Mahmud Khilji II, the Sultan of Malwa. Though the Sultan was captured by the victorious Rajputs, Raja Kumbha treated him with chivalrous generosity and soon restored Mahmud to his kingdom. Hindu rulers appointed Muslims to offices of trust and responsibility and employed many Muslims as soldiers. Rana Sangram Singh had a contingent of Muslim troops under him in his war against Babar.

Rana Hamir of Ranthambhor had employed Mir Muhammad Shah who fought to death bravely and loyally against Allauddin Khilji for the cause of his master. Besides this, Hamir sheltered at the risk of incurring Allauddin's wrath a rebel chief who had fled from the Sultan's court at Delhi. Similarly, Rana Ban Pal of Santur offered shelter to Qutlugh Khan after his defeat at the hands of Sultan Nasiruddin. Even the Vijayanagar Emperors in the Deccan not only employed

Muslims in their army but patronized liberally "the cause of Islam in and outside their capital" These official appointments were more probably due to political necessity than to spirit of toleration or any feeling of accommodation. But undoubtedly they facilitated a healthy growth of goodwill and friendliness between the Muslims and the Hindus.

Islamic Impact upon Hinduism

In the beginning of the period under review, Islam gave a very rude shock to Hinduism. It shattered the Brahmana supremacy and destroyed the royal patronage that Hinduism had been enjoying. Hindu religious monuments and temples were levelled to the ground, and Hinduism, being deprived of state patronage, could not evolve further. Its growth was stunted, but Islam was spread far and widow in the country. The great contribution of the Muslim royal dynasties of Delhi was the introduction and propagation of Islam in India. Besides its doctrinal aspects, Islam brought into Ifiuia a conception of human equality, a pride in one's religion, a legal system which in many ways was an advance on the codes of the time." The strongly egalitarian outlook of Islam and the deep faith and the pride of the Mohammedans in their religion had their repercussions on Hindu society and religion.

The new spirit which the Hindu rulers of Rajasthan and Vijayanagar Emperors displayed as champions of *Dharma* and the upholders of religion, was a direct outcome of contact with Islam. They championed the cause of Hindu religion and society. To support and safeguard religion was the main function of Rana Hamir, Kumbha, Sangram, Krishnadeva Raya and Rama Raya. As a result of propagation of Islam in India religious faith became an active element of policy with Hindu monarchs and chieftains.

Bhakti Movement

Besides this, impact of Islam on Hinduism produced important consequences. Islam gives the message of universal brotherhood, introduces equality in society, rejects caste system and untouchability, is opposed to idol worship, and teaches oneness of God. These Islamic ideas had thrown up a powerful challenge to the upholders of Hinduism and the guardians of Hindu society. In due course, these ideas began to have a conscious or unconscious effect upon the philosophical Hindu mind, and fostered the growth of liberal movements under some saints and preachers who came to be known in history as religious reformers. It led to the revival of anti caste and monotheistic movements in the south, which became the home of religious reforms from the eighth century to the tenth century A.D. The Vaishnava and Saivite saints of the south started *Bhakti* movement and scholar saints like Sankaracharya, Ramanuja, Nimbaditya, Basava, Vallabhacharya, Madhavacharya, formulated their philosophical systems.

These impulses for the reawakening and religious revival were brought to northern India through Ramanand of Varanasi, who was a famous pupil of Ramanuja. Ramanand preached man's equality before God and admitted all classes of people as his disciples. Another mystic saint and reformer of northern India, Kabir, assailed the worship of idols, the authority of the Quran and the scriptures, and exclusive use of a complex learned languages. With some differences in details, these reformers and saints were exponents of the liberal *Bhakti* cult or single minded direct devotion and love to the One. They denounced idol worship and the system, preached the fundamental equality and basic oneness fall religions and the unity of godhead, advocated the monotheistic with, protested against the domination of the priestly class, opposed the complicated, elaborate, excessive ritualism and formalities of religion and emphasized simple devotion, faith and puritan life as the means of deliverance or salvation for all. They held that true religion consisted neither in the sophistries and dogmas of philosophers and doctrines of divines, nor in the practice of meaningless rituals, but in *Bhakti* or a passionate feeling of love for God.

However, it should be noted that oneness of God which

was the cardinal tenet of Islam and which infused a new spirit into the Hindu religious thoughts was not unknown to the Hindus. The monotheistic idea of God which has been the cardinal doctrine of Islam was well known to the Hindus long before it was preached by the Prophet in Arabia. It is explained distinctly in the Upanishads, and the Vedantist philosophers of the ninth century had also expounded it. Even before the Muslim conquest of India, the Hindu reformers had proclaimed one and only one supreme God behind the countless deities of popular worship. But the contact with the monotheistic faith of Islam gave a stimulus to such ideas and reemphasis on the essential monotheistic character of the idea of God and the superiority of the path of devotion over ritualistic sacrifice and mere book knowledge and wisdom. Great stress was laid on the subordination of rites, ceremonies, pilgrimages, fasts and humiliation of the excesses of polytheism. All these had great effect on teachers like Namadeva, Ramanand, Kabir, and Nanak in whom there is a happy blending of Hindu and Muslim influence.

Circumstances Leading to the Bhakti Cult : It is noted above that in their attempt to safeguard the Hindu society against the Muslims, orthodox people in the Hindu society increased the number of social taboos. Disdainful attitude towards girls, ill treatment of the low castes, denial of entry and worship in the temple to the untouchables, were a few of such social abuses enforced as the main content of Hinduism. The lower sections of the Hindu society were being crushed between the milestones of social injustice and religious tyranny of the higher caste Hindus and the politico- religious persecution of the Turko-Afghan fanatics. Propagation of the *Bhakti* cult provided a much coveted relief to the oppressed masses. They welcomed it most warmly.

Hinduism had degenerated a good deal. Masses were sunk in gross superstitions. They believed in supernatural powers, practised numerous complicated ceremonies and meaningless rituals, and worshipped not only the stone and metallic images but trees and rivers also. The Brahmanas enjoyed the monopoly of the sacred lore and numerous social privileges. Hinduism needed purification. The *Bhakti* movement aimed at the purification of the religion and liberation of the masses from priestly thraldom.

Islam with its simple doctrines, democratic organization and absence of rituals was gaining ground in the country. It was a challenge to the religious leaders of the Hindus. They, therefore, felt very strongly the necessity of making Hinduism a living, active force in the life of the common people. The *Bhakti* movement brought the required change. Medieval *Bhakti* cult was in some ways a reply to the attack of Islam. It was a new interpretation of Hinduism in terms of Islam's monotheism and egalitarianism. K. M. Panikkar remarks that the medieval period witnesses many revivalist movements in Hinduism. They were based on *Bhakti* which was the outcome of the feeling of escapism which dominated the Hindu mind as a result of the conquest of its sacred places by Islam.

Thus, Islam's conquest of northern India resulted in strengthening in the Hindu religion. The reaction of the Hindus to the challenge of monotheistic Islam was the rise of the great devotional sects of medieval Hinduism. These sects were based on *Bhakti*.

It is pointed out elsewhere in the book that *Bhakti* cult originated in ancient India and even the Gita preached the *Bhakti Yoga*. The sudden popularity of *Bhakti* in the medieval period is already explained in the above paragraphs. However, it should be carefully noted that all the saints of the *Bhakti* cult were theistic. In the *Bhakti* cult it is the one Supreme God that is the object of the devotee's adoration and it is to His grace that he looks for salvation. In fact all *Bhakti* cults are essentially monotheistic in the sense that the devotees may worship Siva, Krishna or Devi but they all symbolize the One and the Eternal.

Islamic Influence on South Indian Religion : The religious revival in the period under review was first initiated in the South. From the eighth to the fifteenth century the South was the home of religious reforms. It was there that the Vaishnava and Saivite saints started the schools of *Bhakti*. Sankaracharya, Ramanuja, Nimbaditya, Basava and Madhava advocated the *Bhakti* cult and expounded their philosophical system. The philosophical doctrines of Sankaracharya, Ramanuja and others were derived from the ancient system and their exposition was original. But, according to Dr. Tarachand and others, they were influenced by Islam as it was then prevalent in the south. They did not grow up utterly regardless of the new currents of Islamic thought which then flowed in the country. "The elements in their totality and in their peculiar emphasis betray a singular approximation to Muslim faith." But Islam influenced considerably Virsaiva and Lingayat sects. There were plenty of Muslims settled on the sea coast of the south where the great Tamil teachers arose.

They were honoured in societest and the Sate patronized them. In course of time they together with their missionaries and saints propagated religious ideas and encouraged people to think independently on caste system, religious ceremonies and rituals, monotheism, spiritual life, etc. The early commencement of the religious reform movements in the South indicates that they must have received inspiration from Islam. Dr. Tarachand in his book *Influence of Islam on Indian Culture* supports this view and states that the progress of religious thought in the south reveals a *growing absoluption of Muslim ideas into Hindu systems*. But the influence of Islam was in the first stage indirect and selective. This influence on Lingayatism is seen even today.

In spite of being Hindus, the Lingayats do not observe caste system. Widow marriage and divorce are practised by them. They observe neither sacrifices nor *sraddhas*, neither fasts nor feasts. The theory of transmigration of soul is not believed in, their dead bodies are not cremated but buried, and no death ritual is prescribed. All Lingayats eat together, without any distinction, intermarry, and live in unity as a community of brave warriors led by their sanctified preceptor.

Bhakti Movement and Reformer Saints : The earliest reformer saint was Sankaracharya who had a unique success. An account of his life and philosophy is already given in the preceding chapter. Next to him was Ramanuja whose doctrine was the basis of the *Bhakti* cult.

Ramanuja (1060-1118) : He was born in 1060 at Tirupati Perumuer in the vicinity of Madras. He was educated at Canjeevaram and Srirangam. On account of his scholarship he was appointed the successor of his teacher Yamunamuni, the well known Vaishnava saint. He composed the *Vedanta Sangraha,* the *Bhasyas* of Badrayana's' *Vedanta Sutras* and the *Bhagavadgita.* He travelled all over India with his disciple and ultimately settled down at Srirangam where he died in 1118. He was a Vaishnava saint.

The field of his activities was very extensive. He unified the followers of Vaishnavism and established Vaishnavism on a sound foundation. He preached the unity of God under Vishnu's name in the South. The aim of his teaching was the refutation of Sankara's absolute monism, *Mayavad,* and the establishment of *Bhakti* within the philosophy of Vedanta. According to him, *Brahma* is the one supreme reality, and the individual souls are modes or attributes of *Brahma.* The soul attains God by *Bhakti.* He was opposed to *Nirguna Iswara* and proclaimed that love of God was the only way to salvation, and believed in *Saguna Iswara* who is endowed with many auspicious qualities and virtues which a devotee might meditate upon with ecstasy and joy. His teachings are famous under the name of *Visishtadvaita.* He was not only a saint but reformer also. He was opposed to the caste distinctions and opened the way for the Sudras and the outcastes by allowing them to enter temples on certain days. He attached Sudras to his sect.

Nimbarka : He was the younger contemporary of Ramanuja. He carried the doctrine of *Bhakti* or devotion further. Though he belonged to the South he passed most of his life in Brajabhumi (Mathura) in the north. He advocated the principle of self-surrender and the worship of Krishna and Radha. In his doctrine, Krishna comes into prominence as the Supreme Lord of the Universe. According to him the way to eternal beatitude is *Bhakti* for the lotus like feet of Krishna.

Madhava (1199-1278) : Another teacher was Madhava at Kalyanpur in the Udipi district of south Kanara. He was a devotee of Vishnu. He did not attach much importance to Siva. He rejected the qualified monism of Ramanuja and established a system of frank dualism based mainly upon the *Bhagavata Puran."* According to him, knowledge leads to *Bhakti,* and the final aim of man is the direct perception of Hari or Vishnu which leads to *Moksha* or eternal blises.

Many other Vaishnava teachers spread the *Bhakti* cult among the people in the south and expounded the doctrines of Ramanuja, Nimbarka and Madhava.

Ramananda : The next famous teacher was Ramananda who flourished in the last quarter of the fourteenth and first half of the fifteenth centuries. He is responsible to a great extent for the spread of Vaishnava religion in northern India. He was born at Prayag (Allahabad) in a Brahmana family and was educated partly at Prayag and partly at Kasi (Varanasi). He visited all the holy places in northern India and preached Vaishnavism. He advocated the worship of Rama and Sita in place of Vishnu. He rejected the caste system, opposed restrictions with regard to partaking of meals, and admitted to his discipleship men of all classes without any distinction. He taught the doctrines of *Bhakti* cult to all castes without prejudice. Among his twelve disciples, there was a barber, a cobbler and a Muslim weaver. He preached man's equality before God. He was the first reformer saint to use Hindi, the vernacular language for the propagation of his doctrine, and he gained a good deal of popularity among the masses, specially the lower classes. He was the bridge between the *Bhakti* movement of the south and the north. His most valuable contributions to the solution of the religious problems of the medieval period were simplification of worship and emancipation of the people from traditional caste rules. Some scholars argue that Ramananda's contact with Islam and Varanasi enabled him to introduce some novelties in the religion.

Vallabhacharya : Another renowned Vaishnava saint was Vallabhacharya, the most distinguished exponent of the Krishna cult. He was a Telugu Brahmana of southern India. By virtue of his talents, scholarship and deep knowledge of philosophy, he became famous and defeated *Pandits* in a public discussion. He advocated penance, self-mortification and renunciation of the world, and "insisted on the complete identity of both soul and world with the Supreme Spirit" He advocated *Bhakti* to Krishna so enthusiastically that he asked his disciples to dedicate themselves to Krishna without any mental reservation and offer everything to him. This doctrine of Vallabhacharya was entirely saturated with spiritual ideas. His monism later on came to be known as *Suddha advaita* or 'Pure Non-Duality'. But after his death abuses crept in Vallabhacharyanism and it "became in its degenerate from the Epicureanism of the East"

Chaitanya (1458-1513) : A contemporary of Vallabhacharya was the celebrated and popular Vaishnava saint and reformer, Chaitanya of Bengal. He was born of Brahmana parents at Nadia. He was married at the age of eighteen, followed the profession of a teacher, but renounced the world at the age of twenty five, and wandered over the whole country. Krishnadas sums up the teaching of Chaitanya in two sentences: "If a creature adores Krishna and serves his *Guru* he is released from the meshes of illusion and attains to Krishna's feet," and "leaving these, i.e temptations and the religious systems based on caste, (the true Vaishnava) helplessly takes refuge with Krishna." He denounced caste, proclaimed the universal brotherhood of men and the inefficiency of mere *Karma* or ceremonial rites. He preached faith in *Hari*. He held that through love and devotion, song and dance, a state of ecstasy could be produced in which the personal presence of God would be realized by the devotee. Love is the watchword of Chaitanya cult which exercised profound and wide influence on the masses. He favoured the life of a Sanyasi and accepted disciples from all classes, irrespective of caste or creed. Chaitanyanism is even today followed by thousands of people in Bengal and Bihar.

Kabir : He was another famous saint of northern India who made the most earnest effort to foster a spirit of harmony and tolerance between Hindus and Muslims. Though scholars differ in their opinion about the date of his birth, it is certain that he lived in either the closing years of the fourteenth century or the beginning of the fifteenth century. He was a disciple of Ramananda and passed his days mostly in Kasi (Varanasi). He followed the profession of a weaver and suffered a good deal of persecution at the hands of the orthodox Muslims. He did not believe in extreme asceticism and abstraction from the world. He denounced idolatry, rites and cere- monies and laid great emphasis on the equality of man and declared that before God's high throne all are equal, high and low, Muslims and Hindus. He preached a religion of love which aimed at promoting unity amongst all castes and creeds. He was the first saint to reconcile Hinduism and Islam. He denounced the external formalism of both, abandoned the divisions between the two faiths and emphasized their internal unity and common spiritual elements. He was the first to come forward boldly to proclaim a religion of the middle path. According to him, salvation was to be achieved by *Bhajan* or devotional songs and worship, and for this purpose the soul should be free from all sham, cruelty, hypocrisy, dishonesty, insincerity, and external formalities. Kabir's teachings, saturated with mysticism, betray the influence of *Sufi* saints and poets.

Nanak : Another famous saint preacher of the time was Guru Nanak, the founder of the Sikh religion. He was born in 1469 in the village of Talwandi, nearly fifty six kilometres from Lahore. He followed the profession of agriculture, cattle tending and shop keeping but without any success. Later on, he was appointed as the keeper of Daulat Khan Lodi's storehouse of charities. Though he was married and had children, he renounced the world, wandered over many lands, visited all the holy places and gathered spiritual experience. Wherever he went he preached his doctrines of universal toleration and unity of Godhead. He condemned, vehemently and bitterly, idolatry and formalism of both Hinduism and Islam. His mission was to bring to an end the conflict of religions. He urged that barriers of caste and race must give way before the name of God who transcends them all. He exhorted people to give up hypocrisy, selfishness, worldliness and falsehood and lead a pure life of truth, honesty and kindness. His conception of religion was severely practical and sternly ethical. He did not believe in renunciation, but advocated an asceticism of the heart, combined with the fulfilment of the worldly functions of body and mind. He was the reviver of the pure monotheistic doctrine of the Upanishads.

Till his death he endeavoured at the unification of Hinduism and Islam, and among his disciples were counted both Hindus and Muslims. His followers came to be known as Sikhs who were hammered into a military nation by his successors who were known as the *Gurus* of Sikhs. Dado (1544-1603). After Chaitanya and Nanak, the name of Dadu Dayal deserves mention among the saints of the *Bhakti* cult. He was born at Ahmedabad, but he passed most of his life in Naraina and Bharaina in Rajasthan. He was a tanner or *mochi* by caste and his family used to make *mots* or leather bags for drawing water from well. He renounced the world, visited many places of pilgrimage and became a devotee and saint. He rose above prejudices of creed and emphasized the true inwardness of religion. He was a staunch supporter of Hindu-Muslim unity. He raised his voice against idol worship, caste distinctions, the theory of *avatars* or reincarnations of God, the conception of pilgrimage, the external formalities of religion and the practice of worship at the shrines of the departed saints. He insisted upon the unity of God and aimed at promoting unity among different creeds with the sentiments of brotherhood, love, affection and toleration.

Therefore, Dadu established a sect whose followers are known as the *Dadu panthis.* He had no faith in infallibility of the scriptures but in the realization of God *by* individual efforts, and hence, he preached complete surrender to God. He was a great poet and composed his verses in the vernacular of the country where he lived. *Maluk Das* (1574-1682) and *Sunder Das* (1596-1689) were other famous saints, who spread the religion of *Bhakti.* Like other saints, they condemned formalities and rituals of religion, idol worship, work of charities, priesthood, etc.

Raidas : He lived at Varanasi and was a worker in leather. He lived in a dilapidated hut and earned his living by mending shoes. He lived a life of simplicity and contentment and devoted himself to religious men and saints. Instead of indulging in high philosophic speculation about God and nature in his hymns, he aimed at the unity of Hinduism and Islam. His hymns breathe spirit of humanity. He rejected the theory of incarnation, looked upon the world as the play of God and advocated complete surrender to Him. His cardinal doctrine was that "Hari (God) is in all and all is in Hari."

Mirabai : Mirabai holds a very high position among the Vaishnava saints. Though she was a princess of the royal dynasty of Jodhpur and the queen of the renowned Sisodia dynasty of Chittor, she renounced the world for the sake of her *Bhakti* to Lord Krishna. She was considerably influenced by the reformer saints and their *Bhakti* cult. She followed their religion and was a great devotee of Krishna.

Maharashtra and Reformer Saints : The intercourse of Hindus and Muslims produced the same cultural phenomena in Maharashtra as it had been in northern India. The synthesis of the two religions was also achieved in Maharashtra. Their preachers and saints, both Brahmanas and non- Brahmanas, condemned the caste restrictions and formal ritualism, denounced idol worship, advocated *Bhakti* cult and monotheistic creed and aimed to unite people in common love and faith in God. The history of religious upheaval and reformation in Maharashtra begins from *Jnaneswar* who flourished in Maharashtra in the thirteenth century. He set forth noble and divine ideals of the spiritual life for people to follow. His Marathi commentary of the Gita is very famous. After Jnaneswar, Visoba Khechar, a contemporary of Ramanand, had bitterly opposed idol worship. Khechar's disciple Namdev exposed the inefficacy of the external acts of religion. He called upon people to break caste barriers and abandon religious intolerance and narrow mindedness. His cardinal doctrine was that salvation could be achieved by *Bhakti* or love and deep devotion to God. His *Bhakti* to Vithoba (Lord Vishnu) enabled him to perform several miracles in the country.

Eknath was another saint of Maharashtra. He did not favour renunciation and asceticism, but preached that the householder could attain salvation by *Bhakti*. Dasopant was another famous saint contemporary of Eknath. But Tukaram is more famous than these saints. He is next to Namdev. He wields the widest influence in Maharashtra. He was a contemporary of Shivaji and followed the profession of a trader. Being disgusted with the worldly life he abandoned his business and devoted himself entirely to contemplation and devotion. Though he was subjected to severe persecution by the Brahmanas he became famous for his life of piety and selfless devotion. Tukaram's *abhangas* which embody his teachings are recited in every family even today in Maharashtra. He founded a *Varkari* sect. The deity to which all these saints of Maharashtra were devoted was named *Panduranga, Vithoba* or *Vitthal,* and the *Bhakti* movement in Maharashtra centred round the shrine of Vithoha or Vishnu at Pandharpur on the banks of the Bhima.

These religious reformers and saints supplied the spiritual background to the political aim of workers like Shivaji, and they made an ardent and piteous appeal to the God Almighty through their favourite deity to intervene on behalf of the oppressed peoples and bring them relief from Muslim persecution. As a result of their preachings and writings the pulsation of an entirely new national life began to stir throughout Maharashtra.

Sufism and Sufi Saints in India

If Islam had affected Hinduism, the influence of Hinduism on Islam was profound. It gave rise to Sufi movement in the domain of Islam. Islam has a kind of mysticism called Sufism. Its original source is the Quran and the life of Muhammad. Hinduism, Buddhism, Christianity, Zoroastrianism, Manism and Neoplatonism swelled it by a large contribution. Muhammad, the Prophet, was a mystic and the mystical note sounds clearly in the utterances of the Quran. When the Indian and Greek cultures came into close contact, the Greek philosopher, Plato, assimilated some elements of the Hindu philosophy and formed his own philosophy which is known as Neoplatonism. When the Greek works were translated into Arabic, the Neoplatonic ideas passed into Islam in the beginning of the ninth century, such as, contempt for the world, leaning towards divine life, etc. Contact with the Christians accentuated certain tendencies among the followers of Islam, such as, complete detachment from affairs of personal interest, indifference towards suffering, admiration or blame, meditation and repetition of the name of God, etc.

The close and intimate commercial intercourse between the Indians and the Arabs, and the familiarization of the latter with Indian literature and sciences, and their translation in Arabic led the assimilation of Indian philosophical ideas, certain Buddhist doctrines and Hindu *Vedanta*. After the death of Muhammad, the followers of Islam had included such saints who encouraged the growth of certain fraternity of saints by their devotion, renunciation and spiritual life. This has profoundly influenced Islam and encouraged the growth of mysticism in Islam.

All these influences led to new religious tendencies in the

realm of Islam which came to be known as Sufism. Till the ninth century, Sufism was merely tendentious and possessed no system, but later on it developed metaphysical system and the organization of monastic orders. From the twelfth century onwards Sufism began to dominate the Muslim mind, literature, philosophy, etc. The name of Sufi was first applied to Abu Hashim of Kufa who died in 778 A.D. The religious doctrines and spiritual ideas of Husain bin Mansur al Hajjaj of the tenth century have special significance in Sufism. He emphasized the realization of God. He conceived the relation of God with man as the infusion of the divine into the human soul. Shaikh Shahabuddin Suhrawardi and lbn al Arabi of the thirteenth century have promoted a good deal the growth of Sufism by their doctrines.

The former laid emphasis upon the eternal divine light and unison of *soul* with God, the latter explained that the divine knowledge of God can be achieved by faith, devotion and meditation. He advocated religious toleration for all faiths as God is realized by all of them. One of the greatest authorities of Sufi philosophy is Ibn al Arabi. Nearly one hundred and fifty years after him Abdul Karim al Jill had expounded the cardinal doctrines of Sufism. According to him man attains spiritual perfection passing through four stages complete surrender to the will of God destruction of the individual, acquisition of miraculous power and divine attributes and lastly, entrance into Essence becoming perfect (Insan-i-Kamil) godman. He preached that all faiths were thoughts about one Reality, God, and all ways of worship express the same aspects of that Reality and in the end all together contribute to perfection of the whole. This reveals that the doctrines of Jill were profoundly impressed by the Hindu *Vedanta*, the monistic philosophy. Arabic and Persian poets and writers of the subsequent times had propounded Sufi philosophy in their works.

The practical aim of every Sufi is total absorption in God for which there are three stages. The first stage consists of good actions, surrender of will to the commands of God, repentance for sins acquisition of faith, maintenance of cleanliness, performance of prayers, pilgrimage, and fast, giving alms or charity, and suppression of passions by ascetic practices, silence and solitude and curbing of evil propensities of self as pride, envy, anger, narrow mindedness, etc. The second stage is that of attainment of divine and spiritual knowledge and acquisition of detached view of life. Inward light and eternal love transform intellect and will. The third stage is the highest stage. There is complete union with the Divinity and the attainment of the unitive state.

The mystic becomes one with God. Every Sufi who seeks absorption with God always needs a spiritual guide or the preceptor *(Pir* or *Shaikh)* who regulates his disciple's conduct and keeps watch over his spiritual progress and enables him to pass through all the stages leading to the essential unity with God. A Sufi realizes God by constant meditation, contemplation, music, dance and annihilation of self, etc. Dr. Tarachand remarks that "Sufism, indeed, was a religion of intense devotion, love was its passion, poetry, song and dance its worship, and passing away in God its ideal". The Sufist movement afforded a common platform to the more learned and devdut minds among the Hindus and the Muslims. Sufists made no distinction between different creeds and faiths. They preached their doctrines to the followers of all faiths. In fact, Sufism was essentially a faith or rather an intellectual enjoyment reserved for philosophers, authors and mystics free from bigotry.

The above mentioned account of Sufism makes it clear that its doctrines were profoundly influenced by Hinduism. It was on account of Sufi movement that in the medieval age saints, scholars, Hindus and Muslims could intermingle freely without any distinction at one and the same place.

The search of and love for one Supreme Reality have been common to both Sufism and Hinduism. The very conception of loving God and the relations between God and soul as one of the beloved and the lover, peculiar to Hinduism, were adopted by the Sufis in India. Pacificism, and non violence which were imbibed by the Indian Muslim Sufis are conceptions of Hinduism. Some of the ascetic practices which involved the starving and torturing of the body, such as, *Chillah-i-makus* (the inverted *Chillah,* which means the tying of a rope to one's feet and getting one's body lowered into a well and offering prayer in that posture for forty nights), seem to have been borrowed from the Hindu and Buddhist practices. Many other details in the ceremonies and practices of the Muslim Sufis especially of the *Chisti* order, were of Indian origin and were certainly due to the Hindu environment.

The Chistis adopted many Hindu customs and ceremonials in the initial stages of the development of their *Silsilah* in India. The practice of bowing before the Shaikh (head of Sufi Khanqah), presenting water to visitors, circulating Zanbil (a bowl made of dried and hollow gourd), shaving the head of new entrants to the mystic circle, audition parties *(samp)* and the *Chillah i makus* had close resemblance to Hindu and Buddhist practices. Love and liberalism were the key notes of Sufism and Hinduism.

In both, the elements of intellectuality went hand in hand with that of devotion. Mystic discipline in both was canalized towards the moral advancement of the individuals and society by making them rise above the barriers of colour and creed, wealth, power and position. Like Hinduism, the goal of the Sufis was the attainment of not only direct intellectual and emotional communion with God, but also service of humanity. It was on account of such similarity in Hinduism and Sufism, that in the medieval age saints, scholars, Hindus and Muslims, could intermingle freely without any distinction or mental reservation.

Major Sufi Orders

The Sufi saints were organized into various orders or *Silsilah.* Abul Fazl mentions fourteen Sufi orders. Of the various

Sufi orders largely founded outside India, only two, the *Chisti* and *Suhrawardy,* were the first to succeed in establishing themselves firmly on Indian soil.

Chisti Order : The order of the Chistis was founded by Khwaja Abdul Chisti who died in 966 A.D. It was introduced into India by *Khwaja Muinuddin Chisti,* the disciple of Khwaja Usman Haruni, a famous Chisti saint. The following are the Chisti saints of India.

Muinuddin Chisti was born in Seistan in 1143. Seistan is in the east of Persia. Visiting Samarkand, Bukhara and other places of Islamic learning he came to India in 1200 and settled down in Ajmer. He married two wives and died in or about 1236. He preached the philosophy of non-duality. He believed that in the sphere of oneness all is one. Hamiduddin Nagauri and Qutbuddin Bakhtiyar Kaki were his chief Sufi disciples.

Fariduddin Ganj-i-Shakar: Qutbuddin had a famous disciple caned Fariduddin Ganj-i-Shakar (1175-1265). He worked at Hansi and Ajodhan. He is known as Shaikh Farid or Baba Farid. His religious activities and high mysticism raised the Chisti order of Sufis to the status of an all India organization.

Shaikh Nizamuddin Auliya : The greatest and most famous disciple of Baba Farid was Shaikh Nizamuddin Auliya. He was born at Budan in 1236. At the age of twenty he became the disciple of Baba Farid. In 1258, he returned to Delhi and later on moved to Ghiaspur, a village near Delhi. He had witnessed the reign of seven Sultans of Delhi, but he did not attend the Darbar of any of them. His disciples spread all over India. His personality and breadth of his religious outlook assured the popularity of the Chisti order in India. He inspired men with the love of God and helped them to get rid of their attachment to worldly affairs. A characteristic feature of the teachings of Nizamuddin Auliya is the stress he laid on the motive of love which leads to the realization of God. The intuitive insight of the Shaikh readily extended his love of God to the love of humanity without which the former would be incomplete. He died in 1325.

One of the disciples of Shaikh Nizamuddin Auliya, Shaikh Burhanuddin Gharib, who died in 1340, made Daulatabad his head quarters. His successor was Shaikh Zainuddin. In Gujarat, Shaikh Syed Husain, Shaikh Hisamuddin and Shah Barakullah spread the Sufi message of love and humanity.

Shaikh Nasiruddin Chiragh-i-Dehlavi : One of the disciples of Shaikh Nizamuddin Auliya was Shaikh Nasiruddin Chiragh i Dehlavi. He was known as Chiragh of Delhi. He cultivated poverty and resignation. He continued his Sufi missionary activities and died in 1336. He was the last great saint of the Chisti *Silsilah* to have enjoyed an all India reputation one of the disciples of Shaikh Nasiruddin Chiragh-i-Dehlavi, Khwaja Syed Muhammad Gesudaraz, settled in Gulbarga in the Deccan in 1398. Sultan Ahmad Shah Bahmani had great admiration for the Khwaja and followed his discourses on religion and mysticism.

Shaikh Salim Chisti : He was one of the famous Sufi saints of the sixteenth century. But he did not rise to the standard and reputation of Nizamuddin Auliya or Nasiruddin Chiragh-i-Dehlavi. He had his hermitage in a cave near Fatehpur Sikri. Akbar paid visits to him frequently. He preached mysticism and continued the saintly traditions of the Sufi order and won great name and fame. He died in the lifetime of Akbar and was buried in the enclosure of the famous Jami mosque of Fatehpur Sikri. A beautiful marble mausoleum was constructed over his grave.

The saints of the Chisti order had great faith in simplicity and poverty. They observed fast frequently to weaken and control their haser desires. Their clothes were scanty. Their simplicity and purity was instrumental in reforming the lives of their own co-religionists and in spreading Sufism in the country.

After the death of Baba Farid, the Chisti order was divided

into two main sub-divisions, known respectively as the *Nizamiya* and *Sabiriyya* Orders. The *Sabiriyya* Order was founded by Makhdum Allauddin Ali Ahmad Sabir of Piran Kaliar. He was a contemporary of Shaikh Nizamuddin .Auliya. He was a great mystic, but was just opposite to Shaikh Nizamuddin Auliya in disposition and character. If Auliya represented the Jamali (beauteous), Sabir represented the Jalali (majestic) attributes of God and these complemented each other. Shaikh Nizamuddin Auliya by his sympathetic and generous approach towards life attracted thousands towards himself, whereas Shaikh Ahmad Sabir isolated himself from the world and lived the life of a recluse. Even then Sabir wielded tremendous moral influence for the uplift of humanity. In the eighteenth century, Shaikh Kalimullah of Delhi and his disciple Shaikh Nizamuddin Chisti stand out as prominent personalities of the Chisti order of the time. Shaikh Nizamuddin made Aurangabad in the Deccan his headquarters.

***Suhrawardy Order* :** The Suhrawardy order is one of the oldest Sufi orders that established itself in north-western India. This order was founded by Shaikh Shahabuddin Suhrawardy of Baghdad. He was the author of *Awar-i-Jul-Maaril.* He had directed many of his disciples to proceed to India to preach Sufism there. The following are the saints of the Suhrawardy order in India.

***Hamiduddin Nagaury* :** He was a noteworthy disciple of Suhrawardy and was the author of two books, *Tawaliush Shams* and *Lawaih.* He was very fond of music parties and sometimes he formed such parties with Shaikh Qutbuddin Bakhtiar Kaki.

***Shaikh Bahauddin Zakariya Suhrawardy* :** The pioneer of the Suhrawardy order in India was Shaikh Bahauddin Zakariya Suhrawardy. He was born at Kotaror near Multan in 1182-83. He became the disciple of Shaikh Shahabuddin Zakariya at Baghdad. Shaikh Shahabuddin ordered Zakariya to make Multan the centre of his activities. Bahauddin Zakariya set up a Khanqah at Multan and lived there and preached Sufism for nearly half a century. He died in December, 1262. He was a man of great courage of conviction and was a most influential mystic of the thirteenth century. He was on terms of most affectionate intimacy with Baba Farid Ganj Shakar. Zakariya's mystic ideology differed greatly from that of the Chisti Sufis. Unlike them he did not believe in poverty and torturing of the body. He led a balanced, happy and comfortable life. He had no faith in too much fasting and self mortification.

But he was punctilious in the observance of the rules of Islam. He emphasized the external forms of Islam and rejected the Hindu practice of bowing before the Shaikh and other Indian ceremonies which the Chistis had adopted in India. He directed his followers to salute him in the orthodox Muslim fashion, saying *as salam walekum*. Bahauddin Zakariya did not shun wealth. In fact, he accumulated vast wealth unlike Chisti Sufis. He accepted land and gifts from kings and nobles. He was probably the richest Muslim saint of medieval India.

The Multan Branch and Uchcha Branch of the Suhrawardy Order : Shaikh Bahauddin Zakariya's son Sadruddin Arif became a Sufi saint and took up his place in Multan, while his disciple Sayyid Jallaluddin Surkh Bukhari, who had come from Bukhara and had become a disciple of Zakariya, established himself at Uchcha. Thus, the Suhrawardy order in India was split into two branches the Multan branch and the Uchcha branch. The Multan branch of the Suhrawardy order acquired great importance and won wide fame. After Sadruddin Arif's death his son Ruknuddin Abul Fath became the Shaikh of the order. He worked tirelessly for half a century to propagate the mystic ideas of the Suhrawardy order. Many Ulmas flocked to his Khanqah and became his disciples. Sayyid Jalaluddin Surkh Bukhari of Uchcha became a famous mystic and was highly admired and respected both by Sultan Muhammad Tughlaq and Firuz Tughlaq.

Firdausia Branch of the Suhrawardy Order : Another prominent branch of the Suhrawardy order was that of the Firdausia Sufi mystics. The activities of the Firdausia branch were confined to Bihar.

Shaikh Shorfuddin Yahya Manairi : Shaikh Sharfuddin Yahya Manairi, who died in 1380, was a great advocate of the Firdausia order. He was the disciple of Khwaja Najmuddin Firdausi and had made his headquarters at Rajgir in Bihar. He was an excellent exponent of theoretical side of mysticism. In his letters known as *Maktubat* he sought to reconcile the doctrine of the unity of God *(Wahdatul Wujud)* with the law of Islam. Shaikh Sharfuddin Yahya Manairi was not only a speculative thinker, a great scholar of a high order, but also a practical guide to his disciples. He was a prolific writer and had compiled several books for the guidance of his disciples. He laid particular stress on the service of the humanity.

Qadri Order : The original founder of the Qadiri order was Shaikh Abdul Qadir Jilani of Baghdad who died in 1166. The Qadiri order of the Sufis was responsible for the spread of Islam in Western Africa, and in Central Asia. The Qadiri order of the Sufis was first introduced in India by Shah Niamatullah and Makhdum Muhammad Jilani. They lived towards the middle of the fifteenth century. Jilani settled in Uchcha in Sindh and made it a centre of his activities. He was succeeded by his son Makhdum Abdul Qadir. His grandson Shaikh Hamid Ganj Baksh was also a great Sufi mystic. He had two sons, Shaikh Abdul Qadir and Shaikh Musa, who had migrated to Agra in the reign of Akbar. Shaikh Abdul Qadir had become a famous mystic of Agra.

Other famous mystics of the Qadri order were Shaikh Daud Kirmani and Shaikh Abdul Maali Qadri of Lahore. Prince Dara Shikoh, the eldest son of Shah lahan, became the follower of Qadri order. He visited Mian Mir (1550-1635) at Lahore and was much impressed by his saintly personality.

Naqshbandi Order : This order of the Sufis was founded by Khwaja Bahauddin Naqshband 0317 1389). The following are the Sufi saints of the Naqshbandi order. *Khwaja Baqi Billah.* This order was introduced in India by Khwaja Baqi Billah (1563-1603); seventh in the line of succession to Khwaja Bahauddin Naqshband. From the beginning, this order of the

Sufis had laid great emphasis on the observance of the law of the prophet *(Shariat)* and had emphatically denounced all innovation which had soiled the purity of the Islamic doctrine.

Shaikh Ahmad Sarhindi : He was the chief disciple of Khwaja Baqi Billah. He was a contemporary of Akbar and Jahangir and was popularly known as the *Majaddid* and attacked the mystic philosophy of the Unity of Being as expounded by Ibnul Arabi and rejected it. In its place he expounded the philosophy of apparentism *(Wahdat-ush-Shuhud).* He observed that the relation between man and God is that of slave and master and not that of lover and beloved as the Sufis generally think. It seems that Shaikh Ahmad's object was to harmonize the doctrine of mysticism with the teaching of orthodox Islam, and this is why he is known as Mujaddid the renovator and reformer of Islam.

Shah Abdur Rahim was another mystic Sufi saint of the period. Aurangzeb offered him a grant of land, but the saint did not accept it.

Shaikh Abdul Latif and Shaikh Burhan : There are references to two famous mystics Shaikh Abdul Latif and Shaikh Burhan, both lived in Burhanpur in Khandesh Aurangzeb visited them during his subedari of the Deccan.

Shah Waliullah : Another prominent saint of the Naqshbandi order was Shah Waliullah of Delhi (1702-1762). He is famous for his reconciliation of the two doctrines of *Wahdat-ul-Wujud* and *Wahdat ush Shuhud.* According to him "real existence belongs to God alone and that He alone has actual independent being. The existence of the world is not real and yet it cannot be called imaginary either, being the idea of God. God is the only self subsisting; eternal and necessary Being and all else is created and has a contingent existence. In different respects God transcends and indwells. His transcendence and His immanence are united through their different functions in God's total being, in which a reality is included and all distinctions are annulled." There is one Reality which manifests itself in an infinity of forms. Other pluralities are the reflection of the names and attributes of the necessary Being. If at all there is any difference between the two positions, it is insignificant and it can be ignored.

Wahdut-ul-Wujud and *Wahdat ush Shuhud* are relative terms. They are to be used on two different occasions as arguments about the existence of God and His relations with man and the world.

Shah Waliullah was a great scholar and was a copious writer on Jurisprudence, the Traditions of the Prophet and Mysticism. His famous works are: (1) *Hamat,* (2) *Fuuz-ul-Haramain,* (3) *Altaful Quds,* (4) *Anfasul Arifin,* (5) *Tafhimat-e-Ilahia,* and (6) *Faislatul Wahdiltul Wujud Wash Shudud.* He affected a synthesis between the claims of Jurisprudence *(fiqh)* and the Traditions *(hands),* and between the different schools of *fiqh.*

Mirza Janjanan Mazhar (1699-1781) : He lived at Delhi and his Khanqah was a great centre of mystic activity. Mirza Janjanan Mazhar criticized Shah Waliullah for holding *Wahadat ul Wujud* and *Wahadat ush Shuhud* as identical. He initiated hundreds of devotees in the practices of the Naqshbandi order. He was a mystic with wide sympathies and cosmopolitan outlook.

Khwaja Mir Dard : Another great mystic of the Naqshbandi order was Khwaja Mir Dard. Though he was opposed to the doctrine of *Wahdat-ul-Wujud,* he recognized that in the last analysis both the doctrines of the "Unity of Being" and "Apparentism" have one and the same object in view. Both require the devotee to detach his heart from his affiliations of the world. He has expounded his own mystic theory which he calls" *lime llahi Muhammad*" (Knowledge of God based on the teachings of Muhammad). He draws inspiration for his esoteric ideas from the *Quran.* According to him those who follow this path will get self-realization as well as God realization. He was a famous poet of Persian and Urdu and was the author of many works. His chief works are: (1) *Ilmul Kitab,* (2) *Wafdate Dard,* (3) *Nalae Dard,* (4) *Ahe Sara,* (5) *Darde*

Dil, and (6) *Shymi Mahfil*. The chief contribution of Khwaja Mir Dard to the mystic theosophy is the synthesis which he effected between the elements of legalism and love. He considered himself to be both a slave and a lover of God.

The Suhrawardy and the Chisti orders of the Sufis were established firmly in India. Chisti order was the most popular, and its chief centres were Ajmer, Narnaul, Sarwal, Nagpur, Hansi, Ajodhan, Burlaun and other well known towns of Uttar Pradesh. Many followers of the Chisti order could be found in Bengal, Assam and the Deccan. Sindh and Multan had become centres of the spiritual activities of the saints of Suhrawardi order, Firdausi and Shuttaris the offsets of the Suhrawardi order, were active in Bihar and Bengal.

Many other parts of India were within the orbit of the other oraers like Qadiri, and Madari. The Naqshbandi order came later and it became entrenched in Indian soil in about the sixteenth century. The *Bhakti* movement and Sufi philosophy tended to bring, according to Jadunath Sarkar, the ruling sect and the dominated people closer together.

To sum up, the influence of Islam is clearly manifested in the teachings of religious reformers and saints, like Kabir, Nanak, Dadu Dayal and Namdev. They received great impetus from the presence of the followers of Islam in their immediate neighbourhood. The example of Islamic society acted as solvent on Hindu prejudice. Contact with Islam accentuated monotheism of Hinduism, tended to remove the barriers of caste, strengthened the movement of *Bhakti* cult, introduced new elements in its principles about *guru* or the preceptor, minimized the rigidity of the cult without completely abolishing it and promoted the growth of the popular languages.

It also led to the partial reconciliation with Islam and subordination of rites and ceremonies, pilgrimages and fasts, meditation and contemplation to the worship of love and faith.

Reformer Saints

The above mentioned reformer saints not only emancipated the masses from the social and religious tyranny but contributed substantially to the cultural evolution of the country. All the reformers condemned caste system, denounced polytheism and idolatry, pleaded for faith and sincerity and advocated puritan life. They preached that true religion does not mean elaborate ritualism but devotion to and love for God. The cardinal doctrine which they emphasized was that God is the God of Hindus as well as of Muslims, of Brahmanas as well as of Chandals and that before Him all are equal. They asked their followers to devote themselves to their deity whole heartedly, and emphasized that it was a way for salvation. They pointed out that in *Bhakti* it is the Almighty God that is the main object of a devotee's adoration; and it is to His grace that he looks for his deliverance.

According to them, though the devotees worship various gods or goddesses, all *Bhakti* cults are monotheistic in the sense that all deities symbolize the One and Eternal. In fact, they preached the simple religion of love and complete surrender to the immanent God who rescued His true and sincere devotees from their miserable plight. It was due to these saints that the *Bhakti* cult gained the greatest popularity in the medieval period and the *Bhakti* movement progressed with wonderful rapidity in spite of the intolerant fanatic Muslim rulers of the age.

The second legacy of these saints was their religious revival, the aim of which was to synthesize Hinduism and Islam, to ensure the communal goodwill and unity and to create an environment of toleration and cooperation. It was in this atmosphere that the foundation of the Mughal rule was laid in the country. They tried successfully to bridge the gulf between Hinduism and Islam and, thus, paved the way for the liberalism of Akbar. These saints attracted thousands of devotees from the Hindus and the Muslims and exercised an extremely healthy and stabilizing influence on society at a time when the anti social conspiracy of self-seeking Mulas and the fanatic Muslim rulers on the one hand, and the debased priestly class and the higher caste Hindus on the other were driving the helpless masses into utter despondency and desperation. The saints of the period under review inspired the *Bhakti* movement that prepared the ground for the liberal tendencies which found their fruition in the reign of Akbar. It was only then that Hindus and Muslims stood shoulder to shoulder in the service of a common empire, and shed their religious prejudices to an extent never reached before since the Islamic conquest of our country. It was the voice of Kabir and Nanak which spoke through the imperial lips and created storm in the orthodox circles."

The third legacy of these saints was the social and religious reforms. They exposed the futility of all external ceremonies and 'worship, emancipated minds of the people from the domination of the priests and Mullas, minimized the religious favouritism, fanaticism and intolerance, helped the growth of rational life and self-knowledge. They aimed at the abolition of the caste barriers, endeavoured to democratize religion and society, devoted their lives to the uplift of the fallen and the oppressed, elevated the status of women, laid emphasis on *karma* or action rather than birth or rank, and spread such noble sentiments as humaneness, toleration, generosity in the Hindu society which tended henceforth to become more liberal. In short, they brought about the simplication of worship and liberalization of caste rules. They tried, not without a considerable measure of success, to uplift the nation, in the words of Ranade, "to higher level of capacity both of thought and action."

Their fourth legacy was that they safeguarded the Hindu culture, life and literature and kept the torch of Hinduism burning ever in the days of unprecedented political unheavals, oppression, injustice and inhumanity. They enabled the Hindus to withstand the onslaught of propaganda and proselytism of Islam.

Their fifth legacy was that they promoted the growth of vernacular literatures of different provinces. They stimulated evolution and enrichment of the literature, of the spoken languages. They utilized vernaculars as the vehicle of their teachings to make their religious revival nationwide and popular. They rendered the famous scriptures and their cardinal principles into the vernaculars spoken by the masses. Consequently, the vernaculars not only received a distinct impetus and a new dignity but rose in prominence also. The Vaishnavas created a vast lyrical literature in Hindi and Bengali; the verses composed by the saints of Maharashtra enriched the Marathi literature, and the teachings of the Sikh Gurus invented new alphabets and created Gurmukhi literature. We shall now take this opportunity to describe the growth of the vernacular, literatures in the medieval age.

Literary Development

Though the Turko-Afghan kings were primarily military persons, some of them took interest in *belles lettres*, and under their liberal patronage literature of high order was produced during the period under review. The court of Delhi Sultans was well attended by writers, poets, scholars, philosophers logicians, theologians, lawyers and chroniclers. Amir Khusrau, Mir Hasan Dehlavi, Badruddin, called Aadri Chach. Ahmad Thaneswari, Qazi Abdul Muqtadir Shanihi and Amil ul Mulk Multani were the shining lights of the literary firmament during the period of the Delhi Sultans.

The court of Muhammad Tughlaq was adorned by poets, logicians philosophers and physicians. Similarly, celebrated writers, scholars and poets lived in the courts of the provincial dynasties under whose patronage a great deal of literature was produced in the age. Jaunpur was a well known seat of Arabic learning, Islamic philosophy and literature. Its famous ruler, Ibrahim Sharki, patronized scholars generously. His liberal bounty attracted many men of letters to his court. Numerous works on lite nature and philosophy were compiled during his reign. Not only new and original works were written but famous Sanskrit works were also translated into Persian. In the fourteenth century, Firuz Tughlaq got many works on philosophy and astronomy translated into Persian. During the reign of Sikandar Lodi a medieval treatise was translated from Sanskrit into Persian. But it should be noted that the Delhi Sultans patronized Islamic literature. Their patronage was confined to a culture of limited type. The poets and writers of the age looked to Persia and Arabia for their inspiration. Indian life did not figure in these works. The scope of the literary and cultural activity was very much limited. It was confined to the courts of the Delhi Sultans and provincial rulers.

Development of Vernacular Literature : But Islam gave an immediate fillip to the vernacular languages which were in the course of evolution. The great reform movement gave a great impetus to the development of vernacular literatures. The religious reformers and saints wrote, spoke and preached in a language which could be easily understood by the masses. The growth of Hindi, Marathi, Bengali, Maithili, Punjabi, Gurumukhi and other provincial literatures took place in the age. Thus, Ramanand and Kabir, Surdas and Tulsidas preached in Hindi: Mirabai and some other preachers and saints of the Radha Krishna cult sang in *Brajbhasha*. They not only enriched the Hindi poetry but helped a good deal towards the composition of a vast mass of sacred Hindi literature. Namdev, Jnaneswara, Tukaram and others greatly helped the development of Marathi literature. Nanak and his devoted followers promoted the growth of Punjabi and Gurumukhi. Narsinh Mehta and other reformers brought Gujarati into prominence, and Bengali literature owes a heavy debt to the teachers of the Vaishnava cult like Chaitanya, Chandidas, etc. Let us now review in detail the growth of the vernacular literature.

Hindi Literature : The liberal patronage extended by the court of provincial rulers to men of letters has added to the growth of the Hindi literature. The poet Chand Bardai of the court of Prithviraj Chauhan of Delhi and the author of the great epic, *Prithviraj Raso,* was the earliest Hindi poet. This book describes the life of the warrior king Prithviraj and narrates his battle with the Muslims. A distinguished contemporary of Chand Bardai was Jagnak, the author of the *Alha Khand.* It is a lyric describing in stirring and inspiring language the deeds of love and war of two brave warriors, Alha and Udal of Mahoba. Vidyadhar in his book has described the exploits of Jaychand, the king of Kannauj.

In Rajasthan, grew a vast litera ture, rich in heroic ballads and poetry connected with the deeds of Rajput chiefs and warriors. *Hamir Raso* and *Hamir Kavya* of the poet Sharangdhar deserve mention in this connection. They give a glowing account of the gallant deeds of Ranthambhor's ruler Hamir. Similarly, Nath Singh has composed *Vijayapal Raso* which describes the battles of Karauli chief, Vijaya Pal, in stirring language; Narpati Nath had written *Bisaldeva Raso* and Bhat or bard had composed *Khuman Raso* which relates the wars and battles from Sri Ram to Khuman. The period of these *Rasos* is called the age of rich heroic ballads. This is followed by the period of reformer saints and their religious and philosophical literatures.

Gorakhnath and Namdev were the first saints to compose the *Bhajans* and *Pads* or verses in Hindi. But the verses of Kabir, Mira and Nanak are most famous. Kabir's verses, numbering about 20,000, are striking examples of epigrammatic and aphoristic style. His poetry which possessed force and charm is dominated with the sentiment of Hindu Muslim unity. His mysticism has its own prominence in Hindi literature. He popularized Hindi religious literature and vastly extended its influence. Nanak, the founder of Sikhism, has enriched Hindi literature with his verses which have their own poetical excellence. Kabir, Nanak, Dadu Dayal, Sunder Das, Maluk Das, Sundar Vilas, Dharamdas, etc., have created religious literature. Mirabai who was intenselydevpted to her deity, Lord Krishna, expressed her love and devotion in exquisite verses which are famous for their sweet melody and tenderness. *Narsiji ko Mayro, Raj Govinda* and a commentary on *Gita Govind* are her famous works.

Sufi saints have also enriched the Hindi literature. Among these Mulla Daud composed *Chandawat,* Kutban wrote *Mrigawat,* Manjhan *Madhu Malfi,* and Malik Muhammad Jayasi the famous *Padmavat* which deals with the love story of Ratansen of Chittor and Padmavati, a princess of Sri Lanka, and his battle with Allauddin Khilji. Jayasi has expounded the cardinal principles of Sufism in his works. The narration of the growth of Hindi literature would be incomplete if Amir Khusrau is not mentioned. He was a poet of the court of Khilji and Tughlaq rulers. He enjoyed their royal patronage. He was a poet and writer of high order. His many works testify to the boundless fertility of his niuse. His poetry is simple and appeals directly to the masses. He was a man of versatile genius and therefore wrote works on several subjects with marvellous ease and grace.

Marathi Literature : Real Marathi literature begins from the medieval age. Chakradhar, Bhaskar, Bhatt, Narendra and Mukanda raya were the early poets and writers of Marathi. Namdev composed his hymns in Marathi. But jnaneswari, the famous saint of Maharashtra in the thirteenth century, composed his commentary on the Gita called *jnaneswari* in Prakrit Marathi. It appealed to the masses most. Another saint and writer, Eknath, flourished nearly two hundred and fifty years after Inaneswari. His translation of the *Bhagwat* in Marathi and *Rukmini Swayamvar* and *Bhawarth Ramayan* deserve mention. His contemporary was Dasopant the author of *Gitarnava* and *Padarnava.* But the *Abhangas* of Tukaram are most famous in Marathi literature of the period. They are recited in every house even today in Maharashtra.

Gujarati Literature : The early medieval Gujarati literature was enriched by the bards and the Jain monks. To preach the doctrines of Jainism, the Jain monks had composed many works in poetry called *Ras,* among which *Bharatbahubali Ras* of Gunaratna Suri, *Shil Ras,* of Vijaya Bhadra, *Gautam* Swami *Ras* of Udaywant, *Madan Rekha* of Harsewak and *Shant Ras* of Sunder Suri deserve mention. The *Bhakti* movement in Gujarat stimulated the growth of religious literature in Gujarati. Mira and Narsinh Mehta occupy preminent position among the saints and poets of Gujarat. Narsinh Mehta, who was famous for his devotion and love to Lord Krishna, had composed more than one lac of verses and sweet religious songs in Gujarati. His popular works are *Chaturi Shodasi, Sarnaldas no Vivah, Dhan Lila* and *Govind Gaman.* Mehta expounded his mysticism in his works indirectly. He was followed by two famous poets, Bhalan and Bhim. They translated Sanskrit works into Gujarati and composed original ones. Vatso, the author of *Subhadrd Haran* and *Sadhu Charitra,* Vachharaja, the author of *Ras Manjari.* Kushal Labh Vachak, the writer of *Madhavanal Kamkandala Ras* and Tulsi who wrote on *Dhruva* are the famous Gujarati poets of the sixteenth century. Gujarati prose was gradually evolving, and *Panchatantra, Ramayan, Yogavasishtha* and *Gita* were translated in prose in the sixteenth century.

Bengali Literature : The works of Vidyapati and Chandidas, renowned poets of the age, provided stimulus to the growth of Bengali literature. Vidyapati's verses, which express his devotion and love to Radha Krishna, moved the hearts of millions by their sweet melody and earnestness of his *Bhakti.* Vidyapati wrote not only in Bengali and Maithili but in Sanskrit also. He flourished in the court of Shiva Singh of Tirhut. Writers and poets who followed Vidyapati produced a crop of Bengali literature.

The Muslim rulers of Bengal also patronized Bengali. They engaged scholars to translate the *Ramayan* and the *Mahabharat* from Sanskrit into Bengali. Thus, Sultan Nusrat Shah of Gaur got the *Mahabharat* translated into Bengali. Krittivas whose work is the Bible for the common people preached the Bengali translation of the Sanskrit *Ramayan.* He enjoyed the patronage of awking of Gaur." Maladhar Vasu translated the *Gita* into Bengali under the patronage of Sultan Hussain Shah. Kavindra

Parameswar, at the command of Hussain Shah's general Paragal Khan, undertook to translate the *Mahabharat* and brought it down to the *Sri Parva.* Then, Chaitanya enriched the Bengali literature with his songs and *bhajans.* The disciples and followers of Chaitanya made Bengali rich with their sweet songs and *bhajans,* verses and translations of Sanskrit works. In fact, a large volume of Chaitanya literature was produced. But in the sixteenth century Bengali was greatly enriched with the literature about Siva and Durga.

Vernacular Literature in the South : In the south, a great impetus was given to literary efforts by the Saiva movement in the thirteenth and fourteenth centuries, and new original literature was produced in Tamil by the saints of Saivism. Similarly, Telugu and Kannad literatures receive much encouragement from Vijayanagar kings. Great scholars, commentators, poets and thinkers, were associated with their courts. Krishna Deva Raya, the most renowned emperor of Vijayanagar, took keen interest in literature and himself composed a poem, *Amuktamalyada.* Allasani Peddana was his poet laureate. He was a writer of considerable original merit. He wrote many works, the most famous among which is the *Svarochisa Manu Charitra.* Its story is based on the *Markandeya Purana.* Another distinguished poet of the age was Nandi Timman, the author of *Parijat Apaharan.*

During the period under review the Jains also produced a great deal of religious and secular literature. They wrote many independent philosophical and poetical works. Asadhara and Hemchandra Suri are the most famous Jain writers of the period. The former was the author of many commentaries and works on Jain ethics but the latter surpassed him in his monumentary works. The rhyme, which is regarded as a speciality of modern vernaculars, is found profusely used in the *Apabhramsa* works of the Jains. The Jain writers of the Digambar school, by their works, gave a great encouragement to the Kannad and Tamil languages. Hemchandra Suri of Swetamber school who flourished in Gujarat wrote his works in Sanskrit. He was an ascetic, epic poet, lexicographer, teacher and scholar of outstanding merit.

In his works, he made successful attempts to combine the Aryan culture with Jain thought. In his monumental work, *Purusha Charita,* Lives of the Great Men, he had not only narrated the great traditions of the past but ·discussed and popularized, in a Jain garb, the entire mythology of Hinduism. "Hemchandra is one of the makers of Indian mind and takes place with Valmiki, Vyas and Sankara. Other Jain monks also wrote works on several subjects in *Apabhramsa* and Gujarati. It should be noted that owing to the crisis brought about by Islam, literature, like religion, tended to become less the monopoly of the learned scholars and pandits and more a cause of the common people.

Literary Activity in Sanskrit : In spite of the abundant crop of the vernacular literatures, Sanskrit literature did not cease to be cultivated and the period was not entirely barren of works in Sanskrit, both religious as well as secular. About 1300, Parthasarathi wrote many works on *Karma Mimarnsa.* Some works which expounded the doctrines of *Yoga, Vaiseshika* and *Nyaya* systems of philosophy were also .,written in the period under review. The Buddhists at Vikramsil, in Bengal and Jains in Gujarat and at other places assiduously studied logic. A Jain monk named Deva Suri who flourished in the twelfth century was the greatest Jain logician of the age.

The saints of the *Bhakti* movement made valuable contributions to philosophical literature. Great works on philosophic Hinduism were written in the south. Under the patronage of the Vijayanagar emperors, two brothers, Madhvacharya and Sayana, in close association with other learned scholars, wrote famous authoritative commentaries on the Vedas and Hindu philosophy. Their famous work on Hindu philosophy is *Sarvadarsan.* Sayana wrote commentaries on the *Rigveda, Aitareya Brahmana* and other scriptures. Many important Sanskrit dramas were written like *Hammir mada mardan* by Jai Singh, *Pradyumna Abhyudaya* by Prince

Ravivarman, *Pratap Rudra Kalyan* by Vidyanath, *Parvati Parinaya* by Vamana Bhatta Bana, *Gangadas Pratap Vilas* by Gangadhar and *Vidagdha Madhava* and *Lalita Madhav* by Rupa Goswami who was distinguished for his extraordinary learning and power of assimilation. He wrote nearly twenty five works in Sanskrit. This age is noted for a few excellent commentaries. Smriti and grammatical literature flourished in Mithila and Bengal during this period.

Many commentaries were written on the ancient law books on the style of Vijnanesvara, the author of *Mitakshara*, and Jimuta Vahana, the writer of *Daya Bhaga*. From the thirteenth century to the fifteenth, Mithila became so famous in the field that its writers of the Smriti literature came to be regarded as forming a separate school. Smriti studies were revived and developed by Chandesvara and other eminent scholars, and Bhava Datta wrote his famous commentary on *Naisadha*. But Vachaspati Misra, who was a renowned scholar of Sanskrit and Maithil vernaculars, flourishing in the closing years of the fifteenth century, was the most famous among them. Literature of the philosophy of devotionalism *(Bhakti)* and Smriti was also promoted luxuriantly in Bengal. Raghunath Siromani and Raghunandan Misra became most famous there. Similarly, in western India, Nil Kanth Sastri wrote *Vyavaharamayukha* in the sixteenth century.

In Gujarat Sanskrit resurgence was associated with Hemchandra Suri and the magnificent and learned court of Viradhavala revived the traditions of Raja Bhoja in the west. Rana Kumbha's court in Mewar became the centre of Sanskrit learning and culture. Thus, sudden efflorescence of Sanskrit literature in the distant places, like Mewar, Kalinjar, Gujarat and Vijayanagar, was due to the fact that with the Muslim conquest of the Gangetic Valley, scholars and poets took refuge in the courts of the Hindu rulers in distant areas.

Though the works of Sanskrit, compared to those of the vernaculars, were more unreal, ornate, technical and unrelated to the daily life and the social and spiritual aspirations of the people, yet it was Sanskrit alone that united the Hindus during this period. From Kanya Kumari to Kashmir, the language of the scholars and their thought continued to be Sanskrit, and without the continued cultivation of Sanskrit, the Hindus would have lost all sense of unity, harmony and fellow feeling. Again by tying the vernaculars of the country to the thought forms and traditions of Sanskrit a cultural link and spiritual unity was established among the provinces, which was an achievement of the period under review.

The Growth of Urdu : Another important achievement in the domain of literature was the growth of Urdu, "out of the mingling of Persian Arabic and Turkish words and ideas with languages and concepts of Sanskrit origin." It has the words of Arabic, Persian, Turkish and western Hindi, and dialects of the Delhi province. The grammatical structure of Urdu is essentially that of Hindi. "The various necessities which forced the Mohammedans and Hindus to meet each other involved the evolution of a common language," which came to be known as Urdu. It was rather the outcome of the linguistic synthesis of the Hindus and the Muslims, an indigenous product. In course of time it developed new characteristics and the poets, writers and historians of the Muslim courts enriched its literature with their works. It became a good literary language in the north in the eighteenth century. Amir Khusrau was the first poet who used Urdu as the vehicle for the expression of his poetic fancy.

Historic Work : The period under survey witnessed the growth of historical literature under the patronage of the Turko-Afghan Sultans. It is rather a gift of the Muslims to India. The chronological sense was very imperfectly developed among the Hindus, and consequently, they neglected the historical literature before the Muslim conquest. But some valuable historical chronicles were composed in elegant Persian prose during this period. Minhaj ud din's *Tabaqat-i-Nasiri,* a general history of the Islamic world, Amir Khusrau's *Mesnevis* and *Tarikh i Alai,* Hasan Nizami's *Tajul Maasir,* Shams-i-Siraj

Afif's *Tarikh ;.Firuz* Shahi Sarhindi's *Tarikh-i-Mubarak Shahi* and Yahia bin Ahmad's *Tarikh-i-Mubarak Shqizi* deserve special mention. They are standard historical works utilized by the modern historians for writing the history of the literature. The most famous historian of the period was Zia-un din Barani, a contemporary of Muhammad Tughlaq and Firuz Shah. He enjoyed the patronage of both the Sultans. He composed *Tarikh-i-Firuz Shahi* and Shams-i-Siraj Afif completed it. These chronicles not only served as important historical materials of study in themselves but furnished an example which Hindu writers and Hindu rulers were not slow to imitate.

Indo-Persian Literature : The courts of the Turko-Afghan rulers were adorned with Persian scholars, writers, poets, theologians, philosophers and historians. Some of them produced real monumen tal works and left a deep impression upon the Persian literature in general. An account of the distinguished chroniclers and their works in Persian is already given above. The most notable among the poets, writers and theologians were Amir Khusrau and Mir Hassan Dehlavi. Traditions ascribe to Khusrau the composition of ninety nine works. However, it is believed that some of his works are either lost or have not yet been traced. He enjoyed royal patronage from Muhammad Khan, Balban's eldest son, to Ghiyasuddin Tughlaq till he died in 1325. He was a great poet, prose writer, master musician, gifted bard and lexicographer. He was the first Muslim scholar who used Hindi words and adopted Indian poetic imagery and themes. His famous works are *Khazain-ul-Jutuch* and *Tarikh-i-Alai*. Mir Hassan Dehlavi, a contemporary of Khusrau, was another famous Indo-Persian poet. He will be described as 'musical and most pleasing.' Maulana Muaiyyan-ud-din Umrani and Ain-ul-mulk Multani were other shining literary figures. Ain-ul-mulk's famous work is the *Munshat-i-Mahru* which is a collection of letters and despatches. They served as models for official correspondence. Some Muslim scholars were attracted to wards Sanskrit and they translated some Sanskrit works into Persian.

Salient Features

The literary activity of this period had certain salient features which are as follows:

1. The abundant outcrop of the Hindi literature, both in Sanskrit and the vernacular, indicates that the Hindu mind was never sterile as the result of Turko-Afghan conquest of the country. The virility and vigour of the Hindu mind was never extinguished by the deadening effect of the foreign conquest and proselytism of Islam. Though royal patronage was denied to the cultural activities of the Hindus, their literature flourished in many centres and capitals.
2. The literary works that were produced in the age were not of a very high order. They could not be compared to the master pieces of Bhasa, Kalidas, Bana or Bhava Bhuti.
3. To promote the understanding of Hindu culture, translation of Sanskrit works into Persian was encouraged by the Muslim rulers and scholars.
4. Several Muslim poets and writers began to use the spoken language to make the masses understand their philosophy, teachings and thought. Poet Masud used Hindi to express his ideas as early as the eleventh century.
5. Numerous saints utilized the vernaculars to appeal to the people and to attract them towards their teachings. The *Bhakti* movement, thus, led to a rich crop of religious and philosophical literature.
6. Urdu was evolved as a common medium of expression between the Muslims and the Hindus. Its own literature had grown up.
7. A large number of histories, biographies and letters were written in Persian. They formed a magnificent source of history and introduced historical literature in India.

8. As the Kayasthas and Kashmiri Brahmanas entered the lower ranks of bureaucracy during the period of Muslim administration, they were gradually evolving a new language and prose style for official correspondence and later on it came to be known as Hindustani.
9. With the advent of the Muslims the use of paper, love for calligraphy and the system of illustrating manuscripts were introduced in the isphere of literature and they attained their perfection under the Mughals.

System of Education

Though the attainment of the followers of Islam in education were not very high, yet the State encouraged scholars, and learning was held in high esteem. The teaching class occupied a high position in society and commanded respect and confidence of the people. Affectionate relations existed between the teacher and his pupils. Personal service was expected from the pupils.

The Hindu monitorial system was adopted by the Muslims. More intelligent and advanced students were appointed as monitors who assisted the teachers in his work of teaching. Though education was supposed to be incumbent upon every Muslim, the education of average girl was neglected. Though there was no separate department of public instruction, the Muslim kings opened schools and colleges and established libraries and supplemented their educational achievements by patronage of literary works. Poets, writers, philosophers and chroniclers of eminence adorned the Muslim courts. *Maktabs* for primary education and *Madarsahs* for higher education were set up both by the State and well to do persons. Many times *maktabs* were attached to mosques and shrines. Both *maktabs* and *madarsahs* were supported by State grants in cash or land or private liberality. As there was no printing press, books were written by hand and certain persons were especially employed for the purpose. Consequently, penmanship was highly valued in Muslim India. Sometimes technical training was diffused by the system of apprenticeship in *Karkhanas* or workshops under *Ustads* or master artisans. Under the patronage of the Sultan and some Muslim chiefs of the provinces, Sankrit was studied by the Muslim scholars and some important Sanskrit works were translated into Persian.

Though education was mostly religious, the courses of study included grammar, rhetoric, logic, theology, ethics, metaphysics, literature, jurisprudence and elementary science. The medium of instruction was Persian and the study of Arabic was compulsory for the Muslims. There was neither standardization nor degrees and diplomas. Examinations were not the be all and the end all of education. Corporal punishments were inflicted on the students. It is doubtful whether the Hindus and the Muslims studied side by side in the *maktabs* or *madarsahs* or *khanquahs* (schools attached to shrines) without any restrictions of rank, race or religion.

Balban, Allauddin and Muhammad Tughlaq encouraged education. They showed favours to all intellectuals of eminence. Many were the recipients of honorarium from the State. Firuz Tughlaq strove zealously for the spread of education. He not only patronized learning and encouraged men of letters but sent out eminent teachers to reside in different parts of his kingdom for imparting instruction to the people. He repaired old *madarsahs,* built new ones and founded nearly thirty colleges. Firuz Shahi Madarsah was the most magnificent educational institution founded by Firuz Tughlaq big college with a mosque and tank was set up by him in the vicinity of Qadam Shanf to immortalize the name of his beloved son Fateh Khan. Under Khizr Khan and Mubarak Shah, the Sayyid Kings, Badaon and Cuttair flourished as centres of education. They contained many mosques and *madarsahs.* Bahlol Lodi and Sikandar Lodi both took interest in education. Both opened schools and colleges in their kingdom. Sikandar Lodi gave a fresh impulse to the art of writing, compilation and translation, and standard literary works were produced under him, the most famous among them is *Tibb-i-Sikandari,* a book on the science of medicine. According to Farishta it was under Sikandar Lodi that the Hindus commenced the study of Persian and Mohammedan literature.

In the provincial kingdoms of the north and Shia States of the south the Sultans patronized learning and promoted education. Schools and seminaries were set up at Multan under Hussain Shah Dangha and Hussain Mirza. Jaunpur developed as an important centre of education under Ibrahim Sharki. Hundreds of men flocked to Jaunpur from far and near for higher education. There were a very large number of *madarsahs.* It was a university city. There was another famous college in Malwa at Mandu in close proximity to the Masjid of Sultan Hushang Shah. In Bengal, Ghiyasuddin I and II, Hussain Shah and Nusrat Shah promoted education liberally. They founded many schools and colleges and attracted eminent scholars and teachers. Ghiyasuddin II founded the famous college called *Darasbari.*

The Hussain kings of Bengal encouraged Islamic as well as Hindu learning. In Gujarat, the city of Ahmedabad was adorned with magnificent *maktabs* and *madarsahs.* In the south, the Bahmani Sultans were generous patrons of letters and opened schools and colleges in their dominions making ample arrangements for free education. In their benevolent solicitude for the welfare of the poor and orphans, the Sultans of Ahmednagar, Bijapur and Golkonda established many *maktabs* and *madarsahs* in Bijapur, Gulbarga, Bihar, Ellichpur, Daulatabad and Debal. Bijapur and Bihar became seats of learning. The Imperial Library of Bijapur was noted for its rare books.

Art and Culture

The rulers of the period under review were great patrons of fine arts. Consequently, embroidery works, ornamental pottery, metal works, ivory works and calligraphy progressed well. But painting was shunned by the Muslim rulers and nobles as it was prohibited by Quranic traditions. But architecture was very liberally encouraged by them.

Architectural Development

One of the richest contributions of early Muslims was in the domain of architecture. The spirit of synthesis that was expressed in religious thought was also clearly manifested in fine arts. Indo Muslim architecture is a shining example of this spirit of synthesis and harmony. The Muslims had evolved their own art with certain characteristics. Islam has been flourishing in the arid region of scanty rainfall stretching from the Mediterranean coast in the west to the Chinese wall in the east. Here the Muslims have lived and erected the great fabrics of their culture. This vast expanse of land has faced the cruelty and economy of a stem nature. For kilometres together there is no vegetation alive. Scanty pasturage and desert have fostered the nomadic life there. This coupled with emptiness between instances of time and points of space have deeply influenced the Muslim mind.

It led to such mental characteristics as a quiet resignation and a calm submission to divine will, contempt foriconism, absence of plastic feeling, devotion to pure ideas, etc. This has reacted on the Muslim Conception of art. Moreover, for their religious needs the Muslims had to assemble in an open extensive place embodying sublimity, purity, peace and providing shelter for the congregation. Thus, the Muslim art was conditioned by the learning characteristics of the Muslim mentality, practical needs "if their religion and worship, and the geography of their region. Consequently, the salient features of the Muslim architecture were massive and extensive buildings and mosques, aspiring domes, tall minarets, lofty portals, open courtyards, pillared naves, huge walls all bereft of sculpture but adorned with a few mouldings, geometrical patterns and calligraphic inscriptions.

On the contrary, India, the land of the Hindus, has been a country of vast unending plains irrigated by broad rivers, lofty mountains, impenetrable forests, a variety of seasons, abundant vegetation, exuberance of rains, thickly populated towns and villages where the wheel of life moves on with uninterrupted rhythm. Here the whole universe throbs with the intensity of life. Consequently, the Hindus have evolved distinct mental characteristics and system of culture, peculiar and individual. What wonder ,then if such physical features and unique mental set up should have evolved certain system of architecture and we, therefore, find in the Hindu art vastness, stability, majesty, magnificence, sublimity and infinite richness and variety. Like the Indian land, covered extensively with variety of beautiful flowers, leaves creepers, plants etc., every small part of the Hindu buildings and temples was covered with the most elaborate carvings and profuse sculpture, all serving to manifest the Reality.

The spiritual and aesthetic concepts of the Hindus were fully expressed and their art. Hindu religion and art have been inseparably linked together. With the advent of Islam, the Hindu and the Muslim systems of architecture were synthesized. The followers of Islam brought in their train the art of different countries of the western and central Asia, northern Africa and south-western Europe. The happy fusion of these with the different indigenous styles of Hindu art led to the growth of a new Indo-Islamic style of architecture, distinct and different in every province, like Jaunpur, Bengal, Bijapur, Gujarat. Malwa etc.

Blending of two Systems Responsible Factors : The foreign rulers and their followers being military adventurers did not bring with them craftsmen and sculptors. Consequently, for the construction of their buildings they employed Indians. The Indian craftsmen possessed sufficient experience and independence to enable them to work out in their own manner and with their own materials such structures as were required to meet the needs of their new Muslim rulers. They introduced, unconsciously, Hindu architectural designs and decorations in the Muslim buildings.

The early Muslim sovereigns constructed their palaces, mosques, tombs and other structures out of the ready made materials which they obtained by demolishing fortified towns, temples and other buildings of the Hindus. Sometimes the spoils of the Hindu temples were supplemented by a certain amount of new and original masonry under Islamic direction.

Many times the temples of the Hindus were converted by the Muslim rulers into mosques by dismantling their *sikhars* and roofs and erecting in their place domes and lofty minars. Moreover there was a common feature between the temples ,and the mosques. It was the open courtyard surrounded by chambers or colonnades. Temples which were built on this plan were easily converted into mosques to suit the needs of the new conquerors.

The spirit of toleration, harmony and a keen desire for synthesis paved the path for fusion of the two systems of art.

Striking Contrast between the Architectural Structure of the Hindus and the Muslims : The Hindu art was decorative and gorgeous, while the Islamic art was marked with puritanical simplicity. The basis of the Hindu art was trabeate, while that of the Muslim was arcuate. It means that the Hindus used rows of pillars and long beams laid horizontally to span spaces. The Muslims adopted arch to bridge a space and erected graceful domes. Rows of pillars were essential for the Hindus, while the *mehrabs* and the carved bow shaped roofs for the Muslims. Solidarity and beauty were the special characteristics of the Hindu buildings, but spaciousness and simplicity, of the Muslim structures. The Hindu temples had splendid lofty *sikhars,* the Muslim mosques and tombs had magnificent bulbous domes. The walls of the Hindu temples were extremely solid, stable and divided into plinth and basement and stepped by deep projections; the walls of the Muslim buildings were plain and smooth faced.

The temples had "massive darkness" and sombre passages leading to dim shrines and cells; whereas the mosques had vast courts open to light and air coming through many doorways. The Hindu architecture exhibited an infinite richness and variety of sculpture. The Hindus conveyed their meaning by iconography and carved figure compositions. Their monuments were enriched with countless idols of divinities. The walls of their temples and buildings were pulsating with life and imagery. The variety of moulding and the richness of ornament was extraordinary in Hindu buildings. On the contrary, the Muslims were fond of puritan simplicity, and they were iconoclasts. The representation of natural forms and human figures was prohibited by Islamic traditions and practices. For ornamentation the Muslims used colour and line or flat surface carving and ingenious geometric patterns.

Solidarity, stability and beauty were the special characteristics of the Hindu structures, whereas wide conception, massivity, severity and simplicity, of the Muslim buildings. The Hindu art had happy synthesis of sublimity, sobriety, dignity and majesty. The Muslim art had abundance of space. The Hindu art was rich in symbols of *Kamal* (Lotus), *Kalash* etc., whereas the Muslim art lacked these.

Development of Indo-Islamic Architect : Though both systems of art differed fundamentally in their ideals and techniques yet they mingled together giving rise to a new type of Indian architecture. This is described by scholars, like Fergusson, as "Indo-Saracenic" or "Pathan", while some, like Havell, have regarded it as entirely Indian, "in soul and body". They regarded it a modified form of Indian art. Some scholars, like Sir John Marshall and Dr. R. C. Majumdar, disagree with these two views, and point out that the Indo-Islamic 'art is neither merely a local variety of Islamic art, nor it is merely "modified form of Hindu art". In fact, like other aspects of culture of the time, it represented a blending of Brahmanical, Buddhist and Jain styles with those of western and central Asia and northern Africa which the Islamic elements had brought with them in India. Consequently, alterations came about slowly in architecture in the use of arch, style of ornamentation, composition of the various parts of the buildings, addition of certain minor features as *minor* and dome, utilization of wide open space for structures and adoption of plain outlines of surfaces and smoothed walls as distinguished from the extremely mystic and richly decorated walls and pillars of the Hindu temples and buildings.

It is difficult to ascertain how much the Indo-Islamic architecture owed to the Hindu style and how much to the Islamic system. Historians have widely differed in their opinions about the significant question whether the Hindu art or the Muslim art had predominant influence in the synthesis of these two arts, which has exercised far reaching, powerful and distinct influence? It is a controversial subject. The renowned art critic, Havell, remarks that the Hindu influence is abundant and rich in the medieval art. The Muslim attitude towards art was profusely impressed by the Hindu art. The influence of the Hindu art is distinct on many Muslim structures of the medieval age. Fergusson, Smith and Elphinston hold the opinion that the Hindu influence was negative. It was confined to the upper level. Sir John Marshall observes that "Indo-Islamic architecture derives its character from both sources though not always in an equal degree." The Muslims had wonderful capacity to absorb Hindu art. In their own and endowed it with a new and majestic spirit.

Various factors contributed substantially to the evolution of the Islamic art in India. The Arabs who entered India had no liking for art. They could not comprehend the dignity and majesty of architecture. Contrary to this, the Turks were liberal patrons of architecture. They brought into India that art of architecture which was evolved in Persia and it was synthesized with the Hindu architecture. "Wherever the Mohammedans established themselves whether in Asia or Africa or in Europe they invariably adopted to their own needs the indigenous architecture which they found prevailing there." Thus, the Muslim architecture had already become a 'heterogeneous product' before it was introduced in India. Under the patronage of the Muslim rulers it assimilated in India new elements and enriched itself considerably.

The truth is that the Muslims converted invariably Hindu temples, palaces and other structures into their buildings and mosques. They adopted the indigenous style of architecture to suit their own needs. Thus, in transforming the art they had absorbed many ideals and methods of the Hindu art. The Muslim art is indebted to Hindu art for its grace and strength which according to Marshall were significant elements borrowed from the Hindus. Though the Muslim architecture was little influenced by the Hindu style in the vicinity of Delhi due to the numerical superiority of the Muslims, the local Hindu style enjoyed greater ascendancy at Jaunpur and in the Deccan. There it completely overshadowed the Muslim style. In the province of Bengal the Muslims not only adopted the style of building in brick but adorned their structures with chiselled and moulded enrichment, frankly and liberally imitated from the Hindu structures. In western India, the beautiful Gujarati style of Hindu architecture was adopted by the Muslims in its entirety. In Kashmir they did the same with the remarkable wooden structures which had been for long existing there.

The Muslims had added to the Hindu architecture the special characteristics of spaciousness, massiveness, majesty and width. The new foreign rulers introduced *mehrab* or arch, dome, *minor* and tomb in the indigenous architecture. They had enriched design and beauty and adopted the use of coloured stones and glazed tiles to brighten the effect of colours. They endowed the buildings with new beauties of form and colour.

Pattern of subtle curves, intricate and geometrical designs were used for rich decorative treatment. Sometimes the historic inscription and verses of the Quran in decorative, graceful letters were engraved on the Muslim places of worship. The design of the golden *kalash* (the ornate lotus creation and its metal finial) at the top of the *sikhar* of Hindu temple was adopted by the Muslims in placing a stone *kalash* on the domes of the mosques and tombs. The Hindu scheme of profuse ornamentation was applied to decorate the arches or *mehrabs*. The Muslims adopted the Hindu techniques to make the structures more strong, stable and graceful. They learnt from the Hindus the proportionate massing of structures and their different parts.

The Muslim structures are of two types (i) religious, and (ii) secular. The former consist of the mosque and the tomb. The latter include such structures as intended for public and civic purposes, such as, pavilions, town gates, houses, walls, gardens, palace forts etc. The mosque has an open courtyard surrounded by a pillared verandah. For congregational prayers the side facing Mecca is elaborated into a pillared hall or sanctuary with a wall at the back having a recess or alcove called a *mehrab* indicating the direction for prayer. There stands a pulpit on the right side of the *mehrab* and a high tower or minaret rising above the walls to summon the faithful to prayer. The sanctuary where the *mehrab* is enshrined is elaborated into the principal architectural feature with the courtyard and its cloisters leading up to it. There is a central graceful dome over the sanctuary. The tomb, constructed to make the resting place of the dead, is an imposing structure of vaulted halls and towering domes enclosed within a spacious garden enshrining in the centre the grave of the dead. The tomb has a chamber, in the centre of which is the cenotaph, the whole structure being roofed by the dome. In the ground underneath this building is the mortuary chamber called the *maqbarah* or *tahkhana* with the grave *(kabr)* in the middle. Some of the large mausoleums have a mosque as a separating building, the whole being situated within one enclosure called a *rauza;* some important tombs are named as *dargahs*.

Imperial Style : On the whole the buildings of the Pathan rulers were imposing, magnificent and massive. They were beautifully furnished and sometimes were masterpieces of architectural skill. Though in the beginning the Muslim architecture was light and graceful, with the lapse of time it became heavy and solid. Muslim structures were erected in

India from the days of the slaveruter Qutub-ud-din. The style which was used in the vicinity of Delhi is known as Delhi style of architecture. The Qutub Minar, the Quwat-ul-Islam mosque at Delhi, and a mosque at Ajmer called *Dhai Din Ka Jhonpara* belong to the time of the Slave kings.

The materials of Hindu temples and structures have been used in these buildings. In fact, the above mentioned mosques at Delhi and Ajmer were originally Hindu temples. Some of the parts of these temples were demolished and domes and arches were erected there, and Muslim designs and ornaments were added. These two mosques and the Qutub Minar are the best specimens of the Delhi architecture. The Qutub Minar, originally a tower from which the muezzin could summon the faithful to prayer, was commenced by Qutub-ud-din and completed by IItutmish. Percy Brown remarks that the Qutub Minar "as a whole is a most impressive conception, the vivid colour of its red sandstone, the changing texture of its fluted storeys with their overlay of inscriptional hands, the contrast between the alternating spaces of plain masonry and rich carving, the shimmer of the shadows under the balconies, all combine to produce an effect of marked vitality." Its most pronounced quality is that of stability and its very shape decreasing as it rises illustrates "man's highest endeavour to make his handiwork timeless." Fergusson describes it as the most perfect example ora tower known to exist anywhere.

It was purely an Islamic structure, because such towers were unknown to the Hindus in that time. Marshall remarks about the Qutub Minar that "nothing, certainly, could be more imposing or more befittingly symbolic of Muslim power than this stem and stupendous fabric; nor could anything be more exquisite than its rich but restrained carvings." Shamsuddin Iltutmish, a famous Slave king, constructed three buildings at Badaun, 240 kilometres from Delhi. They are the Hauzi-i-Shamsi, the Shams-i-Idgah and Jama Masjid.

The last one is architecturally important as it is one of the largest and most substantially built examples of the Delhi or imperial style another famous building of the period is the mausoleum of Iltutmish at old Delhi. With the exception of Balban's Red Palace and his tomb at Delhi, which is an example of pure Muslim execution, no structures of any importance were produced during the period extending from the death of Iltutmish to the accession of Allauddin Khilji.

Sultan Allauddin Khilji constructed many palaces, forts and tanks, but the most remarkable of them were the palace of Hazar Situm, the fort and city of Siri, the Jamait Khan Masjid at the tomb or dargah of Nizamuddin Auliya, the Alai Darwaza at the Qutub Minar, the Hauz-i-Alai and the Hauz-i-Khas buildings. These buildings indicate that there was great reaction against the Indianization of Muslim architecture and Allauddin made the Arabian style of architecture the basis for his structures. His two well known buildings, the Jamait Khan Masjid and Alai Darwaza or the gateway of Allauddin are other famous specimens of the Delhi or imperial style of architecture; the latter is supposed to be one of the most treasured gems of Islamic architecture in India. Its decorative treatment emphasizes its beauty of form. It has outstanding gracefulness which lies in the shape of arches. It indicates a distinct progress in the evolution of Islamic architecture in India.

The Khiljis were succeeded by the Tughlaqs. Ghiyas-ud-din Tughlaq built the city of Tughlaqabad and his own tomb under the walls of this city. It is remarkable for its simplicity and strength. His successor Muhammad Tughlaq built the fortress of Allahabad and the town of Jahanpanah. But among the Tughlaqs Firuz Shah was a magnificent builder. He had a passion for repairing ancient buildings and erecting new ones. He spent vast sums of money on the construction of many works of public utility and maintained a large number of craftsmen and architects at the cost of the State. He laid out several cities, such as, Firozabad, Fatehabad, Hissar and Jaunpur, and constructed many palaces, mosques, tanks and gardens. But the architecture of the Tughlaq period lost the splendour, luxuriance and variety which characterized that of the Slave and Khilji regimes: it became prosaic, simple, austere and formal.

The Tughlaqs produced at their best a stern, gloomy, spiritless and puritan architecture. If the Khilji architecture is celebrated for the lavish and elaborate use of ornament and richness of detail, the buildings of the Tughlaqs are attractive for a chaste sobriety which was gradually developed into a rigid puritanical simplicity. This was due to the puritan taste and narrow religious outlook of the Tughlaq Sultans and comparatively poor condition of their finances. However, the tomb of Firuz Shah and that of his Prime Minister Khan-i-Jahan Tilangani, the city of Firozabad and its palace fortress, called the Kotla Firuz Shah, are the best specimens of the Tughlaq architecture. The pillars, doors, windows, brackets and other features of the Tughlaq buildings indicate the influence of Hindu architecture.

The Tughlaqs were followed by the Sayyid and Lodi Sultans. The splendour and grace of the Khilji style of architecture was revived under them to some extent, but they could not shake off the deadening effect of the Tughlaq period. Owing to the much diminished influence of the Sayyids and Lodis all forms of enterprise languished and what architecture was produced reflects the broken spirit of the time. Neither mosques of any importance nor public buildings of any kind were produced during their reign. But the best buildings of their period are the tombs of the kings and nobles, especially the tomb of Sikandar Lodi. It is a very finished conception of the art of the period. Beautiful ornamentation in the interior of the dome of Sikandar's tomb and the design of its entrance exhibit Hindu influence. Besides the royal tombs, many mosques of a private nature attached to some tombs were also constructed. *Moth Ki Masjid* built by the Prime Minister of Sikandar Lodi is such independent and notable structure.

It has several conspicuous and attractive features. Among the mausoleums of the nobles the tombs of Bade Khan and

Chhote Khan and *Shish Gumbad* deserve mention. The Muslim architecture under the Sayyids and Lodis was gradually losing its rigid puritan conceptions and assimilating Hindu elements. An art critic remarks that "the architecture of the Lodis was endowed with life and warmth by the magic touch of the Hindu genius." The Hindu features of gates and facade of the Muslim buildings, the external drip stone of the mosque and the plaster ornamentation on the interior of the dome of a tomb bear testimony to the statement. However, the imperial or Delhi style of architecture in the form it finally assumed under the Lodi Sultans, was continued for nearly half a century more, partly due to its outstanding prestige and ancient lineage and partly on account of the disorder in the country during the regime of the early Mughals which precluded any other style taking its place. Ultimately, it paved the way for the Mughal architecture.

Provincial Style

Certain regional manifestations of the Indo-Islamic architecture, distinct from the imperial style at Delhi, were produced in provinces of the country and therefore they are designated as 'provincial architecture'. Though the provincial architecture is subsidiary to the main style, some of its buildings are of remarkable beauty and exhibit definite original qualities. These provincial styles were modified by the Indigenous art of the region, unusual climatic conditions and technical differences, one kind of building material being common in some regions and rare in others.

***Punjab Architecture*:** The earliest provincial style to emerge was in the Punjab. It was there that the first contacts with Islam were made through its two principal cities, Multan and Lahore. Percy Brown holds the opinion that the Muslim structures of Lahore were of Ghaznavide Suljuqian origin, while those of Multan were of an Arab Persian derivation, though Indo-Islamic art at both places had much in common. The structures at Lahore were made of timber and brick, but there are no complete examples of the buildings of this period at Lahore. But at Multan the earliest buildings were two mosques. The first was erected by Muhammad bin Qasim, and the second by the Karmathians on the ruins of temples. Besides these, five tombs of Muslim saints of the period still survive there, the most famous being the mausoleum of the saint Shah Rukn-i-Alam.

Bengal Architecture : The architecture in Bengal assumed a succession of forms which were maintained for a period of two hundred and fifty years. There developed a mixed style of architecture. It combined the Muslim art with the outstanding elements of Hindu art, such as, the use of brick, pointed graceful arches on short solid pillars, Hindu temple style of curvilinear cornices and carved Hindu symbolic, attractive and decorative designs like the lotus. The important Muslim buildings in Bengal are found at Gaur or Lakhanauti, Tribeni and Pandua.

The earliest Muslim structures in Bengal are the tomb and mosque of Zafar Khan Ghazi. But the most perfect examples of the Bengal style are the Adina Masjid built by Sikandar Shah at Pandua and the Dakhil Darwaza built by Barbak Shah. The Adina Masjid presents a certain grave and stately dignity. The Dakhil Darwaza is a triumphal arch, aligned to face the citadel of Gaur. It is a superb example of brick and terra-cotta work and displays a surprising boldness of design and masterly skill. It "shows that the Muslim rulers still retained their grandiose ideals which found expression inspectacular monuments, not however devoid of architectural dignity and ,power. " The other famous structures of the Bengal style are the Chhota Sona Masjid' (Small Golden Mosque), and the 'Bada Sona Masjid' (Great Golden Mosque), the mausoleum of Hussain Shah and the Qadam Rasul mosque. The Great Golden Mosque has the merit of greater simplicity and impressiveness. Fergusson considers it the finest memorial now left in Gaur. The Islamic architecture of Bengal is not a style of a very impressive kind when compared to others design, execution and ornamentation.

Jaunpur Architecture : At Jaunpur, a new style of architecture developed and its typical buildings were produced in the fifteenth century. The Jaunpur style reveals a happy blending of the Hindu and Muslim architectural ideas. It displays the indubitable influence of the Hindu art. Its massive sloping walls, square pillars, smaller galleries and cloisters are clearly Hindu features, designed by Hindu masons. The Atala Masjid, built on the site of Hindu temple of Atala Devi, is one of the brilliant specimens of the Jaunpur style. It has the freshness and vigour of the style and is expressive of the stimulating intellectual influences by which it was surrounded.

The largest and most ambitious of the Jaunpur mosques is the Jami Masjid. Other buildings of the style are the Lal Darwaza Masjid (Red door Mosque), the Khalis Mukhlis Masjid and the broken facade of the Jahangiri and the Khalis Mukhlis. All the Jaunpur mosques have no minars of the general Muslim type, but galleries; beautiful open work screens were provided there for the accommodation of ladies. Fuhrer and Burgess have praised much the Jaunpur style of architecture. Sir John Marshall has admired the rich decoration of the structures of this style. According to Havell, Jaunpur architecture is an interesting synthesis of the creative impulse of the Hindus and the Muslims.

Gujarat Architecture : By far the largest, most important and finest of the provincial styles was that of Gujarat. The Indo-Islamic architecture rose in prominence in Gujarat on account of the assiduous patronage and building ambitions of Gujarat's Muslims rulers, the profound artistic traditions of the inhabitants and the employment of the most accomplished and resourceful artisans of the region. In such circumstances, of all the provincial styles which emerged under the Muslim rule, the. Gujarat style is most indigenously Indian.

The Muslim structures of Gujarat bear unmistakable signs of the influence of splendid Hindu style and its traditions, though modified in certain respects to suit the requirements of the Muslims. The breadth, the spaciousness, the chaste and the graceful elegance of the Hindu style were synthesized liberally with the sense for symmetry and proportion of the Delhi style. Dr. Burgess while admiring the Gujarat style observes that it complines "all the beauty and finish of the not weart with a certain magnificence." Percy Brown remarks that considerable portions of the Muslim buildings of Gujarat "are adaptations and even entire extracts from either Hindu or Jain Temples."

The Gujarat style is noted for its fine wood carving, elaborate ornamentation and delicate graceful lattice work, all elements of Hindu architecture. The earliest Muslim buildings in Gujarat are the mausoleum of Shaikh Farid and Adina or Jami Masjid at Patan, and Jami Masjid at; Broach, a port of Gujarat, and another Jami Masjid at Cambay which is noted for its graceful flying arch, fine proportions and dignified appearance. In the first half of the fifteenth century. Ahmad Shah founded the capital city of Ahmedabad and adorned it with many buildings.

The Jami Masjid of this city having fifteen domes supported on two hundred pillars and finished in 1423, is generally considered the high water mark of mosque design in Gujarat. All the beauties of form and design of local Hindu style have been blended there so that it has become a thing of the spirit, and it is said that this building speaks if that "silent flowering in stone of the souls of men, whose ways of life and thought had flowed into the things made by their hands."

Other famous buildings are the Teen Darwaza (Triple Gateway), a triumphal archway, the central feature of Ahmad Shah's processional route, linking his palace with the Jami Masjid, the tomb of Ahmad Shah at Ahmedabad and the tomb and mosque of Shaikh Ahmad Khattri at Sarkhej about ten kilometres away from Ahmedabad the mosque built at Champaner by Mahmud Beghara and the mosque of Rani Sipari at Ahmedabad are the most striking examples of rich magnificent. Gujarat style exhibiting the profound influence of the Hindu art. Besides the mausoleums and mosques, other secular buildings like *bavadis* or step wells, irrigation works and numerous fruit gardens were also constructed and laid out in Gujarat.

Malwa Architecture : At Mandu, the capital of Malwa, now south western Madhya Pradesh region, the Muslim rulers constructed numerous buildings which are marked by the predominance of Muslim art traditions of design and execution like those of Delhi. The native forms seem to have been suppressed and the Muslim buildings 'clung steadily to the pointed arch style. The Jami Masjid, the Hindola Mahal, the Jahaj Mahal, Hushang Shah's tomb, the Ashiufi Mahal, and the palaces of Baj Bahadur and Rupmati are the specimens of the splendid architecture of Mandu. Hushang Shah's tomb is the first great tomb in India made wholly of white marble. It has certain pleasing features of design and dome. The Hindola Mahal (Swinging Palace) and the Jahaj Mahal are two contrasting buildings at Mandu representing the opposite and extreme poles of the Malwa architecture. Few buildings in India present a more striking appearance or are more solidly constructed than this amazing Hindola Mahal. Its inordinate thick walls slope at an angle of over 77 degrees and, thus, create illusion that the entire structure is swaying, hence, it is designated 'Swinging Palace'.

The Jahaj Mahal instead of having ponderous walling and excessive solidity, has lively and entertaining appearance and is situated between two small lakes like a ship. Its open pavilions, recessed arches, arcaded front, overhanging balconies, arched halls, beautiful reservoirs, pillared compartments and cool corridors make it the most conspicuous building of Malwa. At Dhar, nearly 35 kilometres away from Mandu, there are two well known mosques. One of them was Parmar Raja Bhoj's Sanskrit College converted into a mosque. A few Muslim structures were also erected at Chanderi in northern Madhya Pradesh. The most important of the Chanderi monuments are the Kushk Mahal and the Jami Masjid, which followed the Mandu traditions of art.

Architecture of Khandesh : In the fifteenth and sixteenth centuries the independent kingdom of Khandesh situated in the south of Malwa produced a number of buildings which display original and distinctive features. There is a group of tombs at Thalner in Khandesh. They are a pleasing variation of the Mandu type. The Jami Masjid and the Bibi ki Masjid and the large citadel and palace at Burhanpur are other notable buildings. But the Bibi ki Masjid displays mass vitality and originality in its design and conception than other structures.

Architecture of Kashmir : In the valley of Kashmir the Islamic structures were constructed almost entirely of wood and in due course assumed a singularly distinctive form. Sir John Marshall holds the opinion that the Kashmiri architecture, like other provincial styles, displays the happy fusion of the Hindu and Muslim architectural ideals. The mosque of Shah Hamadan, a typical example of the wooden architecture, the Jami Masjid and the tomb of Zain-ul-Abidin's mother are striking examples of Kashmir art at Srinagar.

Architecture in Deccan : In South India Bahmani Sultans constructed numerous buildings both secular and religious. They bear traces of the native Deccan art. Marshall says that in spite of the Turkish, Egyptian and Persian elements in the architecture of Bahmani Sultans the genius of the Indian artist rose superior to foreign influence and stamped itself more and more deeply on their structures. The buildings of the Bahmani Sultans are mostly found at Gulbarga, Bijapur and Bihar. The earliest prominent Muslim buildings are the Jami Masjid at Daulatabad and Deval mosque at Bodhan (Nizamabad) near Hyderabad, the former was made up of materials from Hindu buildings and the latter was a star shaped Jain temple converted into a mosque. In Gulbarga, the Jami Masjid and the royal tombs, specially the mausoleum of Firuz Shah, are the interesting Islamic Monuments.

The Jami Masjid is a rare example in India of a mosque with no open courtyard as the whole structure is covered by a roof. The tomb of Firuz Shah indicates growing Hindu influence in its carved and polished black stone pilasters and the drip stones and their elegant brackets. In Bihar, some royal palaces like the Rangin Mahal. Zenana Mahal, Mosques and the Madarsah or the college founded by Mahmud Gawan are the most famous buildings of the Bahmani Sultans. Of all the monuments at Bihar the most genuinely expressive of the Bahmani dynasty are royal tombs, the finest among them is the mausoleum of Ali Barid.

The Chand Minar at Daulatabad is equally a celebrated Muslim building. "It is altogether a graceful conception, slender but stable, and exceedingly well balanced." Seven royal tombs and several mosques at Golkonda and the Char Minar (Four Minars), a triumphal archway, at Hyderabad are other striking examples of the Deccan architecture. There is a certain aesthetic excellence in the design and conception of the Char Minar: "it has strength without being aggressive, is dignified yet spirited." But the most remarkable Bahmani architecture is found at Bijapur. Few cities in India have such profuse display of fine buildings as Bijapur. The Jami Masjid, the most powerfully simple, the Ibrahim Rauza (a mausoleum), one of the most elaborate and ornate, the Mithar Mahal, most refined and delicate and the Gol Gumbaz (the mausoleum of Muhammad Adil Shah), showing the Bijapur architecture in its most grandiose form, are the splendid monuments of the Bahmani architecture in Bijapur.

The Ibrahim Rauza rivals even the most splendid and finest Mughat buildings. The Mithar Mahal, a tall graceful building, "has a uniqueness of its own showing the exuberance of the artist's fancy and delight." "The Gol Gumbaz is unquestionably one of the finest structural triumphs of the Indian builders. It creates awe and amazement in the mind of a visitor by its immense scale and majestic bulk." Percy Brown remarks that it is one of the largest and most remarkable single Muslim buildings in India. Besides these buildings, the Bahmani Sultans constructed many castles and fortresses which are admired lavishly by Meadows Taylor.

Architecture by Hindus : While the Muslim Sultans were constructing splendid and dignified buildings all over the country, the independent Hindu princes continued their traditional patronage of art. They lavishly erected temples and Sanskrit colleges and built mighty fortresses, but did not pay much attention to palaces. Consequently, there flourished many local schools of Hindu architecture and sculpture patronized by different ruling dynasties. The distinct characteristics of the medieval Hindu architecture were narrow pillars of circular section with base and capital, pilasters, corbel brackets, cornice or *chhajja,* graceful tapering arch, lavish decorative designs and attractive well proportioned figures. The traditions of the Hindu architecture and sculpture remained uninfluenced by the Islamic architectural ideas till the advent of the Mughals.

However, they were gradually dominated more and more by religious influence and less by aesthetic ideas. They faithfully represented some religious concepts of the country. The conception of Natraj Siva in Hindu sculpture is one of the few rich and valuable contributions of the medieval Hindu art, especially in south India. The Vijayanagar emperors were great liberal patrons of fine arts and they constructed innumerable palaces, council halls, public offices, temples and aqueducts. They are considered by art critics as magnificent works of great beauty, aesthetic sense and craftsmanship, and have been admired lavishly by foreign travellers. Fergusson has described the famous Vithala Temple constructed by Vijayanagar Emperor Krishnadeva Raya as the "finest building of its kind in southern India."

But the best specimens of the Hindu architecture of this period are to be found in northern India, especially in Rajasthan. We come across a considerable number of temples, shrines, palaces, citadels and fortresses all over northern India. But there is hardly any original conception of art. However, the "Tower of Victory, constructed by Rana Kumbha and a Jain tower, both within the fort of Chittor, are extraordinary monuments of medieval architecture and sculpture. The mighty majestic fort of Kumbhalgarh in Mewar and some splendid buildings were also constructed at Amber, the old capital of Jaipur State in Rajasthan. But ruins of Amber now produce an impression of unassailable strength and melancholy splendour.

Music : In the early years of the Delhi Sultanate the art of music did not advance due to the Quranic prohibition and religious conservatism of the Muslims. But later on contact with the cultured Hindus encouraged the Muslims to cultivate the art of music. Three factors further provided stimulus for it. First, the Sufi saints developed their devotional songs and poetry. Second, Hindu converts to Islam did not abandon their traditional *Bhajans*, devotional verses and other types of music. Third, Indian music had such an instutible appeal to the Muslim heart that it could not be shunned entirely. It had very healthy effect on the exuberance of Muslim feelings. All this inspired the Muslim society to take keen interest in music. Consequently, great musicians like Khusrau were produced in the Sultanate age. It is said that he recited his poems in accordance with the Indian tunes and invented new *ragas* like *Qawwali* and *Khyal*. The Muslims had adopted the music instruments of the Hindus and their *Dhrupada Raga*, introduced *Sitar* and *Tabla* for instrumental music. But music made remarkable progress during the Mughal period. However, the trend for synthesis between the Hindus and the Muslims is also visible in the sphere of music during the period under review.

Coinage System : Coinage of the Sultanate period, like music, displays Hindu Muslim synthesis. The earliest Muslim coins had *Nagari* inscriptions. Muhammad Ghori struck coins in imitation of the Hindu kings of Kannauj with the effigy of the Hindu goddess Lakshmi on the obverse. Some Muslim coins had the effigy of Hindu god Siva's Nandi or humped bull and king's name in the *Nagari* script on the obverse and Indian type of horseman on the reverse. In the early days of the Delhi Sultanate the name of Hindu king together with that of Muslim king was inscribed on the same coin.

Conclusion : Thus, in spite of the bitterness in political relations, the impact of Hindu and Muslim civilizations had far reaching consequences. The Muslim conquerors had brought with them definite social and religious ideas which differed fundamentally from those of the Hindus. Long association brought the two distinct groups of the Hindus and the Muslims closer and closer with the result that the evolution of Hindu culture was coloured with Islamic tinge. But Hindu culture in its own turn influenced Islamic elements. In fact, the Hindus and the Muslims have contributed their quota to the evolution of common cultural heritage. The medieval age witnessed the fusion and mingling of cultures but not the absorption of one into the other. There was conflict between the two cultures and their synthesis, though not a perfect one.

The reaction of Islam on Hinduism has been manifold. The conservative elements in Hindu society fortified their social and religious systems by introducing elaborate and rigid caste rules, where as the liberal elements accepted some democratic principles of Islam. The latter manifested themselves in the views of many saintly teachers and preachers like Ramanand, Kabir, Nanak, Dadu and Chaitanya. The growth of Vaishnavism in Bengal and the *Bhakti* cult in the south and Maharashtra are attributed to the impact of Islam on Hinduism. Another result was the spirit of harmony, toleration and co operation expressed in the ideas of the Sufi saints and in the Hindu veneration for Muslim saints. The basis of Sufism has been profoundly influenced by the currents of Hindu thought. Another important feature of the impact was the development of regional literatures and the growth of a new language Urdu. The Vaishnava poetry of the vernacular literature was a miracle of synthesis of Islam and Hinduism. In the society, rigidity of the caste barriers, infanticide, seclusions of women and their dependence on men, early marriage, a new costume, customs and conduct, and fashions and festivals mark the social order of the day. The learned authors of *An Advanced History of India* rightly remark that "the preachings of the saintly teachers of India with their ideal of uplift of the masses, the tolerant ideas of the Sufi saints and scholars and the growth of the Indian provincial literature, might be regarded as signs of modernism appearing as a result of the fusion of the two civilizations.

The Indo-Muslim kings made remarkable contribution in the sphere of architecture. The great art critic Fergusson remarks, "Nothing could be more brilliant and at the same time more characteristic than the commencement of the architectural career of these Pathan kings. "In the domain of art, the foreign conceptions of the arch, the dome and the minaret were combined with the traditions of Hindu art. The Hindu and Muslim elements coalesced to form a new type of architecture. The severity and simplicity of the Muslim architecture was mellowed down and the plastic exuberance of the Hindu architecture was curtailed. The Muslim emphasis on harmony and form blended with Hindu emphasis on splendour and decoration. "The craftsmanship, ornamental richness and general design remained largely Hindu, the arculated form, plain domes, smooth faced walls and spacious interiors were Muslim super impositions."

6

Mughal Culture

Establishment of Empire

Zahiruddin, surnamed Babar, a prince of Farghana in Central Asia, invaded India, and in April, 1526, defeated Ibrahim Lodi, the Sultan of Delhi, and in the following year he won a notable victory at Khanwah over Rana Sanga. This led to the establishment of Mughal rule in India. Babar was succeeded by his son Humayun (1530-1540 and 1554-1556) who had to consolidate his hold in northern India. To achieve this end, he attacked Gujarat and there secured partial victory over Bahadur Shah, but he was defeated in a carefully planned campaign by the Afghan leader Sher Khan and was exiled to Persia.

The Dynasty (1540-1554) and Sher Shah Suri : Sher Khan ascended the throne of Delhi as Sher Shah and founded the Suri Dynasty in 1540. His sound civil administration, original land reforms, works of public utility, and policy of toleration and justice entitle him to rank amongst the greatest sovereigns of India. He was the first who attempted to found an Indian Empire broadly based upon the people's will. He stands as the ideal of new India the India of Hindus and Mussalmans united in heart and spirit. The Successors of Sher Shah were weak.

Utilizing the opportunity provided by the chaotic condition in India at this time, Humayun returned from Persia and invaded India and regained his kingdom of Delhi after fifteen years of absence.

Restoration of Humayun and its Cultural Importance : The restoration of Humayun brought in its train the Persian influence in India. His years of stay in the Persian Empire gave to the empire of his successors a definitely Persian character. The nobles who accompanied him to Persia and the Iranians who returned with him to India formed a nucleus for Persianization. Besides this, there was also the continuous flow of Persian adventurers and the Mughal Empire for the next hundred years, to a large extent, was coloured by the Persian cultural elements.

Akbar as a National Ruler : Humayun was succeeded by his son, Akbar, and soon after his succession he defeated a great rival Hemu in the battle of Panipat in 1556. The Afghan rule came to an end and the Mughal rule began instead. Shaking of the tutelage of Bairam Khan, his guardian, and the petticoat government of his foster mother Maham Anaga, Akbar embarked on his aggressive and ambitious scheme of conquests. After a series of campaigns he conquered and annexed Malwa, Gondwana, Gujarat, Ranthambhor, Chittor, Bengal, Kabul, Kashmir, Sind, Baluchistan, Orissa and Ahmednagar. Within twenty years after his succession he established his sway over the whole of northern India accept Mewar whose Rana Pratap had refused to bend his knees to the 'Turk'. Then he initiated new policies. By his liberal policy of friendship towards the Rajputs and his matrimonial alliance with them, his abolition of the pilgrim tax and the poll tax or *Jizya* on the Hindus and by his policy of religious toleration and employing Hindus in higher ranks, Akbar mitigated the foreign character of his rule and created a national State. His statesman like policy of conciliating Hindus paved the path for a national monarchy. His social reforms, his revenue and Mansabdari systems and good and sound civil administration entitle him to be called the real founder of the Mughal Empire.

The efficacy of his wise policies was seen in the reigns of his successors, Jahangir and Shah Jahan and it was only when Aurangzeb unwisely reversed his policies that the death knell of Mughal Empire was sounded.

Reign of Jahangir (1605-1627) : Akbar was succeeded by Jahangir. He followed the policies laid down by Akbar, brushing aside only the extravagance of Din-i-llahi. His reign on the whole was fruitful of peace and prosperity to the Empire. But on account of the influence of Nur Jahan and her family, the Persian cultural elements crept in the court and the empire.

Reign of Shah Jahan (1627-1658) : After a hard struggle Shah Jahan succeeded Jahangir. Suppressing the revolts of the Bundelas and Khan Jahan Lodi, he waged wars against the Deccan Sultans of Golkonda and Bijapur and succeeded in establishing Mughal suzerainty over them. He unsuccessfully intervened in Central Asia to conquer Balkh as a part of his hereditary dominions. He fully maintained the national character of the State. He never alienated his Hindu subjects and firmly adhered to the political alliance with the Rajputs. Shah Jahan was the greater builder among the Mughals and his reign has been rightly called the golden age of the Mughal period; it marked the climax of the Mughal Empire, but it also sowed the seeds of decay.

Reign of Aurangzeb (1658-1707) : After the disastrous fratricidal war Aurangzeb ascended the throne of Delhi. From the very beginning he reversed Akbar's policy of national State and attempted to restore the Islamic character of the State. By his orthodoxy and advocacy of Islamic principles his active anti-Hindu policy (demolition of temples, oppressive taxes on Hindu merchants, reimposition of the poll tax, dismissal of Hindu officials, discontinuation of the Hindu customs in the court, forcible conversion of Hindus, etc.) and by his severance of the healthy relations with the Rajputs, he created a theocratic State, and the national State ceased to exist. "There can not be a great and lasting empire without a great people, and no people can be great unless it learns to form a compact nation with equal rights and opportunities for all." Aurangzeb was not fitted by his character and ideas to create such a compact nation. Akbar laid the foundation of the Mughal empire and created a national State, but Aurangzeb destroyed it.

Aurangzeb was followed by a long line of weak successors, the last of whom, Bahadur Shah, was deposed and exiled after the mutiny of 1857 by the British to Rangoon where he died in confinement in 1862. *The Rise and fall of the Marathas.* In Maharashtra, the *Bhakti* movement aroused the national spirit during the dark days of the Muslim rule and it culminated in the rise of a leader in the person of Shivaji (1627-1680). He organized the Marathas in a military fold with a sense of national mission, broke away from Bijapur and defeated all attempts of the Bijapur and Mughal armies to bring him to book and later he gave a rude shock to Aurangzeb by escaping from the Mughal custody and set up a Hindu State in the teeth of opposition. As a patriot, general, administrator, and statesman, Shivaji stands very high among his contemporaries. He was the last constructive genius that Hindu India produced.

Shivaji was succeeded by his son Shambhaji (1680-1689). 'During his reign internal quarrels sapped the strength of the Maratha State. In 1689, he was captured and slain by Aurangzeb and his minor son Shahu was brought under his protection. This was followed by a prolonged war with the Mughals for Maratha independence. After the death of Aurangzeb, Shahu returned to Maharashtra and ascended the throne at Satara. Shahu's reign introduced the powerful Peshwa regime in Maharashtra. The Second Peshwa Baji Rao (1720-1740) enunciated the principle of *Hindu Pad Padshahi* the creation of an all Indian Hindu Empire with Maharashtra as its centre. This conception was gradually materialized in the reign of the third Peshwa Balaji Baji Rao (1740- 1761) when the Maratha Empire embraced nearly the whole of India. The imperial authority of the Mughals was totally broken down by the Marathas when they dictated peace terms to the puppet emperor in 1757. Only the shadow of the Mughal Emperor was reigning at Delhi now. This inevitably brought the Marathas in conflict with Muslim powers led by the Afghan ruler Ahmad Shah in 1761 at the field of Panipat. The battle of Panipat went against the Marathas, but they quickly recovered from its shock.

After 1761, the Maratha power in northern India became stabilized under the great Maratha feudatory kings Scindhia at Gwalior, Holkar at Indore, Bhonsale at Nagpur and Gaikwad at Baroda. By the first quarter of the nineteenth century, all these four powers were gradually defeated by the British and the last vestige of independent Maratha power disappeared.

Social Conditions

Structure of Society : Society in Mughal time was organized on feudal basis with the king at its apex. Next in rank to the king were official nobles or Mansabdars who enjoyed special privileges and honours. Though nobility included foreign elements, none of them was allowed to carry the country's wealth outside. Below the nobles was a small and frugal middle class and below it were the lower classes. A wide gulf divided the rulers and the ruled.

Nobility Class : The nobles rolled in wealth, in comforts, and the rich, with abundant resources at their disposal, indulged in luxury and intemperance. "Excessive addiction to wine and women was a very common vice" of the age. Pelsaert writes, "The palaces of the rich were adorned internally with lascivious sensuality, wanton and reckless festivity, superfluous pomp, inflated pride and ornamental daintiness." All this naturally produced vast difference between the standard of the rich and the nobles and that of the common people. A wide gulf divided the two. The most noticeable factor in the life of the Indian courts and of the nobility at this time was the unparalleled sense of luxury. The court of the king was the centre of wealth and culture.

It was Akbar who started the Mughal court on its career of magnificence. When the emperors travelled, the imperial magnificence was in no sense relaxed, and it was the capital in all its magnificence that moved. "Even when directing campaigns in distant parts the court bore no Spartan appearance." The nobles in imitation of the emperor, the court and their patrons led an extravagant and luxurious life. Though the nobles had such virtue as generosity, magnanimity, gallantry, love for learning and fine arts, deep sense of self respect, etc., they were selfish, debased and most luxurious. They exploited the labour community and the lower classes, and misused their wealth.

In dress, diet and methods of living the nobles and the higher classes showed the spirit of luxury. Brocades, printed silk and muslin were the common dress of well to do persons and great nobles. The king and his nobles took great pride in putting on costly dresses and valuable jewellery. We know from Abul Fazl that one thousand complete suits of costly silks were prepared for Akbar every year. Dinners were sumptuous, and dainty dishes were provided as is written by Sir Thomas Roe. The austere and simple food of the Hindus was replaced among higher classes by rich, spiced and special preparations, like pulaos, birianis and the varied and rich foods of the Middle East.

The Hindu nobles began to have great sumptuous feasts in imitation of the manner of the Persian and Central Asian chiefs and amirs. Rare fruits, mysterious decoctions, refinements of the culinary art to suit jaded palates, which the society of Persia evolved, found their way into India and they soon gained popularity with the richer and upper classes among Hindu and Mohammedans alike. Meat became a common article of food and in the summer all the ranks used ice, but the nobles used it throughout the year. Fruits were frequently and commonly used and fresh fruits were imported from Bokhara and Samarkand.

Drink was a common evil confined only to the upper

classes and a large number of persons died of intemperance. All the Mughal emperors except Aurangzeb indulged in liquor. The harems were a common feature of the age and from the king down to the nobles everybody maintained a large number of maid servants and dancing girls. According to Abul Fazl, Akbar had a seraglio of 5,000 women supervised by separate staff of female officers. Thousands of rupees were spent lavishly on the women of the harems and at times sumptuous feasts were offered for mistresses. Women had no independent existence. They were regarded means for sensual pleasures. Though there were restrictions against the use of opium, liquor and other intoxicating drugs and gambling they were not rigidly enforced by the authorities. The nobility and the upper classes frequently and freely indulged in these. Humayun's addiction to opium eating and Jahangir's excessive drinking are well known to us. The houses of the nobility and the wealthy were lavishly decorative and palatial.

With the closing years of the reign of Shah Jahan, the nobles began to lose their old usefulness and grew more demoralized. During the reign of Aurangzeb and in the eighteenth century, further deterioration set in. Their rivalries and conspiracies cast a malign influence on social life.

Middle Class : The middle class people were not given to "ostentatious expenditure" but they lived on a standard suited to their respective professions. The lesser officials of the court lived according to the standard which was determined by the nature of the work they had to do. On the whole, as Moreland Points out, the life these people led was tolerably comfortable. The merchants generally led simple and temperate lives. They used either to conceal their wealth or to lead highly frugal lives lest they be deprively of their wealth by the local governor or a *Faujdar*. The merchants having on the western coast, especially Gujarat, had made much wealth out of their extensive commerce both internal and external. Consequently they maintained a high standard of life and lived in a rich style and Indulged in luxuries. They had no fear of losing their wealth.

Lower Classes : Artisans, labourers, agriculturists, villagers, etc., were included in the lower classes. Their life was hard as compared with that of the two higher classes. Their clothing was scanty; woollen garments or silken clothes and shoes were beyond their means. Under normal conditions there was no starvation, but in times of drought, famine and scarcity, their miseries must have been very great. From the account of Francisco Pelsaert we learn that there were three classes of people whose status was little removed from slavery. They were workmen, peons, servants and shopkeepers. Their food and houses were poor and they were subject to the oppressions of the imperial officers and nobles who exploited them most. The number of servants was large because the wages were low. Honesty was rare among them and they demanded *dastur* to supplement their wages. The shopkeepers and businessmen, though sometimes rich and respected, generally kept their wealth hidden. They had to suffer a good deal of loss as they had to supply various articles to the king, his officers and nobles at less than usual market rates.

During the days of Akbar the peasantry led a comfortable life as the state demand was fixed and the attitude of the king was benevolent. But towards the end of Shah lahan's reign, the peasants were more harassed by the provincial governors, their condition became worse and the evil of pauperism decreased. Bernier is of the opinion that the peasants and artisans in the upper provinces suffered from cruel oppression.

Condition of Women : Though the condition of women as a whole showed a marked deterioration due to the rigidity of *purdah,* the Mughal period produced some notable women in India. The great learned women of this period were Mughal princesses Jahanara, the partisan of Dara ; Roshanara, the partiean of Aurangzeb ; Zebunnisa, the daughter of Aurangzeb, whose verses have come down to us; Chand Bibi of Ahmednagar; Tarabai, the regent in Maharashtra ; Nurjahan, the empress; and Jijabai, the mother of Shivaji. "On the whole, the Hindu womanhood maintained its tradition, receiving its strength from religion and usage, but in proportion to general advancement which the period shows, there is no evidence of progress. Infanticide, child marriage and *sati* were very much in vogue among the Hindus. Polygamy was a common feature of the age.

Means of Entertainment : There were several means of entertainment during the Mughal age. All the Mughal emperors had keen interest in sports and exercises. Gambling, polo, animal fighting, especially elephant fighting, were in vogue and people were fond of wrestling and pigeon flying. Hunting was frequently resorted to. Besides this, people took great delight in chess, dice and other indoor games. In short, there were various kinds of sports and amusements in which the nobles and officials took part.

Cloths and Ornaments : The Mughal age is famous for its fondness of costly dresses. Embroidered or printed silken clothes were put on by the upper classes. Beautiful fine muslin was also used for the common dress. Apart from the caste mark which distinguished the Hindus, the dress cf both the Hindu and Muslim nobles was practically identical." They wore similar dresses and ornaments. The magnificence of the imperial court compelled them to us: costly dresses and valuable jewellery, beautifully designed and gracefully made. Though the ordinary Hindu still put on his *dhoti* as he does now, the higher classes accepted the *pyjama* and the *achakan* as the ceremonial castile befitting their dignity and rank. The Hindus had adopted the dress and manners of the Muslims.

Social Habits, and Customs : "The vice of intemperance was not so common among the ordinary people as among the rich and the nobles." People in general were temperate in their diet, and were civil and hospitable to strangers. Hindus were clever businessmen and the Muslims practised all crafts except dyeing and weaving. Both believed in the maxims and predictions of the science of astrology. People of every class were sunk deep in superstitions. Both the Hindus and the Muslims worshipped the shrines or tombs of the saints. The

Hindus, the Sikhs and the Mohammedans, all the three communities, rendered services to a number of *pirs*, prophets, preceptors and *mahants*, and it was expected that they would display marvellous feats of mysticism. There existed deep hatred and prejudice between the Shias and Sunnis and they caned each other *kafirs* or infidels. Slavery was a common feature of the age.

It was a mark of unprogressive element in society and it hindered the moral and intellectual advancement of the society. The Ganga was considered to be sacred and the pilgrims used to have a dip in its waters. The Muslims worshipped the *pirs* and prophets of their faith and on the occasion of "Id" cows were not sacrificed. As noted above, prominent social practices of the age were *sati*, child marriage, *kulinism* or infanticide and the dowry system. Akbar sought to check such evil social practices as marriage before puberty by either party and marriages between near relatives. He discouraged acceptance of high dowries and polygamy, but in vain. In Maharashtra, widow marriage was prevalent to some extent as among the jats of the Punjab and the Jamuna valley, and polyandry was practised among the latter. The Hindus mainly celebrated *Holi, Rakshabandhan, Dashahra* and *Diwali* festivals. On festival days they wore beautiful dress and valuable jewellery, arranged interesting concerts and offered mutually sumptuous feasts. The principal festivals of the Muslims were *Id, Bakrid* and *Muharram*. Like the Hindus they arranged for various entertainments on their festival days. Caste system and untouchability continued among the Hindus; they were not relaxed in any way.

Travernier who visited India in the reign of Shah Jahan praises the Hindus as thrifty, sober and honest people, and says: "Hindus are morally well, when married they are rarely unfaithful to their wives. Adultery is rare among them and one never hears of unnatural crimes."

Deterioration in Society : In the earlier part of Shah Jahan's reign there was peace and prosperity, but afterwards at the close, the condition of the people became worse. Beggary was prevalent among them. During the reign of Aurangzeb the condition of the people steadily declined. The Mughal nobility lost its moral stamina on account of women, wine and wealth. The standard of public morality was also not high and lesser officials accepted bribe without shame or scruple. The noble conception of public welfare was fast disappearing in the sphere of administration. There was a vast amount of human poverty and misery in the country.

The glittering imperial court became a stronghold of luxurious, jealous, wicked and flattering nobles. Gallantry, scholarship, magnanimity and high tone of morality of feudal lords and courtiers had disappeared. The country was torn to pieces by civil wars and groaned under every kind of domestic confusion. Superstition had taken place of true religion. Worship of *sadhus* and *fakirs* was gaining ground. Villainy was practised in every form. Even the mosques were not free from vices. People began to have great faith in magic, witchcraft and sorcery and sometimes human beings were sacrificed to ensure successful experiments in alchemy. By the end of the eighteenth century and the beginning of the next "in social usage, in politics, in the realm of religion and art, we have entered the zone of uncreative habit of decadent tradition and ceased to exercise our humanity."

The Spirit of Synthesis : But as pointed out by the learned authors of *An Advanced history of India,* one redeeming feature in this age of all round regrettable deterioration "was the continuity of the process of Hindu Muslim approachment and amicable contact between the members of the two communities in spite of bitter political rivalries." Consequently, the spirit of synthesis and mutual harmony led to the growth of a new synthesized culture which was neither purely Hindu nor entirely Muslim, but a happy fusion of the best elements of the two. Akbar's reign is important and instructive for the spirit of Hindu-Muslim synthesis and harmony. Religious synthesis was displayed in Akbar's religious policy of appeasement and the Din-i-Ilahi. He offered a religion which was free from caste restrictions, dominance of the priestly class and external ritualism. It laid emphasis on monotheism and high tone of morality. Religious toleration intimate social relationship and love for each other reached their climax under prince Dara Shikoh. He argued that there existed only verbal differences between Hindu and Muslim mysticism, and wrote his famous *Majm-ul-Bahrain* to explain where the 'two seas' of mystic thought meet.

During the reign of Aurangzeb the Satnami and the Narain sects endeavoured to bring within their folds both the Hindus and the Muslims. The Satnami sect had Hindu as well as Muslim followers. The Satnamis used to offer prayers facing east five times a day; they included Allah in their names for God, and instead of cremating their dead, buried them. In the realm of art the Persian and Indian styles of architecture mingled happily and its excellence was exhibited in the magnificent buildings of Akbar and Shah Jahan. Similarly, the Mughal painting displays the beautiful fusion of the Indian and foreign techniques. Laying out extensive and beautiful gardens is a legacy of the Mughals. Akbar's desire to held the peoples into a unity and social cohesion led to Hindu-Muslim synthesis in dress, diet, etiquette and modes of living.

In the Hindu wedding ceremony *Sehra* and *jama* came into vogue *pyjama* and *Achakan* formed the ceremonial costume and new delicious sweets like *Balushai, Gulabjamun, Barfi, Pulao,* etc., were included in the articles of food. *Hukka* and tobacco were used by the Hindus as well as Muslims. Birth of a male child was celebrated with musical entertainment by both communities. Ladies' ornaments in both communities were identical. Literature could not escape the happy fusion of the two cultures. Vocabularies of the various Indian vernaculars Hindi, Bengali, Marathi, and Gujarati were enriched with Persian and Arabic words. There was a free exchange of views between the two communities, and both freely participated in each' other's functions.

If the Hindus began to observe the Muharram festival, Abdullah Khan, one of the Sayyid brothers, celebrated the *Basant* and *Holi* festivals of the Hindus; Sirajuddaulah and Mir Jafar, Nawabs of Bengal, enjoyed the famous *Holi* festival with their friends and relatives and the *Durga Pooja* was celebrated splendidly at the Mughal court in Delhi till as late as 1825 A.D. In Madhya Bharat, Daulat Rao Sindhia and his officers participated in Muharram celebrations in green dress like Muhammedans. In short as Panikkar remarks, the dress, manners, social amenities and festivals which the Mughals introduced in India ceased to be foreign and were accepted by the people.

The Economy

Babar has given us a description of the economic conditions of the people of India in his *Memoirs*, but it is far from accurate. There is a passing mention in Gulbadan Begam's *Humayun Namah* of the cheap prices of articles that prevailed in Hindustan and it is stated that at Amarkot in Rajasthan four goats could be had for one rupee. The comprehensive economic reforms introduced by Sher Shah must have affected an all round improvement in the economic condition of his subjects. Akbar's reign introduced a period of peace and prosperity. According to Smith, the labourers in the reign of Akbar had possessed more provisions than what their community has today. But in the Mughal age there was an uneven distribution of wealth among the various classes as it is now. The skeleton of society was based on the exploitation of the lower classes. However, the general economic condition of the people was better than what it is today.

Many Prosperous Cities : During the period of the great Mughals prosperity and plenty prevailed in the chief cities. According to the European visitors of the period, Lahore and Agra were among the greatest towns of the world at the time. Burhanpur in Khandesh and Ahmedabad in Gujarat were great cities. In eastern India, there was much opulence in cities like Varanasi, Patna, Rajmahal, Burdwan, Hugli and Dacca.

There was abundance of rice, corn and other necessaries of life. Allahabad, where Akbar created the great citadel, soon assumed importance, because of its strategic position and the value of the riverborne trade to the European trading concerns on the Bengal coast. Agra was the main capital of the empire, but after Shah Jahan, Delhi assumed that role.

Means of Communications : For the vast mercantile traffic there were good means of communications in the form of roads and rivers. With the exception of certain highways, the roads were generally unmetalled, but clearly defined by long avenues of trees, *piaoos* (places for providing water), and Serais (inns) where travellers and merchants could pass the night comfortably in comparative security. Normally, the journeys were safe enough and effective action was taken by local authorities to keep the roads clear of thieves, dacoits, etc., though certain areas acquired a had name in this connection. Strangers in India could take their womenfolk with them while travelling.

The ancient tradition of road building activity in the State was imitated by the Sur rulers and followed by the Mughals. The main centres of the empire were controlled by a reasonable extensive road system. Sher Shah completed the grand trunk road, a legacy of the Mauryas. Communications with Bengal, one of the main provinces, were kept in an efficient state. Another important and long road linked Agra with Ahmedabad in Gujarat and from there to Surat and to the commerce of the world. It was the main commercial route of the Mughal empire. The road to the south was kept in a good state due to the Deccan campaigns, a regular feature of the imperial policy. The rivers afforded excellent means for the carriage of heavy traffic. Along with the Ganges, the waterways were very popular and fleets of river boats sailed down this great highway at frequent intervals from Allahabad to Bengal in the east.

Agricultural Activity : The crops in the Mughal period were much the same as those today sugar cane and indigo, cotton and silk were cultivated extensively in certain parts of the country. Tobacco, introduced in India either late in 1604 or early in 1605, began to be cultivated regularly by the people thereafter. Agricultural implements and methods were very much the same as those of the present day. Adequate means of irrigation did not exist. The peasants were, no doubt, more prosperous than other classes of the population, but they were often subject to the oppression and exactions of local officers. They also suffered most from the chronic wars and military marches which did a great injury to the crops.

Famines and Epidemics : The sufferings and grievances of the peasants and people knew no bounds during the frequent famines, because the Mughal State then made no systematic and prolonged efforts to provide relief and effected no substantial remissions in revenue collection. The little that they did was insufficient to alleviate the acute miseries of the myriads of the people who died of starvation and the pestilence that closely followed it. Cholera and influenza were the common diseases in the country.

Development Industry and Crafts : During the period under review there was extensive and varied industrial activity of the people. It supplied the needs of the local aristocracy and merchants and met the demands of traders coming from different countries of Europe and various parts of Asia. The most important industry of the time was the manufacture of cotton. It was not confined to any particular region, but distributed all over the country. There were many principal centres of cotton manufacture throughout the country, for example, Patan in Gujarat, Burhanpur in Khandesh, Jaunpur, Varanasi, Dacca, and some other places in the U. P., Bihar and Bengal. They were reputed for the manufacture of delicate muslin fabrics. Chanderi in Madhya Pradesh was also famous for its fine cloth. Masulipatnam for its prints, Surat for its borders and Varanasi for its rich brocades. Besides this, shawls at Lahore and carpets at Fatehpur Sikri were also manufactured. Cloth was exported from India to the countries east of the Cape of Good Hope, Middle East, Burma, Malayasia, Java, etc.

The dyeing industry, too, was in a flourishing condition. Coarse cotton cloths were either dyed or printed with a variety of wen shaped and well coloured flowers or figures which were so fixed in the cloth that no water could wash them.

Silk industry received a considerable impetus in the reign of Akbar due to the royal patronage. In addition to Lahore, Agra, Fatehpur Sikri and Gujarat, Bengal was the premier centre of silk production and manufacture. Woollen goods, chiefly coarse blankets, were also woven at many places. Though India lost ancient maritime activity, the ship building industry did not disappear in this age, and there are references to it in contemporary literature. The Mughals had established a centre in the Bay of Bengal where they constructed ships. In Cutch, Cambay and other port towns, ships of considerable size were built. Indian ship building had such a high reputation in India that even the Portuguese had some of their best ships built in India at this time. Saltpetre, which was used chiefly as an ingredient for gunpowder in India and exported outside by the Dutch and the English traders in India, was manufactured in many parts of the country, particularly in the Deccan and Bihar.

Besides these major industries, various other crafts were practised during the Mughal period. Many curious boxes, trunks, standishes (pen cases), ornamental desks draught boards, writing cases, inlaid with ivory, and ebony and simillar other goods were manufactured in large quantities.

Many artisans of all kinds worked for the state in the imperial workshops or *karkhanas* at Lahore, Agra, Fatehpur Sikri and Ahmedabad. In the seventeenth century, Bernier saw many of them. The governors of the provinces patronized local products as they had to supply the Emperor with the choicest articles produced in the area. But, according to Bernier, weavers and craftsmen were not treated well. Nobles and officers forced them to sell goods at low prices and exacted from them forbidden *abwabs*.

Prices of Goods : As the plenty of provisions was very great throughout the country, the prices of articles, mainly those of common consumption like rice, vegetables, spices, meat, live stock and milk, were very low. A Hindustani and Kashmiri sheep could be had for Rs. 1,50 each and a cow in the province of Delhi for Rs. 10, and mutton was sold at 65 *dams* per *mun* which was equal to about 25 kilograms. Wages were also low; an unskilled labourer generally earned 2 *dams* or 5 paise per day, but a highly skilled labourer was paid 7 *dams* or about 18 paise a day. But, it is certain that there was no golden age of opulence for the common people under the Mughals, because though the prices of articles were cheap, their average income was proportionately low or perhaps lower. They did not, however, grovel in misery and smart under discontent.

Mints, Currency and Weights : Sher Shah and. Akbar attempted to regulate the currency of the State. In addition to the imperial mint at Delhi, there were provincial mints in Bengal, Lahore, Jaunpur, Ahmedabad, Patna and later on at Surat. "Akbar issued gold, silver and copper coins, the first having no less than twenty six varieties of different weights and values. Akbar also issued a square silver rupee called the *jalali*. The chief copper coin during the reign of Sher Shah and Akbar was the *dam*, also called *paisa* and *fulus*. It formed the ready money for the rich and the poor, high and low, and was divided for the purpose of easy counting into twenty five parts each called *jital*. Revenue was calculated in *dams*. Business in the empire was transacted in round gold *mohurs*, rupees and *dams*. The coins of the Mughal State, particularly those of Akbar, "were excellent in respect of purity of metal, fulness of weight and artistic execution. "

The common units of weight were *seer* and *mun;* but the *seers* differed in weight under Akbar, Jahangir and Shah Jahan. Akbar's *mun* was equal to about 25 kilograms.

External Trade : During the greater part of the Mughal rule, India carried on a brisk and considerable foreign trade with different countries of Asia and Europe. There were principal land routes on the north-west one from Lahore to Kabul and the other from Multan to Kandhar. Overseas commerce was also carried on. The chief ports were Lahori Bandar in Sind, Surat, Broach, Cambay in Gujarat ; Bassein, Chaul, Debal in the Ratnagiri district and Goa and Bhatkal in Maharashtra ; Calicut and Cochin in Malabar; Nagapatnam, Masulipatnam and a few minor ones on the east cost and Satagaon, Sripur, Chittagaon and Sonargaon in Bengal. Surat was the emporium of western trade and the gateway of Mecca. It was a cosmopolitian city where the merchants of all countries met and carried on their trade briskly, and over a hundred ships of all nationalities were seen daily at anchor in its port.

The chief imports of the country were bullion, raw silk, horses, metals, ivory, coral, amber, precious stones, velvets, brocades, broad cloth, perfumes, drugs, Chinese porcelain, and her exports included various textiles, pepper, indigo, opium and other drugs and miscellaneous goods. The customs duties, fixed by the State, were not very high and this afforded great encouragement to foreign traders. The significant feature of the Indian trade from the reign of Emperor Akbar was the commercial activity of the English and the Dutch merchants who gradually established their factories or trading stations in widely distributed centres throughout the country.

Economic Deterioration : The court revolutions and conspiracies, the incessant wars of Aurangzeb's reign, bankruptcy of the administration and the exhaustion of the imperial exchequer brought about the disappearance of general peace and political order. A natural sequel to this was the economic deterioration and consequently agriculture, arts and crafts were so badly affected that for some time trade came almost to a standstill. The French traveller Bernier dwells at length upon the decline of arts, crafts and industries and the unsettled condition of the country. Sir J. N. Sarkar in his book, *History of Aurangzeb,* Vol. IV, rightly observes: "Thus ensued a great economic impoverishment of India not only a decrease of the national stock, but also a rapid lowering of mechanical skill and standard of civilization, a disappearance of art and culture over wide tracts of the country."

Education System

No Government Education : The great Mughal emperors were patrons of learning and promoters of education. Their example was followed by the Mughal nobility and upper classes. Consequently, education progressed well under the Mughals. Great impetus was given to original research and scholarship, and authorship was rewarded with munificent allowance. But there was nothing like the modern system of education established and maintained by the State in Mughal India. Education was a private concern, a hand maid of religion among the Mohammedans as well as the Hindus.

The duty of the State to educate its future citizens was not recognized by the Mughal State and naturally there was no separate department of education. The Padshah or the Mughal Emperor made large grants of land or money to mosques, monasteries and individual saints and scholars renowned for their knowledge. The Emperor recognized it as a religious and not a political duty and the recipients of these royal favours were not bound to maintain schools or colleges with the money. But in actual practice almost every mosque had a *maqtab,* a primary school, attached to it, where the boys and girls of the neighbourhood received elementary education.

There the Mullah of the mosque also made the children commit the Quran to memory. Elegant penmanship was cultivated and if the boy wished to learn the arts and crafts he was apprenticed to an *Ustad* or master. After leaving the *maqtab,* the more advanced went to the madarsah or college where the curriculum was mainly religious and the chief subjects taught were theology, mathematics and physics. In some places ethics, accounts, geometry, astronomy, logic, natural philosophy, divinity, and history were also taught. Hindu Sanskrit and varnacular schools, in addition to *maqtabs,* continued to function for the benefit of students in the urban as well as rural areas. There were many centres of education like Agra, Labore, Fatehpur Sikri, Sialkot etc. Agra had several schools and colleges where students flocked from far and wide. Sikri was also studded with several schools and seminaries. The famous *Ibadat Khana* at Sikri was the meeting place of the intellectuals of various nationalities and the centre of a set of brilliant scholars of the reign of Akbar. The tomb of Humayun was used as a place of instruction. A college was attached to it,

Individuals also set up education institutions, such as, the college of Maham Anaga and Madarsah of Khwaja Muin in Delhi, the Madarsahs of Maulana Sadruddin in Shahjahanabad and the Madarsahs of Akramuddin, Abdul Hakim and Rafiuddin in the reign of Aurangzeb and the Madarsah of Ghaziuddin, in Delhi founded amidst the waning glories of the Mughal empire. Though some monasteries of Mughal India did not contain scholars and theologians, they were not as a rule seats of learning like the vihars, of the Buddhist Age or monasteries of Christian Europe. There were, however, families of hereditary Muslim scholars living in certain towns whose reputations attracted pupils from all parts of the country and who practically maintained high schools and colleges and imparted the highest instruction in their special subjects, for example, the Madarsah of Shaikb Wajiduddin in Gujarat, the Madarsah of Firuz Jang at Delhi, the Madarsahs of Maulvi Alimuddin and Maulvi Nasimuddin called Fakhr ul Murrabbiin Kannauj, etc.

The innumerable *karkhanas* or manufacturing centres provided technical training and vocational knowledge to those who evinced special interest in and aptitude for handicraft. Raja Jai Singh of Amber (Jaipur) en couraged considerable education in science. He is reported to have founded a number of observatories at Jaipur, Ujjain, Mathura, Varanasi and Delhi.

Medium of Instruction : Though Arabic had become a dead language since the 13th century, the highest Muslim education was imparted through this medium during the Mughal period. All books of science, not to speak of theology, were written in the Arabic language, and Persian was studied only as an accomplishment in the cultured society like French in Europe. The most advanced Muslim students of India used to pay visit to Mecca in Arabia and stay there for one year to give the finishing touch to their education. A Mecca degree commanded the highest respect in India and was often considered as the necessary qualification for Kaziship. The tutors of the princes were frequently chosen from this class of people.

Women Education : Women owing to the purdah system could not attend public institutions, but in nearly every nobleman's establishment a school mistress or governess was kept, and Mughal emperors employed learned Persian women to teach their girls. Akbar is reputed to have established a girls' school in his palace at Fatehpur Sikri. The ladies studied the humanities in preference to theology and Persian rather than Arabic. But all of them who achieved some progress in their studies had to commit the holy Quran to memory seems that many Muslim women were patrons of literature and themselves writers.

The memoirs of Gulbadan Banu Begum, the talented daughter of Babar, are well known, and Akbar's foster mother, Maham Anga, endowed a college at Delhi Some of the Mughal princesses Salima Sultana, Akbar's wife, Nur Jahan, Mumtaz Mahal and Jahanara Begum, the daughter of Shah Jaban, and Zeb un nisa, the daughter of Aurangzeb distinguished themselves in literature. Middle class people usually kept their daughters in ignorance except in very rare cases where the fathers acted as teachers at home. Unlike Persia and Arabia, mixed classes of both sexes were not held in India and the girls of the poor were left in absolute illiteracy.

Royal Patronage : Mughal emperors were patrons of education. Humayun was very fond of books, and he caused a madarsah to be established at Delhi and changed the pleasure house built by Sher Shah in the *Purana Qila* into a library. He assigned a place to the scholar next but one to Emperor in dignity. Sher Shah Suri founded the famous Madarsah at Narnaul in Patiala district. His son and successor Salim Shah followed his footsteps in his educational out look. Akbar's reign marks a new epoch in the progress of education in schools and colleges. He built colleges at Fatehpur Sikri, Agra, and other places and introduced some changes in the methods of studies and in the curriculum. He gave to the existing system of education a national bias. Jahangir had promulgated a regulation in his dominion that whenever a well to do person or a rich traveller died without any heir, his property would revert to the Crown and it was to be utilized for building and repairing madarsahs, monasteries, etc.

After his accession to the throne, Jahangir repaired even those madarsahs which for the last thirty years had been the dwelling places of birds and beasts, and filled them with students and professors. Shah Jahan encouraged learning by granting rewards, and repaired the college called *Dar ul Baqa* (Abode of Eternity) which had been almost in ruins. He also founded the famous Imperial College to the south of the Jama Masjid in Delhi and appointed the teachers of the colleges at Delhi and Agra. He made enduring contributions to education.

In Dara Shikoh the Mughal Imperial family possessed one of the greatest scholars that India has ever produced. He was a voluminous writer. Though Aurangzeb destroyed Hindu schools and temples, he encouraged the education of the Muslim youths in various ways and founded, according to Keene, "numerous colleges and schools." He sanctioned enormous sums of money for the repair and reconstruction of the old maqtabs and madarsahs of Gujarat. The successors of Aurangzeb Bahadur Shah I, Muhammad Shah, Shah Alam II and Bahadur Shah II were all noted for their literary knowledge and were patrons of education. Literature

The Mughals were patrons of literature and gave a considerable impetus to its development in different branches.

Not only emperors but the ladies of the royal household from Humayun's mother to Zebunnisa, the famous daughter of Aurangzeb, were patrons of art and letters. Babar and Jahangir wrote their own memoirs. Many thinkers and scholars flourished and wrote interesting and important works under the patronage of Akbar. At Akbar"s court was gathered a galaxy of poets and men of letters.

The Persian Literature During Mughals : Persian was considerably patronized by the Mughal Emperors and monumental works in Persian were composed under the liberal patronage of the Mughals. The Persian literature of Akbar's period may be considered under three heads *(i)* historical works, *(ii)* translations, and *(iii)* poetry and verse. The famous historical works of the period are *Tarikh-i-Alfi* of Mulla Daud, *Ain-i-Akbari* and *Akbar Namah* of Abul Fazl, *Muntakhab ul Tawarikh* by Badauni, *Tabaqat-i-Akbari* by Nizamuddin Ahmad, *Munshiat of* Abul Fateh, *Akbar Nornah* by Faizi Sarhindi and *Maasir-i-Rahimi* by Abdul Baqi. The most accomplished and greatest writer in Persian was Abul Fazl. He was a poet, essayist, critic and historian. His writings were based on his well digested erudition and politics of the day. He was famous for translating Hindu Scriptures in Persian. By order of Akbar many books in Sanskrit and other languages were translated into Persian to promote free exchange of social and spiritual thoughts between the Hindus and the Muslims.

Different sections of the Mahabharat were translated into Persian by many Muslim scholars and were compiled under the title of *Razm Namah.* Badauni completed the translation of the *Ramayan* in *1589) Atharva Veda* was translated by Hazi Ibrahim Sarhindi, *Lilawati,* a work on mathematics, by Faizi, treatise on astronomy known as the *Tujak* translated by Muhammad Khan Gujarati, and the *Rajatarangini* (History of Kashmir) by Maulana Shah Muhammad Shahabadi. Some Greek and Arabic works were also translated into Persian. The *Jama-i-Rashidi* was translated from Arabic into Persian by Abdul Qadir Badauni and Khan-i-Khanah Abdur Rahim put, into

Persian the *Waqiyat-i-Babari* (Memoirs of Babar) from the original Turkish. A number of poets produced works of merit under the liberal patronage of Akbar, the most famous among them were Ghizali, Faizi, Muhammad Hussain Naziri, writer of many *ghazals* of merit and Sayyid Jamaluddin Urfi, the writer of *qasidas*. Abdur Rahim Khan-i-Khanah, the premier noble, was also a scholar and poet of Persian. Faizi was a poet of distinction but he earned the fame as the translator of Hindu classics into Persian.

Jahangir, who had an excellent literary taste, also extended royal patronage to scholars. His autobiography is famous for its style, frankness and sincerity of views and freshness of the matter. Among the learned men who had adorned his court, Ghiyas Beg, Naqib Khan, Niamatullah and Abdul Haqq Dehlavi were famous. Some well known historical works were also written during his reign. Shah Jahan followed the example of his father in patronizing men of letters. Besides many writers, poets and theologians, there flourished famous historians like Abdul Hamid Lahori, author of the *Pad shah Namah* and Inayat Khan, the writer of *Shah Jahan Namah.*

The scholarly works of Prince Dara Shikoh, who was keenly interested in religious and philosophical studies, were masterpieces of Persian literature. Besides writing a treatise on the technical terms of Hindu pantheism, he wrote a biography of the Muslim saints and he got the Hindu scriptures like the *Gita, Upanishads* and the *Yoga Vasishtha* translated into Persian. Aurangzeb, though a zealous Sunni, was a critical scholar of Islamic theology and jurisprudence. He himself had mastery over simple and elegant Persian as is exhibited by the collection of his letters called the *Raqqat i Alamgiri.* Important histories like Khafi Khan's *Muntakhab ul Lubab,* Mirza Muhammed Kazim's *Namah,* Muhammad Saqi's *Masir-i-Alamgiri,* Sujan Rai Khatri's *Khulasat ul Tawarikh,* Bhimsen's *Nuskha-i-Dilkusha* and *Fatuhat i Alamgiri* by Iswar Das were compiled during the reign of Aurangzeb.

Libraries : The Mughal emperors' fondness for books led to the foundation of the Imperial Library which became a treasure house of every kind of literature. Important works, written by ancient authors of repute, dealing with history, philosophy, science and religion, were collected and placed in the Imperial Library. Humayun himself collected a vast number of books for this library and brought with him his favourite books from Persia. In Akbar's reign it consisted of 24,000 manuscript volumes, many of which were specially compiled out and illustrated for the emperor. Faizi was the librarian. Akbar, Jahangir and Shah Jahan were great collectors of books, and Hindu as well as Muslim nobles followed the fashion of the imperial court. The great private manuscript libraries of northern India have their origin at this time the Anup Sanskrit Library of Bikaner, the Pothi Khana of Jaipur and the great collections of Jaisalmer are the examples of such medieval libraries.

The Vernacular Literatures : The peace, law and order secured by Emperor Akbar, the noble cosmopolitan idea of the religious movements of the age and the preachings of the saintly teachers in the common languages inspired the genius of the scholars that unfolded in manifold petals. As a result of this the sixteenth and seventeenth centuries witnessed the fruition of the knowledge and talents of the Hindus. These two centuries are also called "the Augustan Age of Hindustani literature".

Hindi Literature : The first famous writer of Hindi after 1526 was Malik Muhammad Jayasi, the author of the famous philosophic epic called the *Padmavat.* Akbar's keen interest in and patronage of Hindi poetry and the peaceful and settled condition of the country during his reign gave a great encouragement to Hindi literature. Dr. Ishwari Prasad in his book *History of Muslim Rule in India* remarks that the brilliant conquests and administrative reforms of Akbar inaugurated a new era: and the latter half of the sixteenth century became an age of exuberant imagination, gorgeous display and romance an age of heroic deeds and gallant adventure which called forth the best powers of man. Poets, thinkers, writers and scholars shed lustre on the vernacular literatures. Among Akbar's courtiers; Raja Birbal, Raja Man Singh, Raja Bhagwan Das and Prithviraj Rathor were famous poets. Raja Todarmal also wrote verses in their.

But the most distinguished poet and writer among his courtiers was Abdur Rahim Khan-i-Khanah. His *dohas* in Hindi are even today read with keen interest and great admiration and enthusiasm. *Rahim Satsai,* compilation of his 700 *dohas,* has its own place in Hindi literature. Narhari, Karan, Harinath and Gang were also well known writers and poets of the court of Akbar.

A great part of Hindi literature of the Mughal period was religious, characterized by an exposition of worship of either Krishna or Rama. Most of the poetry of the time borrowed its themes from the cults of Krishna and Rama. Many poets and writers of the Krishna cult flourished in the *Brajbhumi,* corresponding approximately to the Jamuna Valley Notable among them are eight poets grouped under the noble of *Asthachhap* (eight seals), the most renowned among whom was poet Surdas. He, writing in *Braj Bhasha,*described in his *Sursagar,* "the sports of Krishna's early life and composed many verses on the charm of Krishna and his beloved Radha." The verses of Surdas are a part of the most valuable treasure of Hindi literature. They are famous for their sweet melody and wonderful imagery. Other poets of the *Ashtachhap* group were Nandadas, Krishnadas, Parmanand, Kumbhandas and Chaturbhujdas. Raskhan, a renowned poet of the Krishna cult, composed sweet verses, full of *Bhakti* or intense devotion to Lord Krishna. *Prem Vatika* is one of his famous works.

Among the poets and writers of the Rama cult, the most notable was Tulsidas. He wrote in the language of the people and may well claim to be the poet of India. He was not merely a poet of very high order, but a spiritual teacher of the people whose name has become a household world. His notable works are *Ram Gitawali, Krishna Gitawali, Vinay Patrika, Parvati Mangal,*

Janaki Mangal, Dohawali and *Vairagya Sandipani. But* the most famous of his works is *Ramcharit Manas* which is not only an extraordinary and magnificent epic of great poetic genius, singing the great noble deeds of King Rama, but a scripture to which the entire Hindi knowing people of India turn for spiritual sustenance. It has been a code of ethics constantly on the *lips* of all from princes to peasants.

In fact, the *Ramayan* has become the one Bible ora hundred millions of people. (Grierson). "*Romoyan* as a creation in the Hindi literature and as an expression of religion stands supreme." (Kissan Keane). The historical and cultural significance of Tulsidas is unique. Sardar Panikkar remarks that Tulsidas saved Hinduism from schisms and cults; for the religion of the *Ramcharit Manas,* in spite of the exaltation of Rama as the supreme being, was catholic enough to hold all sects and provided the strong motive force of *Bhakti* which has since then remained the basic factor of Indian popular religion.

It was in the Mughal period that the first attempts were made to systematize the art of poetry in the field of Hindi literature by famous poets like Keshava Das, Senapati and the Tripathi brothers who flourished during the reign of Shah Jahan and Aurangzeb. Keshava wrote on the art of writing poetry. His famous works are: *Kavi Priya, Ramchandrika* (life story of Rama), *Alankar Manjari* dealing with prosody, and *Rasik Priya* describing the art of poetical composition. Keshava occupies front rank among the Hindi poets. People even today read his works with keen interest. Among the Tripathi brothers, Bhushan sang the glory and greatness of his own community Hindu and was patronized by Shivaji and Chhatrasal Bundela. The famous works of Bhushan are *Shiva Bhawani, Chhatrasal Shatak* and *Shivaraj Bhushan.* Another well known poet was Sundar who composed his famous work *Sundar Sringar* on poetical composition. Shah Jahan, being impressed by his poetic genius, conferred on him the titles of *Kavi Rai* and *Mahakavi Ray.* Devakavi of Etawah and Biharilal Chaube, author of the well known *Bihari Satsai,* a collection of 700 *dohas* and *sorathas,* also deserve special mention here.

Bengali Literature: The period under review is also noted for a brilliant outburst of the Vaishnava literature in Bengal. Its many branches like *karchas* (notes), the *padas* and songs and, biographies of Chaitanya, have not only saturated the minds of the people of Bengal with feelings of love and liberalism but have also survived as a mirror of the social life of the province during that age. Krishnadas Kaviraj, Brindavan Das, Jayanand, Trilochandas and Narhari Chakravarti have written monumental biographies of Bengal's greatest saint Chaitanya. This period also witnessed the production of many translations of the Great Sanskrit epics and the *Bhagavat*, and books in praise of Chandi Devi and Mansa Devi. Among the poets of Bengal, Kashiram Das, Mukandram Chakravarti and Danaram deserve special mention. Mukandram Chakravarti has gained great popularity and Cowell calls him "the Crabbe of Bengal." The works of Bharat Chandra and Ram Prasad were written after the decline of the Mughals. Besides these, numerous Hindu and Muslim poets had enriched the Bengali literature with their works.

Marathi Literature : Marathi literature was equally enriched during this period by Eknath, Dasopant, Mukteshwar, Vaman Pandit, Tukaram, Ramdas and Moropant. The Marathi works of the age indicate scholarship of the writers and the poets. In the beginning of the age Shridhar Swami borrowed themes from the Ramayan and the Mahabharat and composed his works, the most famous among them being *Bari Vijay, Ram Vijaya, Pandava Pratap* and *Shivalilamrita*. Mukte shwar followed his footsteps and composed his famous *Ramayan.* Among other poets of the age, Raghunath Pandit, the author of *Nal Damayanti Swayambara khyan*, Madhwamunishwar, Amritrai and Mahipati deserve mention. Ramdas a famous saint and poet of Maharashtra, is also the product of this age. His renowned work is *Dasbodh*. Vaman Pandit is the most celebratele among the poets of the Krishna cult in Maharashtra. He is noted for his *Yamak Alankar* and new style of verses. Moropant is the most renowned among the poets of the Rama cult. His work *Kekawali* breathes the spirit of intense devotion. He has composed the whole of the Mahabharat in *arya* metre. Like Tulsidas and Surdas, Tukaram flourished in Maharashtra in this period. He was a celebrated Vaishnava saint whose *abhangas* are recited even today. With the rise of the Maratha power after the death of Aurangzeb, Marathi literature is characterized by a new epoch of *Pauwadas* or ballads. The poets of the age excelled in composing *Lawani* and *Pauwadas* to inspire the Maratha soldiers. Ramjoshi, Anantfandi, Honaji Bal, Sagan, Bhau,Prabhakar, Parashram, etc., are the noted poets and writers of the *Pauwadas* age.

Gujarati Literature : Like Hindi and Marathi, Gujarati literature was also enriched during the Mughal period. Arwa the famous saint and poet of Gujarat, flourished in the reign of Akbar. He abandoned the traditions of the Krishna cult and expounded philosophy and love, critically examined the human nature and exposed the materialistic outlook of life in his works. He is, therefore, renowned as the representative poet of the age. *Chitta Vichar Samvad, Shatpad, Kewalyagita,* etc., are his famous works. He was followed by poet Bhatt Premanand. Credit goes to him for raising Gujarati to the high level of literary excellence. He is supposed to be the author of thirty six works.

Another celebrated Gujarati poet Samal Bhatt flourished after the death of Aurangzeb. He had succeeded most effectively in describing Puranic legends and stories in verses. The stories of his works *Madan Mohan* and *Somal Ratnamal* are very popular even today. Arwa, Paramanand and Samal are the three shining stars of the firmanent of Gujarati literature. They had not only influenced the writers and poets of their own age, but even those of the succeeding generations. Though a few Vaishnava and Jain poets flourished in the seventeenth century in Gujarat, after the death of Aurangzeb, Gujarati literature lacked talented poets and writers, and no work of outstanding merit was composed in the eighteenth century. However, it witnessed the growth of the *Garbha* literature long poems written in praise of goddess Amba or Kali, sung by women and girls while dancing gracefully, moving in circle beating time with rhythmic clapping of the hands.

Urdu Literature : Urdu did not progress considerably under the Mughals, However, Faizi's friend Nuri Azampuri, Hazrat Kamaluddin Makha dum, Shaikh Sadi and Muhammad Afzal were Urdu poets of Akbar's period, whereas Nasir Afzali Allahabadi and Pandit Chandrabhan are considered celebrated Urdu poets of Shah Jahan's reign. But the real progrees of Urdu took place in the Deccan under the patronage of the Sultans of Golkonda and Bijapur who themselves were poets of remarkable ability and distinction. Mohammed Kuli Kutub Shah (1519-1555), the Sultan of Golkonda, was himself a great poet and writer of Urdu.

The poets, Ibra Nisati and Gawasi, flourished after him, under the royal patronage of the Sultan of Bijapur, Muhammad Nasrat Shah, the author of *Ali Namah* and *Gulshan-i-Ishk* and *Shah Hashim*. The writers of *Yusufwa Zulekha Masnavi* flourished' in the Deccan. But Wali of Aurangabad (1668-1744) who wrote *ghazals* (love songs), *masnavis* (narrative poems), *rubaiyats* (quatrains) in simple, natural and elegant style, was the most renowned poet of the age. Urdu poetry received a definite standard of form at the hands of Wali, called the father of Rekhta, credit goes to him for introducing Urdu poetry in northern India. His *Diwan* became very popular in the Mughal court. Many poets composed works in imitation of Wali's works. Among them Hatim, Khan Arju, Abru and Mazhar are most famous and they are known as the fathers of the Urdu poetry in the north. Delhi became the centre of Urdu literature in the beginning of the eighteenth century. After the death of Aurangzeb Urdu progressed considerably and poets like Ghalib, Shah, Nasir, Momin, etc., enriched the Urdu literature.

Sanskrit Literature : The Mughal period is marked by the last efflorescence of Sanskrit literature. Though Akbar's court was adorned with Sanskrit writers, the greatest poet and writer of Sanskrit was Jagannath Pandit. He was honoured by Emperor Shah Jahan with the title *of Kaviraj.* Jagannath was the last of the great Sanskrit poets whose works attain a classic beauty in diction and sentiment." His *Ganga Lahri* and other works have gained great fame and are rightly regarded as classics. There flourished another poet called Kavindra. Though his laboured and ornate literary compositions are 'in no way' on a par with Jagannath's, yet they deserve mention. Rupa Goswami, the writer of the drama *Vidagdha Madhava* and other works, the dramatist Girdharnatha and several others are among the famous poets of Sanskrit during this age. In addition to men, Vaijyanti, who successfully collaborated with her beloved Krishnanatha, in composing the famous work *Anandalatika Ceampu,* and Vallabhadevi, the well known authoress of *Subhashitavali,* were reputed learned women of the period.By the end of Aurangzeb's reign the era of great poets came to a close and the disintegration and dissolution of the Mughal Empire had a disastrous effect on the vernacular literature of the country.

Religious Sects

The sixteenth century, like the fifteenth, was characterized by great religious upheaval, when Vaisnavism appealed successfully to the hearts of millions of people in northern India and Bengal. Tens of thousands began to follow Rama and Krishna cults. The devotees of Rama and Krishna separated themselves into many sects and inculcated worship according to their own ideas. The cult of Krishna was preached by a group of devotees and saints significantly called *Ashtachhap* (eight seals) among whom Surdas was the most renowned. They sang *bhajans* and wrote and preached in *Braj Bhasha* and dwelt with great love, fervour and devotion upon the sports of Krishna's childhood. A person named Hari Vansa founded the Radha Ballabhi sect about 1551 A.D. The followers of this sect worship Radha, the consort of Krishna, and seek to gain the favour of Krishna through her. Other famous Vaishnava saints of the period in Brindaban were Rupa, Sanatan and Jiva Goswami, who founded the temple of Radha Damodar, and Gopal Bhatt.

The Rama cult was preached by Tulsidas who advocated the worship of Rama as an incarnation of God Vishnu. He accepted the principles and practices of orthodox Hinduism, upheld the caste system, emphasized Brahmanical superiority, advocated idolatry, laid stress upon rituals, discouraged the freedom of women, and preached the doctrine of *Bhakti.* He did not found a sect, but he acted as a distinguished reformer and teacher. Besides Tulsidas, there were many other reformers who founded their own sects. Their teachings and writings reveal the impress of Muslim influence. Dadu (1544-1603), a saint and reformer, who denounced idolatry and caste, rejected Hindu ritualism, emphasized simple faith in God and founded a sect known as *Dadupanth.*

The sect of the *Khakis* founded by Kilh arose from among a group of the followers of Dadu. Birbhan, a contemporary of Dadu, founded the famous sects of *Sadhus* or *Satnamis.* The followers of this sect deprecated caste system, adopted one God under the name of *Satnam,* denounced idol worship, maintained a very high standard of morals, disfavoured hoarding of wealth and its inequalities and aimed at the absorption in God. They rose in prominence during the reign of Aurangzeb. Haridas founded a sect called the *Narayanian.*

It confines to the generation of *Narayan* or the Supreme Being. About the middle of the seventeenth century *LaMasi* sect was founded by Laldas whose teachings ran on the same lines as those of Kabir. The *Laldasis* emphasized the importance of Ramanama and sang hymns accompanied with music. *Satnamis* and *Dharamadasis* pointed out the value of repeating the name of God and the duty of leading clean, virtuous and pure lives. Dharnidas, Pran Nath, Budha Sahib; Charandas and Ramcharan were other famous saints who flourished in the seventeenth and eighteenth centuries. Ramcharan founded the *Ram Sanehi* order, Swami Narayan Singh the *Siva Narayani* order and Sahjananda the Swami *Narayani* sect in the eighteenth century.

In Bengal, the followers of Chaitanya preached the *Bhakti*

cult. They held that there could be no *moksha* or deliverance without *Bhakti*. According to them, Krishna is the *Paramatma*, the Supreme Soul and the Supreme Object of worship.

In the Deccan great religious movements also arose in the sixteenth century. Saint Eknath was one of its pioneers in Maharashtra. He emphasized *Bhakti* to God by means of which, according to him, women, untouchables or Sudras and all others could achieve salvation. Another leading saint of Maharashtra was Tuka Ram. He enjoined worship with a clean, pure and lofty heart and exhorted people to be kind to all. Tuka Ram's *abhangas* or unbroken hymns are very popular. Their piety elevates the soul and purifies the emotions. They are still recited in Maharashtra and console millions of people in suffering and sorrow. Ramdas was another saint who had profound influence on the lives of the people of Maharashtra. He was the spiritual guide of Shivaji. He preached Raffia cult.

According to him salvation is attained by devotion to Rama alone. He emphasized that purity in thought and action, unselfishness, truthfulness, forgiveness, sincerity, mercy humility, charity, and generosity are the most certain passports to Divine Bliss. Many of the above mentioned saints came from lower classes. They carried further the great wave of the protestant movements in Hinduism which had arisen with Ramanand and Kabir in the fifteenth century and which spread with wonderful rapidity all over India in the succeeding three centuries. All of these saints were devotees, inspired by the same ideas. Their philosophy was a protest against orthodox Hinduism. But the later saints hardly added anything new to the religiousness or anything of great value to the rich treasures of devotional poetry.

Besides the Hindu saints there were many sufis in the Muslim society. During the Mughal period they advocated intense love and deep devotion to God. They preached that the practical aim of life is to love God and get absorbed in Him. They emphasized complete union with the Divinity and pointed special methods for the spiritual progress. They explained the needs of a spiritual guide or preceptor and laid emphasis on repentance, abstinence renunciation, quiet, piety, contemplation, humility and purity of soul for salvation. They preached their doctrines to the followers of all faiths and persuaded none to give up his creed. Preaching of sufi saints encouraged the growth of religious toleration, harmony and brotherly feeling among the followers of different creeds. Shah Jahan's eldest son, prince Dara Shikoh, was a sufi.

Fine Arts : The Mughal age was not only a period of experiment and innovation but of continuation and culmination of those processes of fine arts that had their seeds sown in the later part of the Turko-Afghan rule. The spirit of harmony and synthesis that commenced in the closing years of the Delhi Sultanate continued in the Mughal period even in the realm of fine arts. The beneficent royal patronage affected markedly the quality ocarts produced by the people. The culture of the Mughal period was the court culture. It was inspired throughout the age by the throne. The masses had no hand in it. The Mughal culture depended almost entirely on the Imperial patronage. When the keen and personal interest of the Mughal Emperor stimulated it, it attained greatest heights; but it languished and faded away when the ruler's interest declined. Con- sequently, under the first five Mughal rulers, fine arts rose to high standard of excellence, but they touched their lowest ebb when the Court patronage was discontinued.

The Mughal Emperors being lovers of fine arts had evolved new styles and techniques which indicate a happy mingling of Persian and Indian elements. This synthesis has left a deep impress on painting, architecture, embroidery, jewellery and metal work of the age. All the fine arts of the period breathe a spirit of luxury. The following factors were responsible for this extraordinary development of fine arts and high standard of production.

1. "The wealth of India dazzled even eyes accustomed to the pomp of Versailles." Immense wealth and the

unlimited power of the empire enabled the Mughals to continue their, ardent, sustained and perceptive patronage and constructed numerous buildings.

2. The relatively settled conditions and a long period of peace that prevailed all over the northern India smoothed the path for undertaking extensive works of art.
3. The Mughal emperors had pronounced aesthetic nature. Each of them was anxious to find expression in some visual arts. The first five rulers were in most respects intellectually superior to those around them. In their cultural outlook and refined taste they had few equals.
4. A strong and wise government, a glorious and rich heritage of culture and sympathetic sovereigns created unique atmosphere for the brilliant output of letters and fine arts.

Architectural Development

With the exception of Emperor Aurangzeb, whose puritan ideas prevented him from patronizing fine arts, all the early Mughal emperors were great builders. In fact, with the advent of the Mughals. Indian architecture enters upon a new phase in which the rugged austerity and simplicity of the work of the earlier Sultans of Delhi is softened and beautified be Persian influence. Architecture under the Mughals attained its most sumptuous form. The unexampled wealth and splendour and great luxury of the Mughals enabled them to construct buildings of supreme beauty, layout extensive pleasure gardens and new cities. Mughal architecture reveals a happy blending of Persian and Indian styles.

The Mughal buildings, unlike those of the Sultanate period, indicate no manifestation of provincial or regional style. They display uniformity in their architectural character and structural principles. The chief characteristics of the Mughal buildings are the bulbous graceful dome, the cupolas at the corners standing on slender pillars, magnificent palace hall and the lofty vaulted gateway. The Mughals introduced the style of constructing mausoleums in the centre of a large park like enclosure, and the innovation of constructing a double dome, the outer and inner one, the latter formed the vaulted ceiling of the mortuary chamber underneath.

There are certain historians, like Fergusson, who believed that the Mughal style of architecture was foreign in origin. This theory of Fergusson has been criticized by E. B. Havell who maintains that Indian culture had a remarkable power of absorbing foreign elements of art. He points out that the art and culture of foreign countries with which India had established relations had their impress upon the Indian art, but it cannot be asserted that the inspiration of the Indian master craftsmen was entirely foreign. Under the Mughals there was a good deal of fusion of culture and arts. According to Sir John Marshall, in a country so extensive and diversified like India, it cannot be definitely said that achitecture ever conformed to a single universal style.

The personal tastes of the Mugbal emperors moulded the types considerably. Much depended upon them. The Mughals provided the elements of grandeur and originality to the grace and decoration of Hindu architecture. After the death of Babar, Humayun's liking for Persian style led to the Persian influence on Indian art and it increased and continued to the end of Akbar's period. But Akbar's genius adopted Persian ideals to the traditions of Indian craftsmanship. During the reign of Akbar's successors, Indian architecture and painting assumed Indian character and in the exquisite and magnificent structures of their periods there is nothing which can be pronounced as distinctly Persian.

Dr. Ishwari Prasad rightly points out that "the Mughal style, which was an amalgamation of many influences, was more sumptuous and decorative than the style that preceded it, and it scilelicacy and ornamentation furnish a striking contrast to the massiveness and simplicity of the art of pre-Mughal days." In design in the use of building materials, in execution, in delicacy and grace, decoration and carving, the structures of the Mughals were radically different from those constructed by the Sultans of Delhi, and they had more of the Hindu and Persian elements than the buildings of the pre-Mughal days.

Before Akbar : Babar, being a prejudiced critic of Indian architecture, was not satisfied with the structures that he found at Delhi and Agra. Consequently, it is said that he invited architects from Constantinople and other centres of Islamic culture to construct his buildings. As no traces of the influence of the Byzantine style are observable in the Mughal buildings, it is very unlikely that the foreign architects, especially the pupils of the famous Albanian architect Sinan, had worked on mosques and other monuments in India.

However, Babar constructed buildings and employed 680 masons daily in Agra alone and 1,941 persons daily on his palaces and other buildings in Agra, Sikri, Bayana, Dholpur, Gwalior and Koal. Though most of the buildings of Babar have perished, three mosques attributed to him, have survived to this day. Two of them are large mosques in Kabul Bagh at Panipat and the Jami Masjid at Sambhal in Rohilkhand and the third mosque within the old Lodi Fort at Agra. Humayun the son and successor of Babar, on account of his anxiety and trouble, did not find enough time to indulge in his artistic fancy.

However, two mosques remain of those built during the reign of Humayun. One is in a ruinous condition at Agra and the other at Fatehabad in the Hissar district of Haryana. The latter has enamelled the decoration in the Persian manner. Percy own points out that Babar and Humayun both had indirectly influenced the subsequent art. "Babar's marked aesthetic sense, communicated to his successors, inspired them under more favourable conditions to the production of their finest achievement, while Humayun's forced contact with the culture of the Safavids is reflected in that Persian influence noticeable in many of the Mughal buildings which followed."

Sher Shah who snatched power from the feeble hands of Humayun was also a great builder. His successors followed his example. They erected mighty forts in the Punjab, Rohtas and Mankot, and constructed a series of tombs at Sahasram in Bihar and in its neighbourhood. Some of them are the finest specimens of medieval architecture. The Sur period is the age of transition in the history of Indian architecture. It was 'in this age that the art was beginning to shake off that puritanical influence which had fettered it since the time of Firuz Tughlaq and was endeavouring to become more ornate in style. Decorating edifice with rich carving was being gradually adopted, and it reached its perfection under Shah Jahan. Sher Shah began to build a new walled capital at Delhi on the site of Indraprastha, but it could not be completed due to his premature death. However, the two remaining gateways of this capital and the citadel, now significantly called the Purana Qila, display "a more refined and artistically ornate type of edifice than had prevailed for some time."

The mosque in the Purana Qila, known as the *Qila-i-Kuhna*, depicts in a most decisive manner the progress that took place in architecture during this age. It occupies a high rank among the Muslim buildings of northern India. It reflects Persian influence in its recessed portal, small minarets round the dome and in its fine masonry, though in other respects it is Indian." The mausoleum of Sher Shah, which stands fouthquare on a high plinth in the centre of a great artificial lake at Sahasram in Bihar, is an immense pyramidal structure of five distinct storeys. On account of its dignity and grandeur it is caused a marvel of Indo-Muslim architecture. Percy Brown remarks that "it is a creation of sober and massive splendour of which any country would be proud." The whole structure exhibits "the aesthetic capacity of the Indian architect at its greatest, and his genius at its highest". Besides this, it also displays a happy blending of Hindu and Muslim architectural ideas. Thus in art, the Afghan ruler Sher Shah paved the path for the great Mughal Emperor Akbar.

Architectural Development During Akbar : Mughal architecture, as we know it for all practical purposes, begins with Akbar. He had insatiable passion for building. Abul Fazl rightly observes, "His Majesty plans splendid edifices, and dresses the work of his mind and heart in the garment of stone and clay." Akbar's reign saw a remarkable development of architecture. He mastered every detail of art and with a liberal and synthetic mind he borrowed his artistic ideas from a variety of sources. The expert craftsmen of his reign gave a practical shape to his ideas. The main elements of the style of architecture evolved under Akbar were the use of red sandstone with insertion of white marble, carved or boldly inlaid patterns and painted designs of the interior walls and ceilings for the ornamentation. The Persian and Hindu influences had their full play in the Akbari style of architecture. While still retaining the Persian ideas which he inherited from his mother, his policy of tolerating the Hindus, sympathizing with their religion and culture and his attempts to win them over to his side made him adopt the elements of Hindu architecture in his buildings whose decorative features were copies of those seen in the temples of the Jains and Hindus.

The Hindu style is remarkably illustrated in the Jahangiri Mahal in the Agra Fort with its square pillars and bracket capitals and rows of small arches, in numerous structures of Fatehpur Sikri, the imperial capital, and in the Lahore Fort. Even the ground plan of Humayun's tomb at old Delhi and the free use of white marble in its external appearance are Hindu elements.

Akbar constructed several forts, villas, towers, palaces, mosques, serais, schools, tanks, wells and gateways. Humayun's tomb is the earliest and noteworthy structure of Akbar's reign. The mausoleum stands on the broad platform formed by the upper surface of a high and wide spread terrace. Two architectural features distinguish this tomb from buildings previously constructed: (i) the shape, design and construction of its dome are according to Persian style: and (ii) the whole building is placed in the centre of a large park like enclosure. Thus, Humayun's tomb introduced new elements in Indian architecture. Other characteristic works of Akbar were the forts and fortress palaces at Agra and Lahore. He enlarged the Agra Fort, a vast structure of red sandstone with walls 21 metres high and lofty gateways and broad octagonal towers. This was "the first conception of red sandstone on such a large scale.

The two imposing and impressive gateways of the Agra Fort display originality and spontaneity and rich and varied ornamentation giving a most attractive appearance. The Agra Fort indicates that the Rajput citadels must have exercised considerable influence on the fort architecture. The Jahangiri Mahal in Agra Fort, intended as a residence for the heir apparent and his family, has fine ornate handiwork. The palace in the fortress of Lahore had the remarkable display of the decoration distributed over its exterior walls. The fortress palace of forty pillars at Allahabad is the largest of those of its kind built by Akbar, as its widest dimension is nearly 900 metres across. It is definitely of Hindu design, "with its projecting verandah roof supported on rows of Hindu pillars."

But the most ambitious architectural project and notable building achievement of Akbar's reign was the new capital city of Fatehpur Sikri and its buildings. Fergusson remarked that Fatehpur Sikri was the reflex of the mind of a great man (Akbar). His most important buildings are his palaces at Fatehpur Sikri which exhibit every characteristic of a completely matured style. The most magnificent buildings at Sikri are Jodha Bai's palace, the residential palaces of Mariam and the Sultana, the house of Birbal, the *Sonhala Makan* or the house of the Princess of Amber, the *Diwan-i-Am* or the emperor's public audience hall of Hindu design, the *Diwan-i-Khas* or the Hall of private audience, the *Panch Mahal* or the palace of five storeys, the Jami Masjid, the Buland Darwaza and the Tomb of Sheikh Salim Chisti. There are numerous other supplementary structures having much the same architectural character. Jodha Bai's palace is the most complete in its design and arrangements, and its carved decoration resembles the Hindu temple architecture. The interior of the palace of Mariam was ornamented with large mural paintings apparently of Persian subjects.

The palace of the Turkish Sultana, a single storeyed pavilion, is noted for its simplicity of design and richness and high quality of its carved decoration. The house of Birbal attracts the eye due to the architectural ornamentation and the exhuberance of its carved decoration, both inside and outside. The *Diwan-i-Khas* which has unique arrangements for the imperial seat has distinctly Indian character in planning and construction. The *Panch Mahal,* a pyramidal structure in five storeys each carved in a wholly different design, exhibits continuation of the plan of the Indian Buddhist vihars which probably survived in the age. All these are secular buildings. But the most impressive part of Fatehpur Sikri is the group of structures of religious nature in which the Jami Masjid predominates. The highest architectural skill was concentrated in the Jami Masjid. Inlaid marble and plaster relief in colour were freely used in this mosque.

The tomb of Sheikh Salim Chisti, a gem of craftsmanship, and the Buland Darwaja are near the mosque. The Buland Darwaza, rising to a total height of 54'2 metres above the roadway with a frontage of 40 metres is a superb structure, equal led by no other gateway in India. It has great dignity and impres- siveness. It was erected to commemorate Emperor Akbar's conquest of Gujarat and has been described as the most perfect architectural achievement in the whole of India. "Each art culture has usually one form of utterance in which it finds the readiest means of expression and with the Mughals it was the entrance gateway."

Architectural Development under Jahangir : The strenuous and unceasing building activity of Akbar was followed by a period of partial inertia. As Jahangir, Akbar's son and successor, had greater love for painting than architecture, the number of buildings constructed by him was poor as compared with the architectural records of his father. The rule of Jahangir was relatively uneventful in the realm of architecture. But three structures of his reign are of great interest and merit. First is the mausoleum of Akbar at Sikandra near Agra, the construction of which was begun by Emperor Akbar himself but completed by Jahangir. The design of this colossal mausoleum was inspired by the Buddhist vihars of India.

It has five square terraces which emerge from the ground rising one above the other, but diminishing as they ascend upwards. The uppermost storey of white marble has a vaulted roof. Originally a central marble dome with a golden ceiling was intended to crown the topmost storey. Had this been achieved, the tomb of the greatest Muslim Emperor of India would have been included among the greatest mausoleums of the world, second only to the Taj Mahal.

The second notable structure of Jahangir's reign is the mausoleum of Itimad-ud-daullah, Nurjahan's father, built at Agra by the Empress Nurjahan herself. Though it is a comparatively small structure, it is wholly constructed of pure white marble with *pietra dura*, that is, inlaying of many precious stones of different colours in most delicate manner, and, therefore it conveys the impression of a rich article of jewellery magnified into architecture. This was a Rajput style of architecture or most probably an older style of India.

This building is noted not only for its rare craftsmanship, 'refined feminism', high aesthetic taste, refinement of architecture, delicacy of treatment and chaste quality of its decoration, but it also marks a turning point in the evolution of architecture under the Mughals. Till now the Mughal buildings were constructed of red sandstone with *opus sectile* ornamentation. But Itimad-ud-daullah's tomb is the first Mughal structure constructed of entirely white marble with inlaid decoration called *pietradura*. It, thus, introduces the age of the sumptuous white marble pavilions and *pietra-dura* of the Emperor Shan Jahan. The third important building of the period is Jahangir's tomb on the opposite bank of the Ravi at Shahdara near Lahore, built by Nurjahan. It lacks the lofty effect of the earlier tombs.

Architectural Development under Shah Jahan : The most magnificent and prolific builder among the Mughals was Emperor Shah Jahan. Numerous buildings, palaces, forts, gardens, mosques and subsidiary structures erected by him are still existing at Agra, Delhi, Lahore, Ajmer, Ahmedabad, Kashmir, Kabul, Kandhar and elsewhere. The architectural structures of Emperor Shan Jahan, as compared with those of the great Akbar, are inferior in splendour, massivity and originality of conception, but they are superior in soft grace, elegance, highly artistic nature and lavish display and rich ornamentation of subtle nature. Consequently, Shah Jahan's architecture becomes, jewellery on a bigger scale.' Shah Jahan's building art gained exceptional elegance. The robust and exuberant style of Akbar gave way to elegant and effeminate style under Shah Jahan. In fact, Mughal architecture reached its climax under Shah Jahan. It was carried to the highest degree of perfection.

Shah Jahan's architecture is noted for certain characteristics. Not only change in the building material but change in the technique and in the architectural elements of style was also introduced in this age. Now marble was substituted for red stone. Shah Jahan founded the Mughal cities of standstone and he left them of marble. It was an age of pure white marble. Technique was also changed. Coloured tiles were rarely used. Rich decoration was obtained by means of Inlaid patterns in coloured stones. The chisel of the stone carver was replaced by the finer instruments of the marble cutter and polisher. As regards the style, instead of rectangular character of the structures of the previous period, there arose the curved lines and flowing rhythm of style under Shah Jahan. Ornamental elements of curvilinear order and marble arcades of engrailed arches became the distinguishing characteristics of the style. Spacious grandeur of design was successfully combined with feminine grace. Then, the Hindu influence, so strong under Akbar, entirely disappeared in Shah Jahan's buildings.

Shah Jahan constructed buildings of the most sensuous and voluptuous order. He largely reconstructed the fortress palaces at Agra and Delhi, and laid out the famous city of Shahjahanabad with a palace-fortress known as the Red Fort of Delhi on the right bank of the Jamuna. But the main buildings of Shah Jahan's time are the Rang Mahal, the Diwan-i-Am and Diwan-i-Khas in the Fort of Delhi, the Jama Masjid, the Taj Mahal and a number of minor buildings in various parts of the empire.

The Rang Mahal is lavishly ornate and is regarded as the crowning jewel of Shah Jahan's seraglio. But the Diwan-i-Khas, which is more highly ornamented than any building of Shah Jahan, rivals the Rang Mahal in an appearance of exuberant grace. It was in this marble pavilion that the great Mughal Shah Jahan, sitting on his peacock throne, gave audience in private to princes of the royal blood, nobles, foreign ambassadors and distinguished visitors. With its costly silver ceiling pavement of polished marble and mingle decoration of gold, precious stones, and marble, it justified the Persian inscription engraved on its walls:

> "Agar Firdaus bar ru-e-zamin ast,
>
> Hamin asto, ham in asto hamin ast;"
>
> (If on earth be an Eden of bliss,
>
> It is this, it is this, none but this).

The Diwan-i-Aam or hall of public audience was not a pleasure resort but a place for the transaction of administrative and official business. On ceremonial occasions the peacock throne was placed in the alcove in the back wall of this Hall for Shah Jahan to sit there. The Jama Masjid, near the Red Fort, intended as centre of public worship is very impressive, dignified and pleasing. On account of its majesty and dimensions it ranks as the largest and most eminent building of its kind in the country. Though it is a nobly proportioned structure, it does not set the emotional chords sounding as do other buildings of this period. The Moti Masjid at Agra, constructed by Shah Jahan in honour of his daughter Jahanara Begum, represents the architectural zenith of Shah Jahan's time from the stand point of true art. Though it does not possess anything like the imposing aspect of Jama Masjid of Delhi, yet it has purity and simplicity, well balanced perfect proportions, and the harmony of constructive designs. Consequently, it is an interesting architectural production and is considered as one of the most elegant buildings of its class to be found anywhere.

Some magnificent buildings were constructed in Lahore during the reign of Shah Jahan. Their chief characteristic was the brilliant exterior decoration on surface with patterns in brilliantly coloured glazed tiles. The finest example of this phase of Mughal architecture is the Wazir Khan's mosque in Lahore and tombs of Ali Mardan Khan and of Sharaf-ur-nisa. Another beautiful specimen of Mughal architecture in Lahore is the Mausoleum of Jahangir built by Shah Jahan and Nurjahan at Shahdara.

But the most important building of Shah Jahan's time is the Taj Mahal, a magnificent marble mausoleum, built by the emperor at a cost of fifty lacs of rupees, over the grave of his queen Mumtaz Mahal. It is the finest flower of Mughal art and most glorious monument of conjugal love, harmony and fidelity in the world. It is a combination of the finest art and the most expert construction. It exhibits the highest artistic merit, extraordinary scientific thought and remarkable technical skill, a splendid layout and the most sensuous charm. For its beauty, magnificence, lavish ornamentation, exquisite appearance, lovely dignity, ornamental gardens, complete lucidity and coherence of external architectural effect, unity of designs and the artistic synthesis of execution, it is rightly regarded as one of the wonders of the world. Percy Brown observes that it marks the perfect monument in the evolution of architecture during the Mughal period.

There is no evidence worthy of consideration to support the belief that an European architect designed the Taj and superintended the *pietra dura.* Vincent Smith, in his *History of Fine Arts in India and Ceylon* discusses all the facts relating to this topic. He holds the opinion that the Taj Mahal is "the product of combination of European and Asiatic genius." But it is a wrong view. E. B. Havell and Percy Brown support the view that it is wholly indigenous and was the logical evolution of the Mughal architecture. It has been proved on reasonable grounds that the Taj is the product of Indian genius.

Another renowned work of art of Shan Jahan's reign was the peacock throne. It was in the form of a cot bedstead on golden legs. The enamelled canopy was supported by twelve emerald pillars, each of which bore two peacocks entrusted with gems. A tree covered with diamonds, emeralds, rubies and pearls stood between the birds of each pair. This throne was removed to Persia in 1739 by Nadir Shah.

Architectural Development under Aurangzeb and After : With the death of Emperor Shah Jahan art declined, because his son and successor, Aurangzeb, being puritan, ceased to encourage it and erect new buildings. In fact, he was more eager to demolish Hindu temples than to construct splendid edifices of his own. However, a few structures of his reign deserve mention. They are the little marble mosque in Delhi Fort for his private use, the mosque and its tall minarets in Varanasi constructed on the ruins of the holy temple of Vishwanath, and the Badshahi mosque in Lahore, almost a copy of the great Jama Masjid at Delhi but inferior to that noble building. Fergusson considers it as the latest specimen of the Mughal architectural style. Aurangzeb's own tomb at Aurangabad in the Deccan is most splendid but extremely simple, devoid of any ornamentation or decoration.

All these structures are but feeble imitations of the older models of the Mughals. In the eighteenth and early nineteenth centuries some buildings were constructed by the Nawabs of Oudh and the Nizam of Hyderabad. The tomb of Nawab

Safdar Jang of Oudh, near Delhi, constructed in 1756, a passable copy of the mausoleum of Humayun, is marred by wretched plaster decoration in the interior. About the architecture in Oudh, Smith remarks that the shoddy buildings of the Nawab and Wazirs at Lucknow are pretentious abominations. Structures erected after Aurangzeb exhibit bankruptcy of taste and poverty of designs.

Mughal Gardens in India : The account of the architecture of the Mughals would be incomplete if their landscape architecture, illustrated by extensive ornamental gardens on certain appropriate sites, is not mentioned here. The Mughals had cultivated deep love for nature. Babar and his descendants revelled in trees and flowers and land scape gardening as a favourite diversion from the toils of political life. Consequently, they laid out extensive gardens. Later on, principal Mughal buildings, especially tombs, were surrounded by park like enclosures.

The gardens of the Mughal emperors and even the gardens of their Amirs like Pinjaur near Kalka show a remarkable sense of beauty and are noted for a continuous flow of water in them. The Mughal gardens were worked out in a regular arrangement of squares, often subdivided into smaller squares to form the favourite figure of the *Char bagh* or 'four fold plot'. There were paved pathways, avenues and ornamental water channels and fountains. In the central place masonry pavilions were erected.

Babar laid out a large garden called the Kabul Bagh at Panipat to commemorate his victory over Ibrahim Lodi in 1526. Jahangir and his consort, the Empress Nurjahan laid out gardens wherever they stayed, and Jahangir in his memoirs records the intense pleasure which he derived from them. The Shalimar, Nishat and other gardens in Kashmir are perhaps the best examples of the Mughal taste for gardens, love for nature and sense of aesthetic beauty. The enchanting scenery in which they are embosomed adds much to their beauty.

The Hindu Architecture : Great Hindu princes during the

Mughal period continued to patronize art. Their building activity manifested in the erection of palaces, forts, *ghats, bunds,* citadels temples, etc. The famous palace called *Man Mandir* erected by Maharaja Mansingh in Gwalior Fort a few years before the advent of the Mughals, is noted for its romantic treatment, outstanding architectural characteristic and joyous colouring. It is a representative example of decorative architecture. But the secular architecture of the Hindus underwent very notable change during the Mughal period. The Hindu princes of this age borrowed many of their architectural forms from the Mughal art of building. While constructing palaces in their capitals they imitated the Diwan-i-Am, Diwan-i-Khas, Shish Mahal and the Baradari of the imperial palaces.

The resultant architecture, therefore, differed both from the earlier Hindu structures and from the Mughal imperial residences. It represented the blending of the Rajput and Persian influences. Mughal foundation breaking out into Hindu exuberance is well illustrated in the palaces at Amber and Jodhpur. The great palace of Bir Singh Bundela of Orchha, another palace at Datia, both in the Vindhya Pradesh region, the Bikaner fort and palace, the Udaipur buildings and island palaces, the Jodhpur fort palace, the Amber palaces, Ajmer lake pavilions and the Lotus Mahal and a garden palace in Vijayanagar are among the surviving examples of Hindu architecture of the period under review.

The Mughal age also witnessed revival of temple architecture in the traditional style. The religious toleration of the early Mughals encouraged the restoration of the old Hindu temples and erection of new ones by Hindu princes, grandees and merchants. Mathura and Varanasi again became the centres of temple building activity. The most notable temple of the age was constructed by Bir Singh but it was destroyed by Shah Jahan. However, the majority of the great temples that survive in northern India today belong to the Mughal period.

Architecture in Deccan : During the Mughal period, the

Sultans of Bijapur and Golkonda had a special claim for remembrance for their architectural achievement which have been already dealt with in the preceding chapter. The Deccan Sultans' beautiful gardens, magnificent public baths, lovely royal palaces, fine mosques and splendid tombs reflect the riches of the Muslim kingdoms of the Deccan, the refined taste of their Persianized Sultans, their spirit of luxury and happy blending of the Hindu Muslim styles.

The Paintings

Painting has always been a speciality of the court in India. Besides the mural paintings which were considered the supreme examples of the painting art, portraiture and pictures were cultivated as courtly hobbies of Hindu rulers and nobles. But the Sultans of Delhi did not encourage the art of painting of portraits and wall decorations.

However, the Mughals revived the art of painting. The Mughal painting represented a happy mingling of foreign (Persian) and Indian elements. A provincialized Chinese art, which was a mixture of Indian, Buddhist, Iranian, Hellenic and Mongolian elements, was introduced into Iran or Persia by its Mongol conquerors in the thirteenth century. It continued to flourish under the patronage of their Timurid successors. The Mughals, being closely connected with the Persian court, imported this art of painting into India. During the reign of Emperor Akbar the salient features of this Indo-Sino Persian art were mingled and assimilated by the contemporary Indian schools of painting which flourished in Gujarat, Rajasthan, Bijapur, Ahmednagar, Vijayanagar, etc. This led to the growth of a particular style of painting called the Indo-Persian school of painting. But gradually the foreign Mongoloid elements disappeared and distinctly Indian ones asserted and predominated. Paintings of the *Khandan-i-Timuria* and the *Padshahnamah* manuscripts in the Khuda baksh Library of Patna, clearly illustrate this change in the art of painting of the period. It was during the reign of Akbar that the art of Mughal painting rose to prominence, it attained its apogee under Jahangir, blossomed luxuriantly with the munificence of Shah Jahan, but under the rule of puritan Aurangzeb its death-knell was sounded. Though it lingered on as a decadent art under the Nawabs of Oudh till the close of the eighteenth century, it practically ceased to exist with the advent of the British rule. Though short its duration was, it was a brilliant episode in the history of Indian art. (Percy Brown)

Before Akbar : Babar, who was a great lover of beauty and art, patronized the art of painting. He employed court painters and the paintings in the Alwar manuscript of the Persian version of the Memoirs of Babar exhibit the kind of work they produced. His successor Humayun developed a good taste for painting during his exile in Persia. While coming back to India he brought with him Sayyid Ali Tabrezi and Khwaja Abdus Samad who were master painters of Persia. They illustrated a copy of the *Dastan-i-Amir Hamzah* and worked with their Indian Assistants and, thus, formed the nucleus of the Mughal school of painting.

During the Time of Akbar : Painting made remarkable progress in the time of Akbar. He created a\ separate department of painting with Khwaja Abdus Samad as its head. His persona] interest in the department and generous aesthetic temperament, his sympathetic attitude towards the foreign artists and his religious toleration and active association with the Hindus gave every kind of encouragement to the art of painting and influenced its course. The result was the fusion of Hindu and Sino-Persian styles in the technique, variety and quality of colours.' A new school (of painting) began to flouish, a school entirely of portraiture and illustration, delighting in animated and crowded scenes in dramatic motives. Akbar invited painters from every part of India and even from outside. Though they belonged to different creeds and castes, they had placed before them the common idea of producing works of great merit. Akbar extended his liberal patronage to Hindu as well as Muslim painters.

It is reported that Akbar had an album of portraits. He got

the walls of his new capital at Fatehpur Sikri embellished with the masterpieces of the art of painting. We are told that more than a hundred painters acquired great eminence while the number of Jesser men rose by hundreds in the time of Akbar. Persian or other foreign painters were few in number in the court of Akbar, the most famous among them were Abdus Samad, Farrukh Beg and Jamshed.

The Hindu artists, the excellence of whose skill was especially admired by Akbar, predominated and out of the seventeen leading painters of Akbar's reign no less than thirteen were Hindus. Abul Fazl considered that few in the whole world are found equal to them. They excelled in portraiture, book illustration and animal painting." Most famous among them were Daswant, Baswan, Sanwal Das, Tarachand, Lal Kesu, Mukund and Haribans. Akbar encouraged pictorial art in all possible ways and engaged master painters to illustrate numerous famous works as the *Chingez namah* and *Zalar namah*, the *Ramayan, Kaliyadaman*, and *Ayardanish.* The best works of painting were undertaken when Akbar was staying at his new capital Fatehpur Sikri.

Akbar tried to give a religious outlook to his patronage of painting by holding that the painter has quite peculiar means of realizing divinity. By thus raising painting in Muslim estimate, by organizing weekly court exhibitions and offering suitable rewards, by giving his own criticisms and suggestions, providing studios for artists, enrolling over a hundred artists in the ranks of *mansabdars, ahadis,* and infantrymen and by improving the production and marketing of art materials, Akbar gave Indian painting a very strong impetus. But painting under Akbar was only an art of the court. It had no profound association with the people or their country. The subjects of painting were taken from incidents associated with the life of the Emperor and the imperial court. Consequently, only portraiture could reach the lower strata of society. Besides this, it should be noted that Akbar's patronage would have resulted in less of value had it not been for the example and opportunity it gave for the revival of indigenous schools of Indian art.

During the Time of Jahangir : The school of painting that evolved under Akbar continued to flourish in the reign of his successor, Jahangir, due to his enthusiastic patronage. Jahangir who was unable to understand 'the largeness and breadth required for architectural effect' had a trained eye for picture. He was an excellent connoisseur, a keen collector of historical paintings and an art critic who possessed the skilled knowledge of an expert. He had gained such rich experience of painting that he could tell the names of individual artists by seeing their paintings. Being a keen student of miniature painting he constantly added to the state galleries the best samples of an the schools of art in India or abroad. His knowledge of the classical aspect of painting and his zeal for the art combined with the skill of his court artists, led to the liberation of the Mughal art of painting from the tutelage of Persian influences and to the growth of art style essentially Indian, leaning more and more to Hindu tradition. Mughal painting may be said to have reached its zenith under Emperor Jahangir and the best art of the period is delightfully fresh and natural.

The artistic intuition and personality of Jahangir, his keen interest in painting and rare judgment of artists, his enthusiastic royal patronage and peaceful and settled condition of the country contributed to the development of Mughal painting to its fullest extent. Jahangir's reign is called the golden age of Mughal painting. Natural scenes, especially hunting scenes and portraitures, were the favourite subjects of Jahangir's painters. They were painted with all their reality. Painting of plants, creepers, flowers, animals, birds and numerous other natural objects reached the highest stage of development. Unusual flowers and rare animals were ordered to be copied or painted by Jahangir. Though they were most elaborate and faithful productions, sometimes doubts arose about their reality. Western paintings which were arriving in India at this time were also frequently copied.

The great painters of Jahangir's time were Farrukh Beg, Mohammed Nadir, Mohammed Murad, Aqa Raiza and Ustad Mansur. It is true that the Hindu painters of the age were not favoured by Jahangir. However, Bishan Das, Keshava Manohar, Madhava and Tulsi flourished at this time and gained considerable reputation. Bishan Das was unequalled in his age for taking likeness. With Jahangir, however, the spirit of the Mughal art died and Percy Brown rightly observed, "With his (Jahangir's) passing, the soul of Mughal painting also departed."

During the Time of Shah Jahan : As Shah Jahan was more interested in architecture and jewellery than painting, the first sign of deterioration in the art of painting was visible in his reign. The number of court artists was also reduced. Consequently, paintings of Shah Jahan's time do not have originality, life and vigour. There is no thing extraordinary in their creation and composition. The quantity of painting executed about this time was maintained but the quality was inferior. Painters confined their art to the painting of imperial magnificence, royal courts, palace life of the luxurious nobles, their valuable jewelled ornaments and dresses. Consequently, such painting had elaborate ornamentation.

Painting under Jahangir had beautiful harmonious mixing of colours; but painting in the time of Shah Jahan had an increased sense of richness and luxury in colouring and the court portraiture and pictures were characterized by rich pigments and a lavish use of gold. Mosaic colouring, the glowing effects of which were heightened with burnished gold, was the chief characteristic of this time. Portraiture is considered to be a special feature of Shah Jahan's reign, but be had withdrawn imperial patronage from 'Mughal Painting'. Consequently, the artists were compelled to seek employment under princes and nobles and set up their studios in the market places to display and sell their pictures to earn their livelihood. They had to work under adverse circumstances for scanty remuneration. However, prince Dara Shikoh (whose album of paintings is found in India Office, London) was a great lover and liberal patron of art, but his premature death gave a set back to painting. A few nobles also patronized the art of painting. Asaf Khan was one of them. His palace at Lahore was decorated with masterpieces of painting. The most famous painters of Shah Jahan's time were Mir Hashim, Anup Chitra and Chitramani.

During the Time of Aurangzeb : With the accession of Aurangzeb the decadence of Mughal painting steadily continued. The final blow to Mughal painting was dealt by Aurangzeb as he regarded its patronage opposed to the precepts of sacred Islamic law. It is said that he had defaced the paintings in the Asar Mahal at Bijapur and got the figures in Akbar's mausoleum at Sikandra white washed. However, painters did not disappear wholly in the reign of Aurangzeb. We have pictures of Aurangzeb's battles and sieges. They reveal that he did not entirely discourage the art of painting. Apart from this, numerous portraits of Aurangzeb in many situations were painted with or without his consent, and he is reported to have inspected periodically some portraits of his unfortunate rebellious son Mohammed Sultan to find out how he fared in his prison cell. It is said that Aurangzeb's expeditions and conquests in southern India introduced the style of Mughal painting into the Deccan.

Painting after Aurangzeb : After the death of Aurangzeb and subsequent decline of the Mughal empire some of the Mughal painters migrated to the provincial kingdoms of Oudh, Hyderabad, Mysore and Bengal. They carried on their old traditions there. But the patronage that they got there and the work that they executed there were far inferior to that of the great imperial Mughals. During the nineteenth century what remained of the Mughal painting was influenced by the European pictures, which were brought into India at this time. Many artists readily adopted the European style to suit the taste of the English merchants and official Percy Brown remarks that the Mughal school of painting originated in the atmosphere of imperial style. "Its existence depended largely on aristocratic patronage and when this was withdrawn the end came. Its roots never penetrated to the subsoil of India properly, but as a splendid pictorial record of Mughal pageantry and power it holds prominent position in the history of Indian painting."

Mughal School of Painting Salient Features

1. The Mughal pictures were small in size. They never attained the dignity and size of the Buddhist frescoes of the Hindu times. Therefore, the Mughal pictures were known as 'miniature painting'.
2. Numerous had been the subjects of the Mughal painting. They were mainly scenes from actual life, hunting, fighting, battles and sieges, imperial court, historical episodes, mythological stories of the Hindus, various objects of nature like birds, trees, plants, flowers, etc. But there was neither mysticism nor real pictures of domestic life.
3. Though the Mughal art absorbed the Indian atmosphere, the Mughal style neither represented the Indian emotions, nor the scenes from the daily life of the Indians. The objects of Indian nature like *pipal*, mango and banyan trees, deer, lion, peacocks, etc., and Indian dresses and ornaments were faithfully painted but the life of the people was never reflected. The art of painting under the Mughals was not profoundly associated with the people. It gave pleasure to princely connoisseurs. It was imperial and aristocratic art, remote from folk sentiment. Thus, the Mughal paintings fail to throw light on the life of the masses in the Mughal age.
4. A keen appreciation of nature was a remarkable characteristic of the Mughal artists and it was fostered by the imperial court, especially Jahangir's. Not only birds and animals were painted after close observation, but broad borders of foliated designs were common in

the Mughal miniatures and in the jungle scenes landscapes were rendered with great feeling and accuracy.

5. The Mughals and their aristocrats speedily developed portrait painting and the Mughal artists revealed a remarkable natural gift for portraiture. The Mughal portrait painter was noted for his rich colouring, sympathetic outline drawing, decorative treatment and the delineation of the actual features. The face, head, hands and fingers were painted with a marvel of likeness, fineness and finish. But, as the portrait painting was controlled by certain laws, bound by traditions, tied to the imperial majesty and magnificence and ruled by the changing fashions of the imperial court, the Mughal portrait became 'stiff and lifeless work, lacking in interest and conviction.' When demand for a cheap and popular form of portraiture arose during the closing years of the Mughal rule, the art had degenerated into a system of stereotyped copying made by careful tracings in a brush outline. However, a good Mughal portrait possessed a charm and quality peculiarly its own.

6. The Mughal artists excelled in colour composition which was generally a beautiful mosaic of reds and blues and gold. As regards their style, they were noted for "the minuteness of the treatment, the decorative composition, the extremely fine and short outline, the free use of gold on costumes and background, and the application of elaborately designed patterns to the garments trappings and accessories.

The Rajput School of Painting (circa 1550-1750) : Traces of fresco painting in the medieval palaces of the Rajput princes of Jaipur, Jodhpur, Udaipur, Bikaner and other places indicate that the indigenous art of painting continued to survive. The ancient Hindu school of painting, direct descendant of the classic frescoes of Ajanta, did not merge in the new developments under the Mughals. Contacts with the Persian and Mughal styles provided strong stimulus to it, and it had an interesting revival. The revived Hinduism, the *Bhakti* cult, the dramatic nature of the temple processions, the picturesque ritual of the religion and keen interest in mythological literature further aided its revival. It flourished in the courts of Hindu princes in Rajasthan and Madhya Bharat. Jaipur, the capital of one of the leading states of the Rajputs, became its famous centre. Consequently, it was known as the Rajput School of Painting.

It rose in prominence in the later half of the sixteenth century and after the efflorescence of two hundred years it declined. But some families of Rajpul painters found shelter and patronage in the Himalayan states. Therefore, an offshoot of the Rajput school of painting manifested itself in small states of the Punjab Himalayan region in the eighteenth and nineteenth centuries.

Some art critics have called it Kangra school of painting as Kangra was the leading Himalayan state; others have designated it as *Pahari* or belonging to the mountains. Rajput painting was noted for decorative detail, while *Pahári* painting was noted for the display of emotions. *Pahari* painting was an art of patient labour and native devotion and was famous for delicacy of line and brilliancy of colour. The subjects of *Pahari* painting covered wider field compared to those of Rajput art. Besides illustrating the mythological and religious stories from the *Puranas* the *Pahari* artists painted portraits, *rag mala* (group of Indian musical compositions) and scenes of farmer's life.

Comparision between Rajput and Mughal Painting : The Mughal art was aristocratic and genuinely realistic, while Rajput painting was democratic and chiefly mystic. The Rajput school of painting was noted for brilliancy of effect. Its themes were popular and familiar. It expressed through line and colour the emotions of a race reputed for its noble qualities and brave deeds. It was largey a folk art. It mirrored the life of simple Indian villager, his religion and its picturesque atmosphere and ceremonies, his pursuits and pastimes. Familiar scenes of the bazar, occupations of craftsmen, fields and farms, ordinary incidents of journey like midday rest or sojourn in the *serai* etc., were painted with grace, charm and sincerity. Many incidents from the Ramayan and the Mahabharat were taken for themes. As the Buddha and stories of his past and present lives became the main subjects of the Ajanta art, Krishna in all his varied character was the central figure of Rajput painting. Together with Krishna, animals like cows, elephants, peacocks, deer, etc., were also represented with a deep knowledge of nature.

The Mughal school of painting dealt with the materialistic aspects of the animal life (the hunting of wild beasts, fighting of elephants, deer, etc.) the Rajput art dignified these creatures by giving them external forms of Hindu deities, for example, the representation of Hanuman, the monkey god. Besides Krishna, Siva and his consort, Parvati, were also represented with reverence. Human passion, pathos, compassion, sympathy, affection, love, mercy and other human virtues were depicted in realistic sketches by the facile brush of the Rajput painters. The lover and the beloved took the form of Krishna and Radha respectively. Love, romance and religion were happily symbolized in popular divinities.

Thus, the Rajput school of painting had so beautifully harmonized and blended the human life and religion that in its spiritual ideology it became superior to the Mughal art of painting. Mughal painting was confined to the majesty and magnificence of the imperial court and it became limited and unnatural in exhibiting the Mughal splendour and luxury. On the contrary, Rajput painting was the art of the people. It closely associated religion with art and with its spiritual and emotional inspirations it superseded the secular and matter of fact Mughal style. If Mughal painting was materialistic, Rajput painting was spiritual; the one aimed at entertainment, the other at reflecting the sweet serenity of Indian life and illustrating the religious beliefs of the people. Like the Mughal artists the Rajput painters painted portraits to maintain the traditions set by the Mughals. Local Rajas, princes and nobles were represented posing at windows or reclining on mats, often smoking *hukka*. Frequently, *sadhus* or saints were also painted. But a Rajput portrait did not possess 'the rich glowing effect or vigorous spirit of the Mughal portrait.' Besides getting their portraits painted, the Hindu rulers, princes and grandees in imitation of the Mughal emperors got their libraries filled with albums of masterpieces of painting and illuminated books, the magnificence of which can easily be imagined from the collection at Jaipur in Rajasthan.

Calligraphic Art

Closely allied with the art of painting was that of calligraphy, which was the only form of art permitted by extreme Islamic orthodoxy. It was cultivated assiduously in many Mohammedan countries. Large sums were paid for the work of famous calligraphists by connoisseurs. "Calligraphy also entered largely into the decoration of the mosques: the ninety nine Divine names and Quran texts are inscribed round the portal and on the wans, and appear in the tracery of the windows. There are various types of lettering from the stiff upright Kufic to the flowing Nastalik beloved of Akbar." The *Ain-i-Akbari* provides us a list of famous penmen of Akbar's court. The most famous and distinguished among them was Mohammed Hussain of Kashmir. The title of *Zarrin-qalam* (Gold Pen) was conferred on him.

Musical Art

The Mughals actively patronized music. Babar was fond of music. He composed songs many of which have survived him. Lane-Poole informs us that the art of improving a quatrain on the spot, quoting Persian classics and singing a good song were highly applauded in the reign of Babar. His successor Humayun loved music and patronized musicians and singers whose company he frequently enjoyed. He fixed two days Mondays and Wednesdays for listening to music.

The Surs like the Mughals extended their patronage to music. Akbar was a great lover of music. He had a good knowledge of the technique of music and played exquisitely on the Indian instrument, *naqqarah*, and he is reported to have composed tunes. His liberal patronage and keen interest in music attracted to the imperial court a large number of musicians Hindus, Iranis, Turanis, and Kashmiris, both men and women. The court musicians were arranged in seven groups, one for each day in the week, and Akbar used to listen to their music with rapt attention.

The most renowned of these was Miyan Tansen of Gwalior about whom Abul Fazl writes that "a singer like him has not been in India for the last thousand years," Baz Bahadur of Malwa employed by Akbar was also noted for his music and Hindi songs. He is described by Abul Fazl as "the most accomplished man of his day in the science of music and in Hindi songs." With the exception of Mubarak and Abul Fazl the *amirs*, and courtiers of Akbar like Abdur Rahim Khan-i-Khanah, Raja Bhagwan Das and Raja Mansingh patronized musicians. This contributed substantially to the growth of Hindustani music. The celebrated singers and musicians composed and introduced new varieties of *Ragas* like *tarona, thumari, ghazal, qawwali*, etc., and some Sanskrit works written on music were translated into Persian language.

The close association of the Hindu and Muslim musicians and exchange of thought between the two also aided much the general progress of music in the period. Some art critics hold the opinion that the synthesis of Iranian and Indian music led to the rise of new style of music which was more refined and charming than the two.

The traditions of Akbar's court were continued by his son and successor Jahangir. He also patronized musicians. Sir J. N. Sarkar in his book, *Studies in Mughal India*, points out that Shah Jahan was a great lover of music. He composed certain sweet and charming Hindi songs and enjoyed vocal as well as instrumental music. Hindu musicians with others were patronized by him. Jagannath and Janardan Bhatt of Bikaner were the leading Hindu musicians of his court. After the death of Shah Jahan, the art of music was disfavoured.

It gradually declined. His successor Aurangzeb was well versed in the science of music. But being a bigoted and puritan Muslim, he was averse to practical performance and therefore he discouraged music, placed a ban upon it and drove away the musicians from his court. Consequently, Mughal singers and musicians sought shelter in the courts of the provincial kings. Bhagdatt who flourished in the court of Rana Anup Singh was the most celebrated musician of the period. After the death of Aurangzeb, Mohammad Shah patronized music and revived it.

During his reign the Mughal court was resounding with the *Khyals* of the famous musicians, Adarang and Sadarang Besides this, Shori Miyan and others introduced new *ragas* and styles. After some years, Sri Niwas had composed his famous work on music *Ragtatwa Nova Bodh.* Apart from Mughals, the Sultans of the Deccan maintained an army of musicians. Golkonda was supposed to have as many as 20,000 musicians. In all the Hindu courts of the period, music was considered an essential part of life.

The Mughal court witnessed a change in the status of musicians. The Hindus regarded music preeminently a religious art. Those who were devoted to it or followed it as a profession were not socially degraded. Even today in the Deccan many master musicians are Brahmanas of the highest social position. Some of the Hindu rulers attained proficiency in all forms of music. But in Muslim courts, music, though greatly patronized, was considered a degraded profession because the main performers were *ustads* and dancing girls of ill repute. As a result of this the popularity of music was reduced with the educated middle classes. They looked upon it as one of the hobbies of the amirs and the luxuries of aristocracy. The ordinary people greatly disfavoured education in music and, consequently, a keen distinction between the music of the schools and that of *ustads* and folk songs and music of the people gradually developed. One can still observe it in northern India. On the contrary, in southern India, "music continued to be the common heritage of prince and peasant alike."

Other Arts

The account of fine arts under the Mughals would be incomplete if other arts are not mentioned here. Though there was the *Quanic* prohibition, sculpture was cultivated to some degree. We are told that the figures of Jaimal and Patta, the defenders of the Fort of Chittor in 1568, were erected and placed outside the gates of the Red Fort of Delhi and the statues of Amar Singh and Pratap, the Ranas of Chittor, beneath the audience window at Agra. The art of jewellery attained a high level of perfection. The famous Peacock Throne of diamonds, emeralds, rubies and pearls and its enamelled canopy marks the crowning triumph of the art of jewellery. Goldsmith's art reached a high degree of excellence, and demand for inlaid work, damascening and enamelling was increasing considerably. Gold and silver ornaments were very popular. The imperial mints at various places produced a fine series of gold, silver and copper coins, generally stamped with calligraphic devices. The art of embroidery made considerable progress. It was patronized in the imperial palaces. The art of weaving and dyeing was cultivated with remarkable success. Excellent carpets of the richest silk brocades, silks, muslins, shawls and chintzes of this age became famous all over the world.

Muslim Legacies

The age of the Delhi sultans and the Mughal emperors had vanished forever, but their relics have survived in numerous forms, visible and invisible. They have become their valuable legacies. The following have been the gifts of the Muslim Age and the Mughal rule in India.

India in Touch of the Outer World : The close commercial and.cultural contact between India and the other countries of Asia and eastern Europe, established in the early Buddhist Age, was lost about the eighth century A.D. But it was restored by the Muslim conquest at the end of the twelfth century. It widened the Indian outlook. Both sea borne trade of India and her navy were also revived. Not only the long streams of caravans passed through the frontier passes of India but ships began to sail from the ports on her coast. Thousands of foreigners began to enter into India and during the hundred and fifty years of the great Mughals, India's name stood high in the world and she was ranked among the most civilized and powerful nations.

Peace Inside the Country : Peace and order reigned internally over 11 large part of India, especially north of the Vindhya mountains. This promoted the growth of industries and brought about general happiness and prosperity.

Administrative Uniformity : Sir Jadu Nath Sarkar observes that nearly two hundred years of the Mughal rule in the country provided to the whole of northern India and to much of the Deccan, uniform centralized administrative system. It gave not only official and coinage but a popular *lingua franca* called Hindustani for the people of all classes except the Brahmanas and the stationary village folk. Some features of the Mughal system of administration are still traceable in India. The Mughal land revenue system and the divisions of the country into *subas, sarkars* and *parganas* still continue under new names. Present provincial and district administrations are derived from Mughal prototype. Even a staunch champion of Hinduism like Shivaji at first imitated the Mughal administration in Maharashtra, but later on he gave a Hindu colour to it by substituting Sanskrit names and titles for Persian ones.

The present civil service, composed of men of *mansabdari* work to administer imperial and local affairs, is the relic of the *mansabdari* system of the Mughals, shorn of its feudal and military character. In the Judiciary some of the present laws are derived from the Mughal codes. A few Mughal canals are still existing and irrigating even today large tracts of agricultural land.

There was one and the same system of administration all over the Mughal Empire. All the twenty *subas* of the vast empire of the Mughals were governed by exactly one and the same administrative machinery. They followed the same methods, procedures, official designations and titles, and used one language, Persian, for official purposes. Many times government officials, soldiers, commanders and governors were transferred from one province to another. Similarly travellers and merchants moved from one place to another, from town to town and *suba* to *suba*. Besides this, the Mughal state was a national state in which all Indians, Muslims and Hindus and foreigners could live comfortably and find employment for their talents. This made all realize the imperial oneness of vast India.

Political Unification : Mughal imperialism was responsible for the conquest of India. Indirectly, it provided political unity to the country and created a feeling of oneness among the people.

Cultural Progress : The Muslim Age and the Mughal rule had considerably influenced the Hindu culture. Habits, manners, dress and social amenities introduced by the Mughals found general acceptance. There arose uniformity of social manners and dress among the people, irrespective of their creed. *Achakan* and *Pyjama* occupied prominent position. Our present day dress, both for male and female, has been the same as we see in the Mughal paintings. In fact, on our dress, etiquette, speech, manners, thought, literature, music, painting and architecture, the impress of the Mughals is clearly visible. They are neither purely Hindu nor purely Muslim but a happy and harmonious fusion of the two. The earlier Muslims aimed at destroying everything that was Hindu, whereas the Mughals assimilated and synthesized Hindu and Muslim things and recreated them in immortal forms. In fact, in the realm of culture, the Mughal period witnessed both a harmonization and a revival.

Social Reforms Activity : The Mughal emperors were as daring in their social reforms and innovations as they were adventurous in the realm of politics. Akbar had great enthusiasm for reforms. He tried to found a new society in India nay, a new nation which would be neither Hindu nor Muslim, but exclusively Indian. He attempted to prohibit cow killing and *sati* system, raise the age for circumcision and marriage, control drinking and prostitution, wipe out communal differences, abolish invidious taxes based on religious differences, appoint persons to the posts of trust and responsibility irrespective of caste, creed or race, and encourage intermarriages between different communities. He aimed at social synthesis and the present-day government of India is directing its activities towards the same.

Art and Craft : The Muslim influence was greatly felt on the articles of luxury and fine arts and the Mughals fostered the spirit of unexampled luxury. The Mughals, who were leading generally a more luxurious life than the Hindus, encouraged several manufactures and fine arts. New articles of food and fruit, new style of cookery and new costumes were introduced. All these were saturated with a spirit of luxury. Consequently, industries of refined kind, shawl making kimkhab, muslin, carpets, etc., were liberally patronized and promoted. Music and painting also received a great impetus. Present day Indian music and musical instruments betray traces of Mughal influence.

The impress of the Mughal music is seen in *qawwali, thumari* and *ghazal* which still survive. Similarly, *tabla* and *sarangi,* two remarkable instruments, are the legacies of the Muslim age. A new school of painting rose in the Mughal period. Indian painting with its delicate touches and delightful hues is but a vivid reflection of those picturesque times." Numerous notable works of the Mughal school of painting now enrich the valuable collection of a large number of museums all over the world. The Persian and Chinese influences in the realm of painting were completely shaken off and the long process of Indianization of painting reached its climax under Emperor Jahangir. Undoubtedly, the highest genius was displayed by Indian artists in the Mughal Age.

Development of Indo-Saracen Art : One of the richest contributions of Muslim Age and the Mughal rule was a new style of architecture (specially palaces, mosques and tombs) and artificial gardening. The greater luxury and the unexampled wealth of Mughal emperors enabled them to erect magnificent structures of supreme beauty, layout very big cities and extensive gardens which even today provide great pleasure to millions of people. Before the advent of the Mughals, gardens were merely jungles of fruits and flowers. But the Mughal gardens represented highly developed art of gardening. A salient feature of the Mughal gardens was that water was brought there through canals and then artificial waterfalls were created in the garden. Another feature was *barahdari* or an open terraced building in the centre of the garden.

The Mughals erected numerous buildings and laid out towns. They exhibit precisely the mingling of Hindu and Muslim conception of architecture, the happy blending of elegance and strength. The city of Fatehpur Sikri, laid out and built by Akbar, has endured as an example of the fusion of Hindu and Muslim ideals of architecture. The distinguished characteristics of the buildings, palaces, tombs and mosques of this age are open courtyard encompassed by chambers or colonmides huge graceful domes, vaulted gateways, lofty minars, well chiselled stones, mosaic work, etc. Of the Taj, the Moti Masjid, the Red Fort and the splendid palaces therein, *Buland Darwaza* and the graceful tomb of Itimad-ud-daullah little need be said.

Development of Vernacular Literature : The Mughals provided a feeling of security which in its turn brought leisure and passion for the working of the mind. Consequently, there was a sudden growth of vernacular literature in all provinces. The *Bhakti* movement and the monotheistic movement in the realm of religion enriched the Indian literature. The literary impulse provided by the peace and prosperity of Emperor Akbar's long and successful reign, his royal patronage and the encouragement by his vassal princes and feudal lords led to a wonderful and remarkable flowering of Indian intellect in the closing years of the sixteenth and the first half of the seventeenth centuries. Varanasi again became famous as the centre of a notable revival of Hindu intellect, a radiating centre of Hindu culture. Once again it flourished as a great university. Celebrated learned scholars, poets and writers like Khanda Deva, Raghunath Siromani and Kavindra Acharya, a friend of Emperor Shah Jahan and one of the *gurus* of prince Dara Shikoh, adorned the great centre of Varanasi. The Mughal Age was noted for a great outburst of literary activities. The literatures of the vernaculars, Indian, Persian, Sanskrit and Urdu have come down to the present Indian generation with the impress of writers and poets who either directly or indirectly enjoyed Mughal patronage and favour.

Indo-Persian Literature on the Helm: A considerable Persian literature was produced in India during the period under review. It is a part of the noble heritage of India, an outstanding contribution by Indian Islam and its followers to the general treasury of Indian culture.

Growth of the Urdu Language : A significant legacy of the Mughals was the development of the Urdu language.. It was the Outcome of the contact between the Muslims and the Hindus. It made considerable progress during the Mughal age.

Growth of Hindustani Language : Another notable legacy of the Muslim rule was the evolution of a common *lingua franca* called *Hindustani* or *Rekhta*. It was an official prose style, mostly the creation of Hindu clerks called *munshis* who wrote in Persian. Later on it was borrowed by Maratha *Chitnises* to serve the purpose of their own vernacular.

Warfare Improvement **:** The age under review witnessed a considerable improvement in the art of warfare and the introduction of gunpowder and artillery, which claimed a decided superiority over the old Hindu methods of war. The steel and the soldier became important factors in warfare. Cavalry rose in great prominence. It eclipsed the elephants of the Hindus. Gradually war elephants fell in disuse. The Hindu rulers imitated the Muslims and replaced their elephant corps with the cavalry units and began to use artillery in battle fields. It was on account of strong cavalry units that the Muslim invaders carried the day frequently. Well equipped artillery and their particular army organization in the battle field enabled them to gain victory over their adversaries quickly. But in the absence of proper arrangements for supplying provisions to the army, plundering and pillaging villages and letting the horses graze standing crops were very common scenes in wartime.

Historical Literature **:** It is due to the liberal encouragement of the Muslim rulers that India owned a good collection of historical literature. Many notable works on history were written in the period under review. Prominent historians of the Sultanate and Mughal periods were Barani, Minhaj-ud-din, Shams-i-Siraz, Abul Fazl, Farishta and Khafi Khan. Historical documents, letters, autobiographies and detailed accounts of the royal dynasties are the gifts of this medieval age. They have been very helpful in writing the history of the period. Thus, new and very useful elements histories, biographies and letters were introduced into Indian literature in the seventeenth and eighteenth centuries.

Monotheistic Religious Revival and Sufism **:** The impact of Islam both creed and society was felt on the Hindu religion, and society. The close mutual contacts between the Hindus and the Muslims had profoundly influenced the social and religious trends in India. This has resulted in the revival of monotheistic and anti-caste movements within Hinduism. Dissenting and reforming movements among the Hindus received a great impetus from the presence of the Muslims and their creed. Ramanand, Kabir, Dadu, Nanak, Chaitanya and a few other sects were the natural outcome of the impact. Apart from this, new superstitions emulated old credulity. *Pirs* and *Shahids, Murshids* and *Shaikhs,* Saints and Martyrs equalled Krishna, Arjun and Bhairava in the number of their gallant deeds and miracles, and this continues even today in the Indian villages. Islam, in its turn, was also considerably influenced by Hinduism.

It gave rise to Sufism in Islam. Sufism has considerable influence of the *Vedant* of the Hindus. It developed rapidly in Hindu environment and under Akbar and his grandson Dara Shikoh, both of whom were noted for their religious toleration. Prince Dara had openly declared that he had found the fullest pantheism *(tauhid)* in the *Vedant* and it was fostered by many Persian emigrants of liberal religious views.

Other Influences : The influence of the Muslim rule for six centuries on Indian culture had been widespread. Many entertainments like hunting, hawking, animal fighting and numerous other games became Mohammedanized in method and terminology. In many other professions Muslim outlook has entered deeply. Turkish, Arabic, Persian and Urdu words have been assimilated in Hindi, Bengali, Gujarati and Marathi languages. In the art of warfare the Hindu princes borrowed a good deal from the Muslims. The imperial Mughal army served as a model which the Hindu rulers imitated. The construction of strong majestic and extensive fortresses, and their defence was considerably improved by Muslims in India as a result of general progress of civilization, introduction of artillery and improvement in the art of warfare.

The influence of the Muslims was strongly felt on the administrative system, the organization of the military and use of arms, the methods of record keeping, the court of princes, the lives of the well to do upper classes, their high standard of living and spirit of luxury, various fine arts especially architecture and gardening and the general etiquette.

In the court life, ceremonials, dress and royal titles and office procedure of the State officials the Mughal empire set the fashion which the Hindu Rajas often slavishly copied. The traditions of the Mughal empire were imitated by many princes. In some Rajput and other Hindu states in Rajasthan and Malwa, the official language up to the third decade of the twentieth century continued to be Urdu. They used Persian script instead of Devanagari.

The Muslims, being more luxurious and easy going, encouraged urban population and more refined and elegant tastes in their daily life. These together with their vices were imitated by the wealthy Hindus and the official class. In aesthetics, perfumery and to some extent in music and dancing the Muslim royal families shaped the outlook and guided the taste of the Indian society.

It were the Muslims who introduced paper in India and consequently books could be multiplied in a more attractive and durable form than the palm leaves on which the letters were scratched with a sharp steel point. Several manuscripts were illustrated during the Mughal period. India owes to the Mughals the art of illustration of manuscripts. From Akbar's reign onwards many Hindi and Sanskrit works were beautifully copied and charmingly illustrated for the Hindu princes. The art of Persian book illustration and calligraphy reached such a high level of excellence under the Mughals that it not only continued in India for a long time but won fame even in Europe. It is to the Muslims that India owes the practice of diffusing knowledge by copying the manuscripts and circulating them widely. Another significant legacy of the Muslims that continues even to this day is the *Unani or* the Graeco-Arab system of medicine.

7

Impact of Christianity

Portuguese Power

An oceanic sense was altogether absent from the policy of the Indian rulers in the medieval age. Consequently, in 1499, Christian naval power the Portuguese with its base in Europe entered the Indian waters after the arrival of Vasco de gama at Calicut. Within a period of hundred and fifty years they established in India not a territorial empire but the empire of Indian commerce with a few territorial possessions on the western coast. Though, the so called Portuguese empire faded away after the advent of other European sea powers in India, they made some contributions to the cultural life of India. They have enriched Indian vocabulary and medical science to some extent. "Garcia da Octa's treatise on the medical plants of India is the first systematic study of an important subject.

The introduction of printing and the establishment of seminaries for the training of Indian priests at Verapoly and at Goa are notable contributions to enlightenment. The ornate Manuelesque architecture which they popularized on the west coast and the bungalow type of building they introduced are also worthy of mention."! The Portuguese as ardent catholic missionaries "brought the majority of Syrian Christians into the Catholic Church and made India the most Catholic country in the East, outside the Philippines." It is due to these missionaries that the Catholic Church maintains its primacy in India and has more numerous members than all other Christian sects put together. The ecclesiastical architecture of India, especially in the Deccan, is Portuguese. The Cathedral at Mylapore and many other churches on the western coast testify the enthusiasm of the Portuguese in matters of religion. Again the Portuguese then were world famous merchants; their trade monopoly provided a good world market for Indian goods, especially spices and muslin, on a scale unknown before, and it brought into India the products of other European countries and China mainly chinaware. Another significant element of the Portuguese trade was the supply of Persian horses to Vijayanagar kingdom whose external trade was practically in their hands.

The Dutch

In the beginning of the seventeenth century the Dutch established their trading centres on the Malabar and the Coromandel coast and conquered Lanka (now Sri Lanka) in 1654. This sounded a severe blow to the Portuguese power and trade monopoly. But the Dutch never acquired any formidable military power in India where their possessions grew in significant before the rising of English settlements and were eventually conquered by the English.

English and French

The East India Company of Britain was established in 1600 for trade with the East. After overcoming opposition of the Portuguese, it succeeded in establishing its trading centres in India and secured some commercial privileges from the Mughals. France also entered the fray with the establishment of the French East India Company in 1664. It acquired settlement on the Madras coast. A succession of wars, known as the Cranatic Wars, were waged between the French and the English for the control of southern India in the middle of the eighteenth century. Both sides enlisted rival factions of Indian powers to help them and the success of the British was due partly to the genius of Clive and partly to the loss of the sea by the French navy. Pondichery, the capital of the French settlement, was captured by the British in 1761, from which the French never recovered. It was a death knell to their power. With the disappearance of the French and the death of Tipu Sultan of Mysore, South India passed under British control. Meanwhile, in northern India the right of collecting revenues of Bengal, Bihar and Orissa had been ceded to Clive in 1765 by Mughal Emperor Shah Alam. By this act, the East India Company became in effect a sovereign power on the mainland of India.

India under British Empire

This right of acquisition of revenue was followed by England's regular fight for supremacy in India. Warren Hastings, the first Governor General of India (1774-1785), to consolidate the Company's possessions, waged wars with the Marathas, Haider Ali, Tipu Sultan and the Rohillas and swept clean the Augean stables by his administrative reforms. Cornwallis, his successor, continued the work of consolidation, purified administration, evolved order out of chaos and introduced the famous Permanent Settlement of Bengal. With Wellesley (1798-1805) new era begins. In short campaigns he crushed the power of Mysore and reduced the Maratha leader, Peshwa, to the position of a subordinate ally. By his subsidiary alliances he made the Indian states dependent on the English Company. Later on, Marquis of Hastings (1813-1818) reduced the powers of the Maratha chiefs Holkar, Bhonsle and Sindhia brought the Rajput states under British control and deposed the Peshwa and annexed his territories in the Deccan. In 1845-1848, the Punjab was also annexed after the wars with the Sikhs and then the territories of Oudh were brought under the direct rule of the Company. In the meanwhile, Dalhousie's Doctrine of Lapse brought under the British sway many states like Satara, Jhansi, Nagpur, etc. By 1856, from the Indus to the Brahmaputra, from the Himalayas to Kanya Kumari the Union Jack flew in unquestioned supremacy.

In 1857, a great national uprising the Mutiny took place. Its aim was the expulsion of the British and the recovery of national independence. Though it was crushed ruthlessly, it is important only from two points of view: (1) It was the last effort of the old order to regain national independence and honour; it was a heroic effort of a dispossessed people to reassert national dignity; and (2) it is the great dividing line in Indian history as the policy practice and ideals of the government that followed differed fundamentally from the government of the East India Company, which it displaced. The Crown took over the government of India in 1858 and the company disappeared from the stage of Indian history. That Government of India from 1858 to 1922 confined their activities mainly to the collection of revenues, maintenance of peace and the defence of India's frontiers, and undertook schemes neither for the reorganization of society, nor for raising the moral and the material standards of the people, nor for increasing national wealth of the country. They provided the appurtenances of the civilization but did not undertake the work of civilization themselves. Since the beginning of the twentieth century Indians launched a vigorous campaign for achieving their national independence. After determined and prolonged struggle under Gandhiji's leadership Indians compelled Britain to accept finally the principle of India's complete freedom and a new chapter in history opened with the withdrawal of the British and the achievement of India's political freedom in August, 1947.

Material Development in India During Birtish Rule : The British rule in India has brought in its train material developments which can be described under the following heads:

Transport and Communication: As late as the middle of the nineteenth century the means of communications in India were comparatively defective. The railways were unknown and the few trunk roads constructed by Indian rulers were inadequate. The improvements wrought in this direction dating from the time of Lord Dalhousie have brought a social and economic revolution.

(i) *Railways* : The construction of a network of railways the most important part of India's system of communications and transport is credited to the British rule. The military need of the railways in India was felt during the Sepoy Mutiny and their economic value during the famines. Consequently, on the recommendation of the Famine Commission of 1880, the Government of India took to railway construction in right earnest. Due to the profits accruing from the railways, "they have changed from a suckling baby to a milch cow." On the recommendation of the Mackay Committee of 1908 a network of railways has linked up distant parts of the country and since then railways are being extended considerably.

(ii) *Roads Transport:* During the British rule inadequacy of roads was clearly realized and good metalled roads have now been driven through the plains and hills of every part of India, besides thousands of serviceable *kachcha* roads.

(iii) *Water Transport* : Though some rivers have been navigable, the inland waterways and marine transport could not be developed satisfactorily.

(iv) *Post, Telegraph and Telephone* : The Post and Telegraph Department provides people easy and rapid means of communication all over the country. The first telegraph line was laid out by Dalhousie and the half-anna postage was his reform. The Post Office acts as a banker and agent of the people enabling them to deposit their savings from all distances. The telephone exchange has totally annihilated distance so that a person in any town in India can now speak on the phone to a person in another town.

(v) *Wireless and Aviation Facilities* : These are the two marvels of the twentieth century that have been introduced into India by the British Government. The aviation branch is now counted as a significant factor of Indian communication and the country is linked by airlines to all important countries of the world.

(vi) *Radio* : The introduction of the Radio has placed India in touch with the whole world. A large number of radio stations have been set up in the country. Now radio is being used for various aspects of national progress.

Agriculture and Irrigation Facilities: During the British rule nothing was done for agriculture for a long time. It was Lord Curzon who set up the Department of Agriculture and since then progress has been continuous. An Imperial Research Institute at Pusa has been opened, agricultural colleges have been setup in some provinces and experimental farms have been started for the education of farmers. Great progress has also been made in irrigation and networks of canals have been constructed in many provinces and vast tracts of barren lands have been reclaimed. Public works like Sukkhur Barrage, the Mandi Hydro Electric Scheme, Sutlaj Valley Project, the Havellian Project and a few others have been marvels of engineering skill.

Industry and Trade Development : The protectionist policy of England in the eighteenth century and her free trade policy of the nineteenth century operated very unfavourably to Indian industry and trade. Few attempts were made by the British Government in India to develop the industries and trade of the country. But the last two World Wars gave a great impetus to industry and trade in India. Cotton and Textiles, Iron and Steel, Jute, Coal, Petroleum, Gold, Manganese, Silk, Paper, Cement, etc., are the chief industries of India. Though today capital is shy, labour is insufficient and industrial and technical education is defective, Indian industries have progressed with wonderful rapidity.

System of Education : Seeds for western education were sown during the British rule. Many universities and colleges were set up on the western model. Western literature, science, politics, economics, history and other branches of learning have been introduced in Indian educational institutions which have been established all over the country.

British Contribution

The British rule of nearly two centuries has left certain gifts to India. These gifts are as follows:

Administrative Skill : During the time of the East India Company, a great administrative machinery had been gradually built up, the foundations of which were laid by Conrwallis. The period that followed the Mutiny witnessed the growth and development of this administrative machinery, both at the centre and in the provinces. The great all India services, the Indian Civil Service, the Indian Police Service, the Indian Audit and Account Service, the Indian Medical Service, the Indian Education Service and the great provincial services (particularly Revenue and Judicial Services) created an administrative machinery that shouldered the heavy burden of governing four hundred million people which no government actually faced before. Such a vast machinery felt itself competent enough to deal not ,only with the work of government on a large scale but also with food, famine, plague, means of transport and communications, agricultural projects, etc. Law was administered under an enlightened and comprehensive system of jurisprudence. The settlement and assessment of lands and the Government demands from the riots were clearly defined. In fact, for a hundred years India had enjoyed a peaceful administration, though from the point of view of organization for national welfare, the British Government's work fell far short of legitimate expectation. It followed a system of veiled commercial and economic exploitation that drained the wealth from India.

Growth of Popular Political Institutions : Credit goes to the British Government for the establishment and growth of popular political institutions. They fostered the conception of national State in India. In 1853, the Legislative Council was set up and later enlarged in 1861 to include some nominated members. With the Minto-Morley Reforms the provincial legislative councils began to reflect popular opinion and provided a most valuable training ground in parliamentary work. The Montague Chelmsford Reforms took a step further by introducing the principle of direct election for democracy in the provinces and the centre, and partial responsibility in provincial governments known as dyarchy. Later on, by the Government of India Act 1935, the provinces became autonomous. Besides this, Lord Ripon's reforms of local self-government laid the foundation of local and municipal self-government which provided ample training for democratic and self governing institutions in higher spheres.

Unification of India : One of the most notable gifts of the British rule was the unification of India. After the Mutiny, the British set afoot a conscious process of unification, the main aim of which "was not merely to secure the effective exercise of British authority in Indian States, but weld the whole of India into one country." Railway, post and telegraph, telephone, currency, salt administration, import and export duties, income tax and defence measures were the main external forms through which this unity was achieved. By their doctrine of paramountcy the British reduced the independence of the Indian States to an absolute and open dependence on the British power. Deposition of some of the Indian princes by the British Government, the assumption of the Imperial title by Queen Victoria and the three successive Imperial Durbars held at Delhi clearly demonstrated to the world the glorious achievement of this unity.

Peace Descries: Another important gift of the British to India is universal peace or freedom from foreign danger and internal disorder. A peace so profound and spreading over extensive territory had never before been seen in India. It is said that it was the peace of grave. But such a peace is very valuable for national growth. The British completed and carried to perfection the task undertaken by the Mughal Emperor, Akbar, but reversed by the dissolution of the Mughal Empire.

Outer world Restoration : The British restored our contact with the outer world. Sir J. N. Sarkar rightly observes that the English have admitted us to the entire outside world, not only in Asia, but in all other continents as well; and they have admitted the rest of the world to us, in a degree not dreamt of under Muslim rule. India has now been switched on to the main currents of the great moving world outside, and made to vibrate with political, economic, social and cultural changes. An isolated self contained life is no longer possible even for the remotest Indian villages.

People Homogeneity : The uniformity of the British administration and the subsequent universal peace have been tending to fuse the various races and creeds of India into homogeneous people and to bring about social equality and community of life and thought which are the necessary basis of nationality. Under the British rule people of various races living in India for centuries together felt oneness and resolved for their political emancipation.

Modernization of Society : Another great gift of the British is the modernization of the Indian society. The modern western social practices, customs, manners, dresses etc., are due to the British rule.

Progressive Spirit : The direct action of the State and the indirect examples of the British people and the contact with the western peoples have infused a spirit of progress into Indians. The best Indian thinkers now feel grave discontent with the present social, political, religious and economic set up. They are eager to translate their progressive ideas into action and are endeavouring to make our state and administration, society and religion, education and industry, life and thought better and still better. Our best thinkers and most effective leaders are opposed to the oriental passivity and fatalism; their gaze is fixed forward and they accepted the principle of progress in practice. It has resulted in increased efficiency and purity of administration, and formation of several associations of social service and economic regeneration.

Indian Arts on Revival : A notable achievement of the British rule was in the field of arts. In 1860, Alexander Cunningham was appointed the first Director of Archaeology and later on Fergusson wrote his famous work describing the magnificent architectural monuments of India. These two factors paved the path for revival of Indian interest in arts. The appointment of Dr. Hultz as first eminent epigraphist to the Government of India was the beginning of the great work of reclamation of Indian history. The deciphering of the scripts of ancient India and the official search for old inscriptions and documents all over the country and their publication provided India the first corpus of source material from which her history was constructed. It soon created among Indians a historical sense, a pride in their achievements and nationality. The story of the great ages of the Mauryas, the Guptas, the Vakatakas, the Chalukyas, the Pallavas and the Rashtrakutas of Indian history was recovered to us by the devoted labours of many European scholars who were in the service of the British Government in India. Our Indian history was thus recovered under the British. Indian Buddhism, its profound philosophy and Pali literature were brought to light again by the European scholars. Panikkar observes that "even the revival of Sanskrit studies on modern lines in India is due largely to the activities of the British Government and the scholars patronized by them. The Queen's College at Varanasi was the first serious attempt to teach Sanskrit in a "systematic way to young India." It was through the good translations of European scholars that the great religious classics of India the Vedas, the Sutras, the Upanishads, the famous Epics and the Dharmashastras like those of Manu and Baudhayana have been made available to a much wider circle of people in India than ever before.

In the field of architecture Indians have been completely ignorant of the rich heritage of their country. Ellora, Ajanta, Bagh and Mahabalipuram meant nothing to Indians in the beginning of the nineteenth century; nor had the magnificent and charming sculptures of Elephanta, Sanchi, Bharhut, Amrawati, Mathura and the temples of Orissa or the Chola Bronzes any significance for Indians. They had become strangers to their own inheritance. "Hindu Stuart" was perhaps the first European to appreciate the beauty and charm of Indian sculpture. In due time, the taste spread first among the European critics before India awoke to her own artistic treasures. It is to such men as Cunningham, Havell, Coomaraswamy, Fergusson and Marshall that Indians owe the revival of their artistic sense. These are undoubtedly great achievements to the credit of Britain. All this brings us to the new aspect of our history Renaissance.

8

The Renaissance

Renaissance or reawakening marks the nineteenth century of Indian History. But the Indian Renaissance is not like the European Renaissance a return to India of the past ages. It is the attempt of a reawakened national spirit to explore a new creative impulse of self-expression that shall give the spiritual force for a magnificent reshaping and reconstructing. Indian Renaissance, therefore, is the rejuvenation of Indian cultural life that puts on a new garb without completely being adrift from old moorings".

The ancient Indian culture provided the basis on which modern renascent India has been constructing a magnificent edifice. Thus, Indian Renaissance has been essentially a matter of spirit producing striking changes in the realm of religion, society and culture along with a demand for national regeneration. A new self consciousness in many walks of life has come to the surface.

The soul of India is 'unfolding itself and India is shedding her shackles of the past. The rapid evolution of modern India is but an aspect of the Indian Renaissance that commenced in the nineteenth century. This Renaissance has profoundly stirred the Indian soul to its very depths and produced far-reaching remarkable changes in several spheres of Indian life. In fact, modern India owes everything to the Renaissance.

"No reformation," remarks E. B. Havell, "is possible without renaissance" and it may safely be added that no radical changes or revolution in any broad policy or plan can be effected except on the basis of a social and religious reformation and extensive nation wide cultural renaissance. In India, Renaissance was followed by reformation movements all over the country. It paved the path for national regeneration. During the latter half of the nineteenth century many spheres of Indian life were permeated with the spirit of renaissance and reformation.

In the eighteenth century India had degenerated considerably. Indian religion became a bundle of superstitions, society had grown rotten at its very core, and culture appeared like a pool of stagnant water. In the nineteenth century many directed their efforts consciously towards the general redemption of India from this all round nationwide degeneration and degradation. Broadly speaking, these efforts are designated as Indian Renaissance. The spirit of Renaissance and the subsequent reformation movements have been comprehensively affecting almost all departments of national life. The spirit of reawakening, revival and recreation spread from sphere to sphere of national life. It profoundly affected society, religion, literature, industries, crafts and politics. In fact, there have been new developments in religious, social and political life, new trends in the realm of education, literature, fine arts and science. In all these spheres there have been rising in prominence great distinguished persons who have added lustre to India. Any progressive nation in the world would have been undoubtedly proud of them.

Sir J. N. Sarkar observes that the Indian Renaissance was at first an intellectual awakening, and profoundly influenced our literature, education, thought and art; in the next succeeding generation it became a moral force, and reformed Indian society and religion; and in the third generation from its commencement it has brought about the economic modernization of India and ultimately the political emancipation.

India before Renaissance

Political Condition : When the English power was first established in India after the Carnatic Wars and the battle of Plassey in the middle of the eighteenth century, India had touched the lowest point of molal degradation, political degeneration and weakness. Prof. R.G. Rawlinson remarks that "general condition of India in the eighteenth century was perhaps the unhappiest in the chequered history of the country." The break up of the Mughal Empire caused widespread anarchy and misery. Northern India became a scene of plunder and slaughter. The Marathas like a swarm of locusts swept down upon the plains of the north and carried fire and sword in the countryside. Predatory bands of Pindaris carried on the evil tradition of raid and slaughter. There was no government worth the name.

The disintegration of the Mughal empire drove all powerful, ambitious and brave persons to earn their livelihood by joining the profession of soldiers of fortune or that of dacoits. Consequently, there were thousands of mercenary soldiers, eager to serve any prince who would pay them liberally. They had neither deep loyalty nor intense patriotism, nor sound military discipline. In southern India things were no better. The dissolution of the.. Sultanates of Bijapur and Golkonda left Deccan an easy victim to the contending but weak authorities. Ceaseless civil wars were fought in the Deccan by the families of the Nizam, the Nawab of Arcot, the royal dynasty of Mysore, the Maratha intruders and masterless vassals. The whole country was ravaged with the wars which denied peace and prosperity to the troubled country. In the territories of East India Company there was neither a settled government nor a regular system of administration. Power was divorced from responsibility with disastrous consequences. Due to Subsidiary Alliances the native rulers became sensualists. They became notorious for their carelessness and laxity of morals.

Society and Religious : In society, after the dissolution of the Mughal empire, material prosperity had been destroyed, misery and disorder spread far and wide, trade and communication interrupted, culture thrown backward, and painting, architecture and other arts and crafts declined by incessant warfare among small. States and the incursions of the predatory bands like the Pindaris. The condition of the common people was miserable. "In social usage, in politics, in the realm of religion and art, we had entered the zone of uncreative habit of decadent traditions and ceased to exercise our humanity." Normal civilized life among the people was decayed. Indian civilization and culture had been almost moribund, decadent and effete.

It lost its vitality and assimilative tendencies. It had been touching the lowest point of decline for over a hundred years from about the middle of the eighteenth century. It was a dark age and consequently nothing of first rate importance was produced in any Indian language. Almost all indigenous arts languished and disappeared in the absence of liberal patronage and several old works of art were lost owing to the ignorance, indifference and carelessness of the people and the rapacity of the foreigners who carried them away from India. All attempts to seek beauty and delight in life were decried.

Reason was absent in the realm of religion which was identified with cults, elaborate meaningless ceremonies and rites, several superstitions, intellectual dogmas and rigid moral codes. Pessimism was developed as a philosophy of life. It bred fatalism, inertia and passivity and developed a truncated life and a narrow vision.

In the closing years of the eighteenth century, Indians

came in close contact with the western people especially the English and the French. The inrush of a totally different civilization for the time being ended all creative power of Indians in religion, art, science, philosophy and other branches of knowledge. An uncritical lavish admiration for all western things took possession of the mind of educated classes in India together with contempt for things of native origin. There was recoil against the Indian life as lived by the majority. Perhaps this was the first time when the Indian mind was completely thrown off its balance.

Thus, anarchy and chaos prevailed in the sphere of social life. There was no safety for life and property. The countryside witnessed scenes of ravages and slaughter by mercenary soldiers of fortune. Agriculture, industry and trade were ruined. The rottenness at the core of the society first manifested itself in the form of military and political weaknesses. India appeared merely a geographical expression. There was no strong political power and, consequently, the country could not defend itself against the attacks of the aggressive sea powers. Widespread corruption, inefficiency and treachery disgraced all branches of the public service. Life became dull and dreary and fatalism determined the actions of the people. In the midst of such decay, anarchy and confusion, Indian literature, fine arts and even true religion perished. In fact, the old order was dead with nothing to replace it when the British conquest began.

The Seed Time of New India (circa 1784-1830) : During the period extending from Warren Hastings to William Bentinck the old order was dead. India was no longer ruled by Indians. They were even excluded from the public service. The old government of the Mughals and the Marathas was completely shattered. The normal, social and cultured life had entirely decayed. It was an indispensable operation for the new order, like the burning of the stubble on the reaped field as a good preparation of the next luxuriant crop.

The period, following the Governor Generalship of Lord Cornwallis (1786) was the seed time for new India. At the end of this period, that is, Lord William Bentinck's time (1828-1835), Indians began to assert themselves for their rights. They began to guide in a responsible way the thoughts of their countrymen, shape the national life and participate in the government of their country. They commenced the protestant movement in the realm of religion, and new trends in the field of literature. But these Indians of new breed drew their inspiration and power not from the East but from the West. They had acquired English education and complete grasp of the western thought. They were fairly well acquainted with the reasons and sciences of the West and therefore properly equipped for the work of the modern age.

Now India passed from the medieval to modern age. It was the lovely dawn of a new era, the commencement of new India. The period that followed is noted for the extraordinary outburst of intellectual activity and a radical transformation in India's religion and society. It was the beginning of Indian Renaissance.

The Causes : The following causes prepared the ground for the Renaissance :

British Advent : The political rottenness of India enabled the British to establish their foothold in this land. With their political and territorial extension there was the economic expansion. The industrial revolution and the immense growth in commerce, wealth and power which accrued to Britain from the adoption and development of new mechanical appliances were of major significance to Britain. The tremendous improvement of communication through the steamship, the railway, the telegraph the telephone and later on the radio and aeroplane facilitated travel and commerce. Its extensive monopoly of the new machines for industrial and manufacturing concerns gave Britain an enormous advantage in both the economic and political fields. Being properly equipped with these new appliances, the armies and navies of Great Britain made short work of the opposition of the Indians who did not possess them. This political supremacy and economic superiority of the British coupled with their high notion of western civilization and culture enabled them to give a rude shock to the old Indian order which was crumbling fast all over the country. Gradually the age old conceptions and systems began to yield place to new ones of the West. Moreover the British and their strong imperialism in India provided administrative uniformity and established peace and political unity in the midst of innumerable other discordant elements. All this paved the way for nationwide reawakening.

Western Effect : The close and intimate contact with the West effected through the advent of the British, the exertions of the well known educationists like David Hare, enthusiastic missionaries like Carey, and experienced administrators like Macaulay brought about a radical change in the political, social and religious outlook of the Indians. The contact with Europe, U. S. A., and Japan revealed to Indians a panorama of immense possibilities in every walk of life and roused the Indian intelligentsia for creative spirit.

English as a Medium of Instruction : The extensive spread of the English education specially through the medium of schools and colleges has gone a long way in transforming the ideas and mentality of the Indians. English education broke the intellectual isolation of the Indian mind and quickly brought it into close contact with the science, literature, philosophy, economics, politics and history of the West. Consequently, there appeared a great mental expansion similar to that which the nations of Europe experienced when the classical learning was revived there during the fifteenth and the sixteenth centuries. An entirely new world of ideas and plans revealed itself to the admiring and wondering gaze of the young Indian students in educational and social institutions. In place of the extravagant mythical geography, religion of superstitions and rituals, legendary history, tyrannical monarchy and pseudo science with which they had been familiar came sober and correct ideas about the configuration of the earth, new progressive social and political ideas of the West, rise and fall of the nation states and unalterable laws of nature and science. All this served to awaken in Indians a keen desire for national regeneration on the basis of the best in the past. In fact, Indian Renaissance began with the study of English literature, modern philosophy and science.

Missionaries Role : The nineteenth century witnessed a Christian missionaries movement from Europe, Canada and the United States unequalled in the history of Christianity. Thousands of missionaries, Roman Catholic and Protestant, inspired and impelled by a great revival of Christianity, carried their faith to India and at a number of points in education, medicine and various other forms of philanthropy as well as religion, touched the culture of the country. They set up many hospitals and schools in India. Both in the government and missionary schools, Indians had new western education. Along with the new western knowledge came the fierce attacks of the early Christian missionaries on Hinduism and Hindu society.

The zealous Christian missionaries who never failed to point their fingers of scorn at ancient Hindu religious and social institutions were educators as well as crusaders in India. They established many English schools and colleges. They not only imported freely the new secular knowledge but also taught systematically Christianity as the only true religion in the world. As a result of this a thorough going scepticism or a partial leaning towards Christianity for the time being was produced in the minds of the educated middle classes. Many were drifting towards Christianity and some distinguished persons like M. Madhusudan Datt had embraced it. But in the long run vigorous activities of the missionaries and their vehement criticism of Hindu religion and society served to rouse Hinduism from its slumber: The innate vitality of

Hinduism began to assert itself. Innumerable religious movements like Brahmo Samaj, Arya Samaj, Ramakrishna Mission, Radha Swami Satsang, etc., appeared.

Role of Indian Press and Literature **:** Indian press and literature acted as very powerful stimulants for the Renaissance. Monumental works were written and published. Ancient heritage of India was discovered through the efforts of a group of Europeans who keenly devoted themselves to the study of Indian history and literature and published their works. Many western scholars and art critics through their praiseworthy works aroused in Indians the consciousness of the true value of the fine arts of India. Various newspapers and periodicals were started and they not only brought Indians into close contact with the external world but also made them aware of the sense of great responsibility to solve the numerous problems that the country was facing. All this smoothed the path for the progress of Indian Renaissance.

The above mentioned elements stirred the people and roused them from the slumber of ages. It was the beginning of Renaissance. "A critical outlook on the past and new aspirations for the future marked the new awakening. Reason and judgement took the place of faith and belief, superstition yielded to science, immobility was replaced by progress and zeal for reform of proved abuses, over powered agelong apathy and inertia and a complacent acquiescence in whatever was current in society. The traditional meaning of the *Shastras* was subjected to critical examination and new conceptions of morality and religion remodelled the orthodox beliefs and habits." The new spirit and ideas, at first confined to a small group of people, gradually spread among the large sections of the people and ultimately their influence reached the masses.

Indian Renaissance Common Features

Different Factions **:** In the beginning, Renaissance led to the repudiation of Indian values and slavish imitation of all that the West stood for. It seems that the influence of the West in all spheres of life has been so overwhelming that Indians have lost their own and become 'sedulous apes'. They were becoming Europeans in everything except the colour. There was an extreme drift towards western ideas and things. This may be called 'progressive group'. It freely and liberally borrowed from European ideals of life and sociological, political and Marxian theories of the West had endeavoured to lead India along the paths quite at variance with those of Indian culture and civilization. Such a state of things roused in due course a strong reaction. Consequently, a spirit of revival commenced and everything savouring of the past was supported whole heartedly, welcomed warmly and honoured enthusiastically. It was a defensive mechanism against extreme reaction.

It was symbolized in the religious messages of Dayanand Saraswati, Rama Krishna Paramahansa and Vivekanand. It may be designated as the 'revivalist group'. It stood whole heartedly for the dogmatic acceptance of all that the old and past stood for. Between the two movements arose a new one. It sought compromise between the two. It was led by Raja Ram Mohan Roy and propagated by Rabindranath Tagore, Dr. Annie Besant and Ramakrishna Mission.

It looked upon the past with a clear and self discerning eye, admiring the past where praise was due, criticizing the old where it was essential and learning new things from the West to satisfy the demands of the people and of the times. This 'middle group' aimed to assimilate the best and enduring features of European culture with those of Indian without eliminating or discarding the essential ingredients of the Indian culture and civilization. Consequently, the group produced intellectual giants like Rabindranath Tagore in literature and painting, Dr. S. Radhakrishnan in philosophy and Jawaharlal Nehru in politics.

But the first decades of the twentieth century witnessed the birth of another unique spiritual movement in India. It was led by Sri Aurobindo. It interpreted Indian Renaissance as the rebirth of the soul of India into a new body of enthusiasm and energy, a new form of its innate and ancient spirit. It lays emphasis on the greater and nobler action of the spiritual motive in every sphere of Indian life. It aims at more magnanimous achievements and higher activity which ends in the discovery, expression and manifestation of the Divine Self in the human being. The mental, the emotional and the aesthetic parts and inborn potentiality of human beings are to be unfolded and developed fully for their greater satisfaction and finer nature of human beings. In other words, this movement has found "in all round spirituality the master key not only to unlock the treasures of the past but also to remould the present on the basis of true appraisal both of the East and the West."

Awakening of Hinduism : At the first flush of the Renaissance ardent youths of the country became utterly indifferent to Hinduism. They discarded it and rejected its dogmas and rituals. Soon they were attracted towards Christianity, because the inner spirit of Hinduism was neither taught nor its vitality and spiritual force explained to them. They could find nothing but unreason, superstitions and repulsiveness in the rituals of Hinduism as practised in their time. The reform of such a religion seemed an impossibility to them. Consequently, many highly intelligent and educated Bengalis of the pre-Mutiny days like Krishna Mohan Banerji, Lal Behari De and Govind Dutt (the father of the famous poetess Toru Dutt) embraced Christianity. But before this tendency could spread allover the country it was arrested by religious movements aiming at the revitalization of Indian religious and social life. The Brahmo Samaj of Bengal, the Prarthana Samaj of Bombay, the Arya Samaj, the Theosophical Society and the Ramakrishna Mission are the most outstanding of these movements, a detailed account of which will be given later on.

As a result of these religious movements the innate vitality of Hindu religion with its great and glorious past began to assert itself. "At first the revived Hinduism was on the defensive, rather cautious and timid in maintaining its position and inclined to compromise with the enemy. But soon it took the offensive, marched forward and even entered the hostile camp and asserted in ringing tones its right to live as one of the civilizing influences of mankind." This was new Hinduism that has been clearly the fruit of the Renaissance.

On, account of these religious movements there arose in the period a number of reformers, teachers, saints and scholars who have purified Hinduism by denouncing some of its later accretions, separated its essentials from non essentials, confirmed its ancient truths by their own experience and have even carried its message to Europe and America. They have been able to view their religion apart from the mythological, ritualistic and sociological forms in which it was embedded. They successfully interpreted Hinduism and its religious philosophy and main principles independent of Indian caste system, mythology, external rites and ceremonies. It was due to all this that today Hinduism is as fresh, vitalizing and vigorous as it, was in any of the periods previously.

The old fear that Hinduism might be overshadowed by Christianity or eclipsed by western civilization and culture exists no longer. It has successfully outlived the Christian missionary propaganda of modern age as it survived, the Muslim religious persecution of the medieval periods and the religious schism caused by Buddhism and Jainism in ancient times. It is now capable enough to meet any of the modern religions of the world, on equal footing as their friend and ally in a common cause. If the world in its present distracted state needs spiritual message and looks for a light to guide its footsteps in the darkness that has enveloped its path, renascent India is in a position to give it through the greatest of her prophets.

Reforms in Society and Religion : As a result of the religious movements and their leaders, like Brahmo Samaj and Raja

Ram Mohan Roy, the Prarthana Samaj and M. G. Ranade, the Arya Samaj and Dayanand Saraswati, the Ramakrishna Mission and Vivekanand, Sri Aurobindo, Maharshi Raman and Mahatma Gandhi, our social system under went a great transformation. It brought about a great upheaval in Hindu society, promoted the growth of wider social and religious outlook and stimulated the development of individual and organized efforts for speedy social reforms. The new Hinduism with great pleasure began to serve in many ways the suffering humanity and minimize its miserable plight. Many Hindus directed their activities with missionary zeal towards the social and religious regeneration of India. Today thousands of women and men are working enthusiastically in noble religious spirit not only in the Ramakrishna Mission, the Arya Samaj, the Indian section of the Theosophical Society, but also in innumerable fields of social services inaugurated by Gandhiji, Acharya Vinoba Bhave and others; social regeneration and reform formed a pretty large part of the present Renaissance in India. ,

In fact, the movement of Renaissance commenced with the social reforms. Consequently, the *Sati* system and the practice of infanticide had disappeared. They have been incredible things of the past ages. Women are being educated freely and liberally. They are given equal rights and privileges with men. Child marriages have been declared illegal. Widow marriages have been made possible and have been legalized. Monogamy has been the order of the day and polygamy has become extremely rare. *Parda* is a dead custom and social equality between the two sexes is now well established. Women have entered the economic field and they have taken to several professions. Today many of them are holding posts of trust and responsibility. If some of them have been active in the political field, a few are distinguished leaders of thought. Foreign travel is no longer discarded. Now it has become very common. Radical changes have been introduced in the social institutions. Not only inter-caste but also inter-community marriages are being performed and the ban on inter-dining lifted. Many social taboos have lost their rigidity. The reactionary features of the Hindu society have been disintegrated. Attempts are being made to wipe out social evils like drinking, illiteracy, poverty, etc. The rigidity of the caste system is dissolved and thanks to Mahatma Gandhi the demon of untouchability has been overthrown. Thus, the Renaissance has enabled India to pay more attention to life on earth and promote the general material and moral prosperity of the people. It has made Indians conscious of their social ills and goaded them to uproot these evils. It has rescued Indians from a philosophy of fatalism and listless passivity, which had taken a strong hold on them in the preceding period of great decadence.

Glory of Indian History come in Light : The Renaissance not only awakened and fortified the sense of Hindu greatness, but brought the glories of the Indian history to light. The slow and patient labour of many European scholars helped a good deal in the reconstruction of the lost story of India's greatness. The work of archaeologists, epigraphists, numismatists and art critics like James Fergusson, Dr. Buhler, Dr. Fleet, Percy Brown, Sir John Marshall and Dr. Anapda Coomaraswamy revealed the glory of India's numerous ancient monuments scattered all over the country. They made Indians take pride in their past history. Gradually, the Hindus were awakened to the sense of their greatness. They came to know that they had to their credit achievements in every sphere through many centuries of the past and they could no longer be conquered and subjugated by foreign imperialist people.

The names of great monarchs of Indian history, like Chandragupta, Asoka, Samudragupta, Chandragupta II, Harsh, etc., whose memory had died out long ago, were brought to light. The discovery of rich and prosperous Indus Valley civilization, the deciphering of Asoka's inscriptions, the history of the religious achievements, and the story of establishing empires, of the extension of Indian civilization and culture across the seas, of the unique world famous monuments of architecture like Borobudur, Angkor Vat, etc., gave to Indians a sense of national pride which they had lost for many centuries. Renowned historians like Jadu Nath Sarkar, R. Bhandarkar, Har Prasad Shastri, M. G. Ranade, Rajwade, Sardesai, V. A. Smith, Macdonell, Rapson, Rawlinson, Cot. Tod, Grant Duff, Elphinston, Lanepoole and historical societies and research institutions like the Bhandarkar Oriental Institute and the Bharat Itihas Sansodhan Mandal not only intensified Indian national pride in the history of India but smoothed the way for reconstructing the past history of India's greatness and glories.

The Recovery of India's Ancient Literature : The Renaissance enabled Indians to recover their ancient literature Vedic, Buddhist and Jain. The Vedas and their commentaries had almost totally disappeared from India, the land of the Aryans, where no one could interpret them rightly and explain them correctly. Worst of all, none had the fortune to possess a complete authentic manuscript of the text. Similarly, for a thousand years Lord Buddha had been forgotten and the great literatures of Buddhism in Pali and Sanskrit were totally neglected and ignored. It were the English who printed the Vedic and the Buddhist literatures of India and revealed them to Indians. The enterprise and scholarship of Europeans restored to Indians the ancient literature of Buddhism from Nepal, Tibet, China, Central Asia and Japan. Many English, French and German scholars had sent the lost and forgotten Buddhist works to European countries, and they have made them available to Indians in the printed book forms.

European scholars who cultivated the study of Sanskrit literature opened the eyes of the Indians to the great rich heritage that their ancestors had bequeathed to them. It was the enthusiasm of European scholars, like Sir Charles Wilkins, Sir William Jones, Cole brooke, Wilson, Muir, Monier Williams, Max Muller and others for the culture of India that provided the first great impetus to the modern study of classics in India.

They did much to introduce ancient Sanskrit classics to the western world. Wilkins translated the Gita. Jones edited the *Shakuntala* and several other Sanskrit plays and works. Colebrooke wrote extensively on various aspects of Indology and edited numerous Sanskrit texts, such as, the Grammar of Panini and *Hitopadesh.* Glassenhap of Germany wrote commentaries on many Sanskrit philosophical texts including one of Madhavacharya. Stanislaw F. Michalski, the great Sanskrit scholar of Poland, devoted his whole life to the study of the Sanskrit and ancient Indian literature.

Under the inspiration of Max Muller, a great German scholar in England, sacred books of India were translated and published, and Indian philosophy was studied with keen interest in the West. All this restored India's classics to Indians, enabled the new middle classes in India to know of nobler and higher things in their own thought, and helped to rouse the world's interest in India and provided a great impetus to the sense of nationalism among Indians.

Development of Indian Vernacular Literature : A significant feature of the Renaissance was the rapid growth of India's vernacular literatures. At first there was the flowering of certain versatile genius and it was followed by the phenomenal growth of the vernacular literature. Bengal took the lead in this sphere. The first great distinguished writers in Bengali were Ram Mohan Roy, Akshay Kumar Dutta, Ishwarchandra Vidyasagar, Devendranath Tagore, Madhusudan Dutta, Rajnarain Bose, Dwijendralal Roy and Bankim Chandra. There arose around these a class of men. They formed a kind of seed bed for the future creative genius, accomplished persons of fine critical ability and appreciative temper. They were men of scholarly habits, learned in many branches of knowledge, art as well as sciences; in short, men not only of culture but of original culture. All these writers were a prelude to the rise of Rabindranath Tagore who has contributed to all aspects of culture and literature prose, poetry, drama, novel, essay, short story, music, painting, dancing, etc. He has been the acknowledged king of literature. So extensive and deep rooted was his influence in the realm of literature that the new literary impulse in Andhra, Gujarat, Maharashtra, Uttar Pradesh and the Punjab has emanated from him in greater or less degree. Mohammed Iqbal of Urdu and Persian, Premchand of Hindi and Sarat Chandra Chatterji of Bengali have been other most distinguished figures of the Indian literature. They introduced new style, new techniques and secularized the themes in the realm of prose.

As regards the different Indian vernacular literature, it is a matter of great pride that the works of centuries have been crowded into a few decades in the evolution of modern literatures of India. Some of the vernaculars were unimportant as vehicles of modern expression till the beginning of the nineteenth century. After the growth of English education they began to develop considerably. Before the Renaissance all the vernacular' literatures dealt with religious subjects. Mythological or heroic narratives figured very much. Prose was hardly existing. Expression was through poems and songs. Poetry was very popular.

It was the only medium used except for pithy saying and business correspondence. Worst of all, there was an absolute lack of good, standard and suitable vernacular text books for schools and colleges. Even for adults story, novel and history of the type popular in Europe for centuries before 1850 were unknown in India. The Renaissance provided a strong stimulus to the vernacular literatures to progress. All branches of literature were developed considerably. As a result of the Renaissance, Indian languages have become both simpler and harder at the same time for the expression of modern thought. Not only their vocabulary has been immensely enlarged but they have gained flexibility, variety and naturalness of movement. Their old classical pedantry and stiffness have disappeared. At the earlier stage of the Renaissance a prose style was gradually evolving when the Christian missionaries translated the Bible into Indian vernaculars and propagated their religion through the spoken languages of the people. The establishment of the printing press, the publication and circulation of the Indian newspapers and the study of western literatures further contributed to the growth of new styles and evolution of literature. Numerous writers, poets and literary figures rose in prominence. They showed clarity combined with beauty of expression and flight of imagination. Many of them were noted for the strength and purity of their diction.

Various aspects of vernacular literature were changed and improved considerably. The Indian drama has been completely transformed since the middle of the nineteenth century. It closely imitated the modern European drama. It gained a good deal from the adoption of many European features. In fact, in novel and drama Indians have been wholesale borrowers from the West. It is from the West that they have taken the art of criticism in the realm of literature. Similarly, other aspects of vernacular prose literature were shaped on the western model. If the Indian Press has considerably popularized the vernacular literatures, the study of western literature has secularized them. Before the commencement of the Renaissance, the themes in Indian literature were borrowed from scriptures and epics. They were mainly mythological and religious, but now they are reflecting many sides of life. They are closely related to all aspects of human life.

The influence of Europe has also enriched Indian literature by developing a keen interest and deep regard for the historic past of India and be kindling the spirit of patriotism among the Indians. It awakened sense of nationality and has undoubtedly added a noble and glorious element to the Indian literatures. The following examples will make it clear. The novels of famous Bengali writer Bankim Chandra and the plays of well known dramatist Dwijendra drew their inspiration from the Indian history. The songs of harati, Tagore, works of famous Hindi poets, Bharatendu Harishchandra and Maithilisharan Gupta and the early songs of celebrated Urdu poet Iqbal were intensely nationalist. Bengali acquired the standard of a modern literature with a comprehensive outlook on life.

It became rich in its varied aspects and produced writers, poets and dramatists of world significance. It is a matter of great pride that Hindi, Gujarati, Marathi, Urdu, and the great Dravidian languages of the south Telugu, Tamil, Malayalam, and Kannad had equally important developments in all branches of literature. Consequently, the best literature of India had gained an international status and a universal appeal. The healthy growth of these different languages led to an integration of linguistic nationalities in India. However, it may be remarked that this development fostered the fissiparous tendencies of particularism which ultimately led to the demand of linguistic provinces or States. Probably it may prove detrimental to national solidarity.

Scientific Approach : One very striking feature of the Indian Renaissance is manifested in the scientific spirit of research and discovery.

Since the foundation of the Asiatic Society of Bengal in 1784, a large number of European as well as Indian scholars have been devoting themselves earnestly to the work of research, excavation, exploration and discovery. They have also concentrated their attention on study. Their labours have produced marvellous results. The works of art critics and archaeologists inspired many to cultivate the spirit of research. The Ancient Monument Preservation Act of Lord Curzon provided an impetus to the cause of study and research. Under the guidance of the Archaeological Department of the Government of India and a few other research institutions and historical associations valuable scientific excavations, which have considerably modified the views of scholars about the ancient history of India, have been undertaken on the prehistoric sites like Mohenjodaro, Harappa, Nalanda, Kaushambi, Hastinapur, etc. Numerous museums and good centres of study, research and education have been established at various places. Much attention is being devoted to them. Striking progress in the study of science and philosophy has been made and independent institutions are established for the purpose.

India has contributed considerably to general advancement in the realm of modern science. The discovery of Ramanujam in the field of pure Mathematics and those of Jagdish Chandra Bose in another branch of science were real and substantial contributions of new India to the world of knowledge. Now an Indian name is associated with Einstein's Theory of Relativity. There are some renowned Indians among the luminaries in the realm of Physics and Chemistry. Einstein s epoch making work on Mathematical Physics is now mentioned with that of S. N. Bose. C. V. Raman and Dr. Meghnad Saha made remarkable and outstanding contributions in Physics, while P. C. Ray, J. C. Bose and S. S. Bhatnagar were well known all the world over for what they have achieved in the sphere of chemical science. S. C. Ray and B. Sahani have also earned a wide reputation for their prominent discoveries.

In the realm of astronomy, S. Chandrasekhar stands as the most distinguished and notable person. Today he has become an international scientist due to his original work in Stellar Dynamics. A good deal of attention is also devoted to philosophical studies through the inspiration of distinguished teachers and philosophers like B. N. Seal, S. Radhakrishnan and others. The scholarly works of Radhakrishnan and his world wide tours and lectures have enormously increased the interest of European and American countries in Indian thought. His brilliant and masterly exposition of the philosophical, religious and cultural Ideals of India has undoubtedly made a stirring appeal to the mind of modern man. And all this has considerably raised India in the estimation of the world.

Development of Art : The spirit of Renaissance has also produced a finer appreciation and better cultivation of the fine arts, such as, painting, music, dancing, architecture, etc. A new era of considerable importance has dawned upon India through the reawakening of her consciousness. The aesthetic eye of man has been opened to the immense splendour of ancient Indian art.

(a) *Development of Painting* : Sister Nivedita, Havell and Percy Brown are among those from outside India who caught the true spirit of India's artistic and masterly expression and revealed it to the admiring gaze of humanity A striking and stirring revival of this spirit has been observed in the works of many modern Indian artists. Havell and Abanindranath Tagore laid the foundations of the new, spiritual and creative art of painting. Havell had successfully grasped the essential principles of ancient and medieval Indian art by his aesthetic temperament and innate sympathies for Indian culture and civilization. Consequently, he had encouraged the revival of Indian painting and he worked hard for it. Among Indians the influence of Abanindranath was decisive. It revolutionized Indian painting. It was the Indian Society of Oriental Art, founded by Abanindranath Tagore, that started a new art movement to revive the ancient art traditions of India. Abanindranath Tagore together with the group of his faithful disciples Surendra Gangoli, Nandlal Bose and Asit Kumar Haldar have done a great deal to further the cause of reawakening in painting. Other distinguished artists of the period who earned international fame are Abdur Rahman Chughtai and Amrita Sher Gil. A great deal of credit goes to Rabindranath Tagore and Dr. A. K. Coomara swami for the renaissance in fine arts. If Rabindranath had inspired a group of artists, Coomaraswami had done much to preach the majesty, splendour and glory of Indian art and had completely revolutionized the western attitude towards Indian art. Besides this, the Schools of Arts in Mumbai, Kolkata, Lucknow and

Indore have been throwing new talent in the revival of painting. The Mumbai School of Arts has tried to develop a new style by applying western technique and methods to the current Indian conditions.

(b) *Development of Architecture and Sculpture :* As with painting there has been a revival of sculpture and architecture also in two ways firstly, buildings constructed by the indigenous 'master builders' to be found chiefly in the erstwhile Indian states particularly in Rajasthan and Madhya Bharat, and secondly, structures based on imitations of the western models. The well known Assembly Hall in New Delhi and the Victoria Memorial in Kolkata belong to the buildings of the second group.

(c) *Development of Music and Dance :* A new spirit in the cultivation of music and dancing has also been abroad in India. The Sangit Samaj of Calcutta and the Jnanottejak Mandir of Mumbai roused a new awakening in the realm of Music. Pandit P. N. Bhatkhande, a member of the Jnanottejak Mandal, inaugurated new education in music and infused a new spirit for music among the people. He organized a music school at Gwalior and later on the first All India Music Conference at Baroda in 1916. Another distinguished person for the revival in the work of music was Vishnu Digambar. His notable disciples have spread all over northern India and Mumbai. Rabindranath Tagore has also revived Indian music. He has made his own contributions to it by flexibility, varied compositions and accompaniments. For the detailed scientific study and practice of Indian music, new societies, institutions and schools have sprung up in Mumbai, poona, Kolkata, Channai, Baroda, Delhi, Lucknow, Gwalior, Indore, Jaipur, etc.

In the realm of dancing also there has been a great reawakening. If Dilip Kumar Roy by his brilliant exposition and masterly demonstration of Indian music in the west won admirers in the western countries, Uday Shankar by his charming and scientific dances, not in India but abroad also, revived a keen interest in Indian dances. Eminent art critics showered on Uday Shankar rapturous and lavish praises not only for his mastery of the art but also for his marvellous and happy fusion of modern ideas about dancing and music with the traditions and techniques cultivated and built up by India for centuries together. Other famous exponents of Indian dances are Rukmani Devi, Ramgopal, Birju Maharaj, Sitara Devi, Damyanti Joshi, etc. Earnest efforts are being made to revive indigenous types of dramas and dances in various institutions like the *Prachin Kumari Nritya Sangha* of Assam, *Vishwabharti* of Belpur, the *Kerala Kalamandalam*, *Bhartiya Vidya Bhawan* of Mumbai, *Kalakshetra* of Chennai, etc.

Industrial Growth : Renaissance fostered a new spirit of awakening in the economic sphere by making the Indians feel keenly the poverty of the masses and industrial backwardness of the country. They began to realize the drawbacks of the economic policy followed by the British Government in India and the great evils of excessive dependence upon agriculture. Industrialization has been suggested a remedy for this. Consequently, a new outlook has been inaugurated in the economic sphere. New elements, new techniques and economic motives are being introduced. As a result of this, new spheres of struggle have arisen between capitalism and labour on the one hand and landlords and agriculturists on the other. New problems have sprung up in the economic life of the nation. All this has provided fruitful fields for the socialists and communists.

Rise of New Middle Classes : After the Mutiny of 1857 the British deliberately prepared a class of quislings. They prepared a table of salutes and a vain dictionary of titles for those Indians who were most loyal to them. Magnificent titles as *Farzand-i-khair-i-daulat-e-Englishia* (the beloved son of the British Empire), *Inder Mahinder* (the supreme lord of lords). *Siphara-*

e-Saltanat (the shield of the Empire), Khan Bahadur, Rai Bahadur, Knight, etc., were created by the British Government. They were liberally conferred on the aristocracy and princely order. By these methods the conservative aristocracy was rallied to the British Empire.

The princes, business magnates and great landlords vied with one another to be considered the most loyal among the British subjects. Great rulers and top ranking officials became petitioners for decorations and high sounding titles from the British Emperor. They felt themselves honoured when empty ranks were conferred on them. Rai Sahibs, Khan Sahibs and Knight Commanders considered themselves to be the pillars of the British Empire. They regarded it as one of the greatest privileges and honours that they could achieve in life. Thus, the British endeavoured to shatter the solidarity of the upper classes and the princely order. They created a wide gulf between the masses and the aristocracy. If the aristocracy was thus won over, the British fostered the growth of middle classes which looked upon the British Empire as an opportunity more than a burden.

During the medieval ages, the Indian bureaucratic classes the Kayasthas, the Brahmanas, the Khattris, and others were always dominated by feudal nobility or warrior classes. With the rise of the British Empire the feudal nobility sank in popular estimate and it lost its importance. The Rajas, Maharajas, Princes and Nawabs in the British provinces had no power left to them. They were mere decorative figures. The warrior classes like Rajputs, Jats, Mewatis etc., fell into discord since in the Indian armies they had to be content with lower ranks. Therefore, substance, power and influence now passed to those classes from whom the large army of clerks and officials was recruited.

When English education spread far and wide the differentiation of these classes from others became very clear. Great lawyers like W. C. Bannerji, Phirozeshah Mehta; teachers like Surendranath, Gokhale, Tilak, Radhakrishnan;

administrators like Raja Madhav Rao, T. Raghvacharya, Dutta and journalists like G. Subramanya Iyer, Motilal Ghosh etc., came from these classes. They left their own mark. The liberal professions and the higher officials were also frequently recruited from these classes. Besides the Government service, the only openings then available to them were those of law, medicine, teaching, government service, and journalism. These classes being better educated than others, having wider appreciation of the immediate requirements of the nation, more intelligent grasp of the problems of the day and a greater sense of solidarity, began to stand for modern India. They came to be known as middle classes.

The old nobility and proud aristocracy, living on their glorious past, began to lose their ground everyday. Soon they lost the sympathy of the people giving chance to middle classes to rise. Western influence poured into India through these classes. Their views were propagated considerably by the Indian press. Panikkar observes that building of a new India in all spheres except the industrial one was the work of the middle classes. "They were the advocates of new learning and the torch bearers of new India that was shaping." It were those who fostered the spirit of the Renaissance, encouraged numerous social reforms and organized the nationalist movement. All these will be described in the next chapter.

The Impact : The meaning of the Renaissance, its importance, its causes and various phases all have been dealt with above. Now we take the opportunity to describe in brief the effects of the Renaissance. They are as follows:

The Renaissance revitalized all spheres of life and reawakened the nation from the slumber of ages. It brought about a marvellous reawakening and wonderful progress in the realms of politics, society, religion, literature, philosophy, science and industry. The reawakening in the world of politics caused widespread nationalism and created anti-British sentiment. It led to the long freedom struggle. Consequently, under the leadership of Dadabhai Naoroji. Phirozeshah Mehta,

Surendranath Bannerji, Gopal Krishna Gokhale, Bal Gangadhar Tilak, Mahatma Gandhi, Madan Mohan Malaviya, Sardar Vallabh Bhai Patel, Subhash Chandra Bose, Jawaharlal Nehrn, Maulana Abul Kalam Azad, and others, India regained her freedom after a prolonged struggle.

The reawakening in the social sphere transformed entirely the social life of the country. It brought about a great upheaval. At the advent of the British rule there were numerous social evils, like the *sati* and *parda* systems, child marriage, enforced widowhood, devdasi system, illiteracy, untouchability, rigid caste system, etc., which led to national degeneration. But the Renaissance removed these evils. They now began to lose their tyrannical hold on the minds of the Hindus. It smoothed the path for social progress. Reason and scientific judgment took the place of superstition and blind faith. Liberality and independent thinking overpowered rigidity and conservatism.

The religious reawakening made Indians realize the widespread decadence in the realm of religion. People were entangled in numerous superstitions, meaningless elaborate rituals, expensive ceremonies, rigid traditions, orthodox habits, etc. Nationwide movements were started to emancipate the country from these evils. Raja Ram Mohan Roy, Maharshi Devendranath Tagore, Keshav Chandra Sen, Swami Dayanand Saraswati, Ramakrishna Paramahansa, Swami Vivekanand, Sri Aurobindo, Maharshi Raman and others reinstalled the ancient truths of the country.

They remodelled morality and religion. They gave a new divine and spiritual message of India to the materialistic world. Now the Indians began to have an unflinching faith in their religion and strong hope in future. While reasserting the fundamental faith of Hinduism, great emphasis was laid on the principle that all religions are branches of the same tree, that same sap flows in all of them and that, therefore, mutual toleration is of the utmost importance in all matters affecting religious belief and practice." Moreover, the teachings of

Hinduism have been adjusted to the scientific thought and the political and social philosophies of the West. Hinduism had been well interpreted in the light of modern scientific thought. Consequently, the Hindu philosophy and religion have come home to Indians with a new meaning and a fresh application to the nation's social problems.

A new feeling of unity had dawned. A feeling, that the whole of the Hindu society in all provinces and states has been one community with common temporal and spiritual interests, has begun to grip the minds of the Hindus. The Arya Samaj, the Ramakrishna Mission, the Hindu Mahasabha and even Gandhiji all have fostered and strengthened this feeling of unity.

Reawakening in the realm of literature led to the study of Sanskrit by western scholars. This stimulated interest in India. Indians came to know the glories of their own literature and history, and therefore they determined to reconstruct their own history and preserve their culture. Western education through the medium of English led to intellectual awakening which was well expressed in the development of Indian vernaculars. Bankimchandra, Rabindranath Tagore, Saradchandra, Premchand, Iqbal, Maithilisharan Gupta, Trimbak Bapuji Thomare, Vireshlingam, etc., have enriched the vernacular literatures of India.

The prophets of Renascent India turned attention towards the fine arts of the country. Painting developed a new technique; the old tradition and types in music and dance have been revived. Music now has become a salient feature of education. In the realm of science Profulla Chandra Roy, Jagdish Chandra Bose, Shri Nivas Ramanujam, Chandra Shekhar Raman, Meghnad Saha, Birbal Sahani, Sri Krishnan, etc., have revived this self-confidence in the Indians that science is not the monopoly of the western scientists alone. They have developed the spirit of scientific inquiry and research among the Indians.

So far as economic effects are concerned attempts have been made to industrialize India on the basis of scientific inventions and new machinery. Consequently, numerous manufacturing concerns were set up, general output was increased and industrialists like Tata, Dalmia, Birla, etc., rose in prominence. It introduced in India the western economic theories and new political thought and soon India became the battle field of conflicting ideologies of socialism, communism, individualism, capitalism, idealism, etc. In fact, this is the legacy of the West to India. The evolution of the Indian culture has been considerably influenced by the western thought in modern age. This brings us to India and the West.

Contact with Western World

The Christian sea power in India brought with them western civilization and culture into the country. It not only introduced many new elements into the Indian cauldron but also disturbed the existing disposition of various forces in Indian society like the last stone which starts an avalanche; a process of change began, but it has not yet ended and its future no one could yet foresee.

Challenge of the West and its Results : In the closing years of the eighteenth century channels of Indian culture were getting dry. The culture of the country had become moribund, decadent and effete. The creative spirit had disappeared from fine arts; literature, science, philosophy and religion. The intellectual life had become dull and sluggish. Knowledge was petrified. Society with all its evil customs was like a pool of stagnant water. The traditional charms of Indian society collapsed. India needed a violent shock and a rude challenge to remedy this state of affairs. This was provided by the people of western countries and their culture. It is a mistake to think that this shock, challenge and effect of the West in India were due to the advent of the British. Sometimes the British endeavoured to hinder the healthy influence of the West by reactionary elements. In fact, the western influence in India was the outcome of the forces of time and history, as it happened in China and Japan. In course of time the western influence would have entered India even without the advent of the British.

It was in the closing years of the eighteenth century that western civilization and culture challenged all old values and beliefs of India. Consequently, old rites and rituals, customs and traditions crumbled. Social, religious, economic and political institutions collapsed at a terrifying pace. The very roots of the national life were very violently shaken. India was literally in the melting pot. When the edifice of Indian culture was collapsing the western culture attempted to superimpose its structure on Indian soil. It changed the vision and revolutionized those who came into contact with it. Its immediate result was the indiscriminate imitation and adoption of western mode of life and habits. In fact, some went so far as to endeavour to build up a new Europe on the soil of India. Fortunately this process was quickly arrested by the forces of the Indian Renaissance which has been already described above. However, western civilization and culture have left their permanent marks on Indian culture.

Extensive Cultural Impact : The advent of Islam influenced chiefly the Hindu princely order, aristocracy and town dwellers. They determined the tendency and not the tone of the social whole. But the revolutionary changes which the western culture initiated did not stop in the towns. They gradually filtered into remote villages in ever widening circles of influence. This process was hastened with wonderful rapidity by the conquest of space and time through improved means of transport and communications which solved easily the problem of distance and immobility. Thus, the influence of the west spread far and wide among all classes of people in towns and villages.

Influence in Education : The first influence of the west was felt in the realm of education. Western culture began to spread through English education which was commenced by the Christian missionaries and encouraged considerably by the decision of Lord Macaulay and declaration of Lord Hardinge that preference would be given to the knowledge of English in all public services. The western system of education introduced in India the study of western philosophy, sciences, literatures, history, economics, sociology, etc. It created literate classes which derived their ideas not from the age long traditions of the land but from the west. They looked to the west for every aspect of their life and imitated a good deal of the western culture. This had the effect of developing a wide gulf between the educated and the uneducated classes in India. Apart from this, the new literates brought into existence the middle class with its manifold problems and privileges.

On the Vernacular Literature : The impact of the west and English education was keenly felt on the vernacular literatures of India. Contact with European minds, benefited Indians considerably. Through the English language the western literatures were thrown open to Indians and a flood of ideas was let loose. It had an intensely stimulating effect. Before 1919, Indian nationalist leaders received inspiration from the western literature of freedom. They modelled their speeches and articles on the western thought and borrowed a good deal from British leaders and orators of repute.

Numerous works in the English language provided new trends of thought and action in India. The western literature offered several brilliant specimens in the different branches of literature and Indian writers copied them. The best of the writers of the Indian vernacular literatures have been western in spirit, in outlook, in literary devices, in the choice and treatment of the subjects, though they retained a close connection with the west in the literature and life of ancient India. They represented the spirit of the west clad in a half oriental garb.

The Indian prose literature begins with the translation of English prose works. Our prose writers wrote essays in the light of the western ideology. They imitated western style and theme in their writings. They applied western methods of study to oriental literature. Even Rabindranath Tagore is no exception to this. The Indian drama was considerably influenced by the western drama. The details about the stage and the distinct analysis of the individual and social problems in modern Indian drama are the outcome of the study of the western drama. The style, technique and theme of the western play writers, like Ibsen, Galsworthy and, Bernard Shaw have been imitated by the Indian writers. The growth of One Act Play in Indian literature is the result of the western literary influence. The works of well known writers like Laxminarain Mishra, Upendranath Askq, Harikrishna Premi, Udaishanker Bhatt, Kailashnath Bhatnager, Seth Govind Das, etc., betray the influence of western drama.

Indian story and novel also were profoundly influenced by the western literature. They were absent in the realm of Indian literature till the first half of the nineteenth century. With the translation of western stories and novels, original works were also composed. Western theme and style were liberally followed in the original works. In the sphere of criticism western elements were freely adopted.

Like prose, poetry was also considerably influenced. English *Sonnet, Ode,* and *Blank Verse* were imitated. Madhusudan Datt in Bengali and Ayodhya Singh Verma in Hindi achieved marvellous success in *Blank Verse* English lyrics were freely followed. In long poems on love and mysticism, English thought and style were imitated. In the sphere of essay western models were adopted. Western scholars played prominent role in composing dictionaries and grammars of Indian vernaculars. Christian priests and missionaries set up Indian vernacular press to spread the divine message of the Bible, and for learning the Indian vernaculars they wrote their authoritative grammars. Later on the western scholars not only wrote history of the Indian literatures but established institutions for their rapid evolution and expansion.

Under the influence of the west many Indian vernacular printing presses were set up and many newspapers in Indian languages were started. In 1780, Hickey commenced the publication of the *Bengal Gazette* in English. It was followed by the publication of first Indian vernacular newspaper *Bengal Samachar* in 1816 and the *Bombay Samachar* in Gujarati in 1822. The first Hindi newspaper, the *Banaras Akhbar* was started in 1845. The newspapers and periodicals of the Indian languages not only brought us into close contact with the various countries of the world, but provided opportunities to us to study the literatures and know our political, social, religious and economic evils.

Our ancient language, Sanskrit, was restored to us through English. The first Englishman to learn Sanskrit was Charles Wilkins and the person who clearly realized the significance of Sanskrit was William Jones who came to India in 1783 as the Chief Justice of the Supreme Court at Calcutta. He founded the Bengal Asiatic society for the study of the Oriental Literature. The result was that European scholars were encouraged to take up the study of Sanskrit. It has been said that the years 1828-1870 witnessed the flowering of oriental scholarship and the period between 1870- 1900 saw the publication and circulation of many Sanskrit works like the *Sacred Books of the East* in fifty volumes, the *Harvard Oriental Series, Trubner's Oriental Series* etc. Wilkins, William Jones, William Hamilton, Cole brooke, Wilson, Williams, James Prinsep, Max Muller and other scholars began to study Sanskrit, and edited, translated and published famous works of Sanskrit and, thus, focused the attention of the Indians towards the rich heritage of their Sanskrit literature.

Western Polities and Contemporary India : In the sphere of politics the western thought and administration have given us the conception of political unity and constitutional law and revolutionary notions of liberty and equality. Western thoughts have fostered in India the growth of the spirit of deep nationalism. Political consciousness and aggressive patriotism were borrowed from the west and it profoundly effected the course of Indian history. We received inspiration for intense nationalism from Washington, Cromwell, Mazzini, Garibaldi, Napoleon, etc. Political awakening and growing nationalism unified heterogeneous elements in the country. But the British introduced communalism and separate electorate. It poisoned the national springs. As a result of these evils, our country was partitioned.

The uniformity of British administration, universal peace, political unity, constitutional development and spread of western political ideas led to an increasing emphasis on democracy and institutions of local self-government in India. Though democracy was known to India in the past, the western emphasis on institutional democracy brought something new to the Indian consciousness. The growing spirit of intense nationalism and the popular idea of democracy sowed the seeds of discontent in the congenial soil of India. The growing impoverishment of the country, increasing population, the feeling of political subjugation and slavery and dehahilitation of the old social order made the discontent deep and widespread. Consequently, the middle classes became often restless, aggressive, self-assertive and loud in their demands for the rights and privileges. Besides this, they began to embrace western political ideologies of socialism, communism, individualism, idealism, humanitarianism, etc. This threatened the political edifice of British imperialism in India.

Western Civilization and Indian Society : We are witnessing a silent revolution in Indian society due to the impact of the west. On one side there is the group of conservatives and reactionaries who warned the people of the invidious encroachments by the west, hindered all kinds of progress and persuaded the people loudly to follow old traditions and customs and maintain social solidarity. On the other side, there is the group of progressive persons. They focused the attention of the people on the major social evils like the untouchability, inequality, backwardness of women, child marriage, *parda* system, illiteracy, polygamy, *devdasi* system, etc., and induced people to accept good things of the west. This has aroused our social consciousness and helped in the growth of middle classes. It were the middle classes, which imbibed many western ideas and followed numerous western customs and manners. They have the snobbishness of the west. Being well educated, restless, critical and individualistic, they played a prominent role in moulding the destiny of the country. They provided pioneers and guided the political emancipation and social regeneration.

On account of the impact of the western civilization and culture our moral ideas are changed beyond recognition. Through actions and reactions, through antagonism and assimilation, western ideas began to penetrate into Indian thoughts and habits. Our manners and methods, dress and diet, modes of thought and ways of living reveal western traces. The caste system which has been the bedrock of Hindu society for centuries together is itself collapsing : its rigidity is slackened. Many social evils are disappearing fast. A new view of life and conduct has been introduced in India by the west. A new note of individualism, socialism, revolt and scepticism is surging through the Indian society. The younger generation is becoming individualistic in its outlook. The emphasis upon the individual has tended to loosen our social bonds and shake our social solidarity and cohesion. Our institutions of joint family and caste system have received very rude and violent shock. Previously the individuals surrendered to the society and sacrificed for the social good. But now the individual exalts himself above the society and, therefore, old patterns have lost their balance and are crumbling.

But, as noted above, the influence of the west has been beneficial for the uprooting of our social evils. Inspiration for social reforms is derived from the west. A significant result of impact of the west are the countrywide bold attempts to have social reforms especially to liberate Indian womanhood from the bonds of social tyranny. The All India Women's Conference came into existence and its activities soon assumed a wide national range.

Indian Religion, Philosophy and the Western Culture and Civilization : The impact of western civilization and culture introduced radical changes in the realm of our religion. Superstition was replaced by reason, and conservatism yielded to independent thinking. The traditional explanations of the *Shastras* were subjected to critical scientific examination. A new conception of religion appeared in the light of western rationalism. Old beliefs, habits and traditions were critically and rationally examined. Many of them were denounced as they came from the past encumbered with effete practices and conceptions. Hinduism appeared to many a bundle of superstitions and they began to embrace Christianity and assimilated many western ideas.

They began to study the Bible and follow its principles. This produced a reaction. A revivalist group rose in prominence. Religious reformers and saints like Raja Ram Mohan Roy, Swami Dayanand Saraswati, Swami Vivekanand, Sri Aurobindo and others arrested the growth of Christianization in India.

In the realm of philosophy we received from the west philosophies of materialism, realism and idealism. It created intellectual ferment in the educated classes.

The European missionaries brought Christianity to a direct confrontation with Hinduism. It had two results: first, the missionaries gained considerable number of converts to Christianity, and they created a small new class or group with in the existing socio-religious structure of India. The second impact 'of Christianity was significant. It created among the Hindu intellectuals a deep sense of inwardness to discover in the inner core of Hinduism the conception of monotheism, and all other higher philosophies to feel proud of. The Christian ideas influenced the traditional Indian society to take a fresh look at their own set of values.

Scientific Invention and Research : In the medieval age India lost her spirit of scientific invention and eagerness for research. In the modern age contact with the west made Indians realize that scientific inventions lie at the root of the marvellous progress of the West. From the inventions, discoveries and the lives of the scientists of the west, Indians had learnt the progressive outlook, rational and detached way of thinking, scientific approach to problems and the utilization of science in various walks of life.

The west has given us a spirit of inquiry, Jure for exploration, method of scientific experiment and invention and boldness of enterprise. We have regained from the west not only great eagerness to seek truth and new knowledge but the capacity and power to probe in the mysteries of human life and universe which were lost to us in the dark medieval age. As a result of this, proper arrangements have been made for the advanced study of sciences in Indian educational institutions and universities. Many institutions and laboratories have been set up for the scientific experiments and inventions. The Indian Institute of Science at bangalore deserves mention in this respect.

Western Effect on Art : It is the west which has restored to us our ancient fine arts and made us know the glories of our past We have completely forgotten them in the medieval period. European scholars like Sister Nivedita, Havell, Fergusson, Hindu Stuart etc., have revealed to the world the salient features of the fine arts of India. Cunningham, Coomaraswamy, Marshall, Percy Brown, Smith Tod, Max Muller and others have written monumental works on the greatness and glories of our past.

They laid the foundation of our knowledge of Indian art, epigraphy and archaeology. Many English and European scholars deciphered Indian inscriptions, explained their meaning and interpreted them successfully. They had undertaken excavation works and provided numerous authentic source materials for constructing the history of India.

All this has aroused in us the consciousness of the value of our arts and inspired us to write the authentic and scientific history of our country. Thus, the successful efforts of the west enabled us to regain our cultural heritage.

Economic Impact : In the domain of economic life the high standard of living of the materialistic west has changed the Indian standard of living based on the deep sense of contentment and spiritualism. Consequently, the old and easy ways of life began to crumble fast. Hereditary occupations could no longer guarantee the individual subsistence or comfort. New types of employment and castes came into existence. As a result of this the old economic standards are gone.

The economic and industrial policy of the British destroyed the ancient industries of India and forced the country to rural economy. In fact, her traditional economic structure in agriculture and industries fell to pieces. But on account of the increased population and absence of new large scale industries, agriculture could not be the sound means of subsistence. All this multiplied existing difficulties and created new problems. In the meanwhile, the industrialization in Japan and America and the growth of capitalism reawakened Indians. Close contact with the western countries revealed to Indians a panorama of vast possibilities in the realm of economic life. The abundance of minerals, raw materials and labour inspired Indians to industrialize their country.

In course of time under the western influence new industries and manufacturing concerns were gradually set up, and sound measures were adopted for the industrialization. Consequently, ancient economic values of life were changed considerably. Material prosperity was promoted and the standard of living rose gradually. Changes in the material conditions of existence have brought about profound changes in the mental outlook of the people. They have become aware of the economic backwardness and poverty of the country.

Now they began to adopt measures for rural and urban development. In other words, the economic life of the country is being modernized.

But the greatest economic and political event of the west that has influenced economic, political, social and moral development of India is the *Russian Revolution*. The assumption of power by the proletariat not only in Moscow but in Peking also had a profound effect on the youths of India. They were now favourably inclined towards socialism and communism. Before 1920 there hardly existed any labour or peasant organisation in India. But the period between the two world wars and after witnessed the phenomenal growth of the labour movement, the establishment of trade unions, commencement of peasant agitation and the foundation of the socialist and the communist parties.

The social ideology of the movement, derived from Marx and Engels, is revolutionary to the social, political, economic and religious organization of India. The new western ideology has changed our economic outlook, introduced a desire for liberty, a passion for social justice, a sense of revolt and a rebellious and anarchic mood. It has aroused the Indian intelligentsia to demand self-government for industrialization. All this has changed the sway of religion, society and capitalism. A new demand for modernization for all avenues of progress and for equality and justice has been springing up. Consequently, a different type of national sentiment based on economic divisions has been rising.

Influence of India on Western Culture and Civilization : The above account makes one feel that in the modern age the west has profoundly influenced the course of Indian civilization and India has been overwhelmingly dominated by the west. It is a fact that India witnessed reawakening due to the impact of the west. But India also considerably influenced the western outlook in many ways. In the medieval period the Arabs and the Italians together with their goods from the east carried the ingredients and thoughts of the Indian culture to Europe. Later on European travellers like Sehastein Friar Manrique, Pietro Delta Valles, Bernier, Travernier, Thevenot, Nicolo Conti, Hawkins, Sir Thomas Roe, Peter Mundi, and other Jesuit priests had travelled all over India and taken to Europe in abundance the cultural inspiration from India. Sir Thomas Roe's idea of India provided inspiration for Milton's picture of Satan sitting exalted in his book *Paradise Lost*. Dryden was also so profoundly influenced that he composed a drama *Aurangzeb*. In 1671, the French traveller Bernier had taken with him to Europe Mughal prince Dara Shikoh's manuscript of *Upanishads* translated into Persian. Later on French and German Jesuit and Christian missionaries had studied Sanskrit and got some Sanskrit works published. In 1732, a Jesuit compiled the first grammar of Sanskrit in a European language. As a result of this a famous revolutionary writer of France. Voltaire, and later on Amiel emphasized that the soul must be 'Brahmanized' for the spiritual progress of humanity.

In the closing years of the eighteenth century European scholars endeavoured collectively for the systematic study and dissemination of Sanskrit literature. A group of orientalists encouraged the first regular study of Indian culture. Three Englishmen, Sir Charles Wilkins, Sir William Jones and Colebrooke "aimed at a union of Hindu and European learning" and had done a good deal to introduce the ancient Sanskrit classics to the western world. Wilkins was the first European to translate the Gita. William Jones founded in 1785 the Asiatic Society of Bengal. It was under the patronage of this Society that authoritative translations of many Indian Sanskrit classics were published and they "have reverberated the fame of the Indian culture throughout the whispering galleries of Europe." Jones edited, among other Sanskrit works, several Sanskrit plays including the *Shakuntala* of Kalidas. He also translated *Manu Smriti* in English. He was the first to declare to the west "that Sanskrit was the most scientific language and contained works common both to Latin and

Greek languages:' Thus, it was he who laid the foundations of the science of comparative philology and paved the path for the evolution of the theory of Max Muller. The study of phonetics, encouraged in Europe, revealed that the races which spoke Sanskrit, Latin, Greek, and 'land', the language of Persia, had a good deal of resemblances in religion, rites, mythology and social customs and institutions. This has thrown a flood of light on the theory of the original home of the Aryans. Another valuable work of Jones was in the realm of chronology of Indian history which gradually aroused interest in the study of Indian inscriptions and coins.

In the first quarter of the nineteenth century, H. T. Colebrooke translated the largest number of Sanskrit works, studied widely Hindu law, philosophy, grammar, astronomy and religion, wrote extensively on various aspects of Indology and edited many Sanskrit texts, such as the grammar of Panini and *Hitopadesa.* It is said that an Englishman, Hamilton, taught Sanskrit to some German and French scholars and therefore it led to vigorous researches in Sanskrit literature and deep study of Indian culture in Germany and France. But Germany was the first country in Europe to discover the hidden treasures of Sanskrit literature and German scholars endeavoured hard to bring into light several Sanskrit texts. Consequently, profound influence was exerted on the German thinkers and philosophers by Indian religion and culture. To the German scholar Schopenhauer the *Upanishads* came as a new gnosis, as a revelation. He said that the study of the *Upanishads* had been the solace of his life and it would be solace of his death.

The well known German philosopher Kant's central doctrine that things of experience are only the phenomena of the thing in itself has been acknowledged as essentially a doctrine of the *Upanishads.* The Indian poets influenced the German writers and poets; for example, the influence of Kalidas' *Meghduta* (the Cloud Messenger) on the *Maria Stuart* of Schiller is most distinct. The famous German poet Goethe had lavishly admired Kalidas' Sanskrit drama *Shakuntala* and he had modelled his Prologue to Faust on the prologue of this particular drama. Later on, another German scholar, Max Muller, had completed and published the translation of the text of the *Rigveda* after strenuous labour of thirty years. He had derived such inspiration from India that he convinced the western people of the magnificence and majesty of Indian culture by his original works, translations and compilations of Sanskrit texts. By attracting scholars' attention to the study of comparative philology and religion he introduced revolution in the domains of philosophy and religion.

Like Europeans, American Scholars could not but be influenced by the Indian culture, religion and philosophy. The famous American writer and thinker Emerson, poet Walt Whitman and Alcott were profoundly influenced by Indian philosophy. Emerson used to read and reread the Gita and the *Upanishads* to a group of poets, authors and thinkers of America in Concord, Massachusetts. Emerson's essays like "the Over Soul" and "Circles" and poems like "Brahma" are nothing but Upanishadic thought. Poet Walt Whitman's poems "Passage to India" and "Leaves of Grass" reflect distinctly the spiritual life of India and the mixture of the *Upanishads* and the *Bhagavad Gita* of the Hindus. The American Transcendental Movement, of which Emerson was the leader, was the outcome of the impact of Indian culture.

After the extensive tours of Swami Vivekanand in America, Indian Vedant was well studied and today there are many Vivekanand Ashrams which have been the radiating centres of Indian culture and religion in that country. They have grown and expanded into a network of organizations of social and spiritual service. J. Krishnamurti, an Indian thinker and philosopher, has been explaining to Americans, Indian philosophy and spiritual ideology, and it has been profoundly influencing the west. If the 'California Group' is established for the study and observance of the esoteric teachings of Indian Vedantic Philosophy in North America, Circles Esoterico da communhao da Pensamanto in Sao Paulo, Brazil (South America) is founded 'to comprehend the spiritual wisdom of the world and particularly that of India. It has recently organized researches into Vaishnavic thought. Besides this the India Society and the International School of Vedic and Allied Research, organized by a group of Indians in America, has been furthering the cause of Indian culture in an admirable way. Under the auspices of these the depth and profundity of India's aesthetic expressions and their psychology and motivation have been unraveled to big American audiences.

Like the poets of America and Europe, the poets, writers, thinkers, philosophers and scholars of England have also been influenced by the Indian religion and philosophy. The works of Shelley, Wordsworth, Carlyle and Robert Browning are full of traces of Indian Vedanta. When Emerson first visited Carlyle, he received a copy of Gita as a present from Carlyle. Tennyson, the famous poet laureate of England, has referred to Indian topics in some of his own poems. Sir John Woodruff was so much attracted by the Tantrik cult of India that he followed it and edited in a masterly way a number of Tantrik texts. It was through his exposition of Tantrik thought that the ideas of Tantras entered the west in modern times. But the influence of Indian thought is most obvious in the philosophical writings of famous modern English thinkers, like Gerald Heard and Aldous Huxley. It is said that the thought of Gerald Heard clearly exhibits Sri Aurobindo's teachings. The greatest English novelist, Somerset Maugham, favoured visit to India to acquire knowledge of the higher values of life.

Ireland is considerably influenced by Indian religion and culture. The famous jurist, Maine, has shown that "the old Brehon laws of Ireland are derived from the Vedic laws of India." The new Celtic revival in Ireland is influenced by the Hindu philosophy and religion. The British literary and dramatic revival bears traces of Indian ideas. George Russell and Yeats who were the two chief inaugurators of this Irish movement were deeply influenced by the spiritual thought and life of India. The poetry of Russell is soaked in Indian mysticism.

During the British rule many British officials, businessmen and Christian missionaries lived in India and came in close contact with the Indians. Many of them were so profoundly influenced by the Indian culture that they wrote many authoritative works about India. Historians like Elphinstone, Tod, Malcolm, Smith, Duff, Rapson, poets like Edwin Arnold and Kipling, and novelists like Thackeray are such Englishmen who endeavoured to interpret India to the west. The School of Oriental and African Studies in London is trying to encourage the study of Indian culture and philosophy. Prof. Turner who is its chief advocate has mastery over Sanskrit. Dr. Bake is well versed in classical music and folklore and folk dances of India. In the nineteenth century the daily English life was so much influenced by the Indian ideas that Indian *hukkah, pulao* and *chutney* became very popular and many Indian words, manners and dishes entered the English society. The India Society and the Society for Cultural Fellowship with India prove that England recognizes the majesty and splendour of Indian culture and desires to deepen her cultural relations with India.

In the present century many European countries are taking keen interest in Indian culture. The famous French savant, Romain Rolland, is well noted for his 'deep understanding of the intrinsic meaning of Indian culture'. He has written with great reverence works on Sri Ramakrishna, Swami Vivekanand and Mahatma Gandhi. The renowned French mystic Paul Richard, was considerably influenced by the doctrines of Sri Aurobindo. A group of French scholars, among whom Sylvian Lewy is noted, has done valuable work in the realm of Indology. Institute de Civilization Indianne is a famous institution in France which has been promoting the study of Indian culture and understanding of Indian life. The Leo university is also encouraging research on the *Satpath Brahmanas*. Louis Renon of the' Paris University, a famous Indologist and Sanskrit scholar, during his talk at Shantiniketan, in 1949, remarked that the best writers and thinkers of France had been influenced by Indian thought and culture.

The well known German thinker, Count Hermann Keyserling, was so much influenced by Indian mysticism and spiritual ideology that he recognized 'the absolute superiority of India over the west in philosophy.' As the German people consider themselves an off shoot of the Aryans, they take a keen interest in Sanskrit, the language of the Aryans. Munich and other University centres have been patronizing the study of the Sanskrit literature. Many Sanskrit texts including the Vedas have been translated in German language. Some authoritative works are also edited on Buddhism, Jainism and Hinduism. Glassenhap is famous for his commentaries on several Sanskrit philosophical texts including one of Madhvacharya. There are many oriental libraries in Germany. In the Russian region of Germany there exists the famous institution 'Biblio Theckder Dentslben Morgenlandischen Gessell schaft' which contains 40,000 books ,"in oriental culture, literature and religion.

The Summer School form Spiritual Research in Ascona, Switzerland, has the religions of modern India as one of its special subjects of study. The Kern Institute in Holland and the Oriental Institute in Italy are famous centres where original work is being carried on Indian fine arts, archaeology and literature. A renowned professor of the Kern Institute has success fully edited the Bhishma Parva of the Mahabharat, the Garud Puran, the Brahmand Puran etc. Research work is also being undertaken on Pali and Sanskrit in Denmark, Norway, Sweden and Finland. Sten Konow of Norway is renowned for his original researches on the evolution of religious thought of India. Winternitz of Czechoslovakia is well known for his monumental work on the growth of Indian literature. Prof. Tucci has made Italy famous by his researches on Sanskrit and studies in Vaishnavic thought. He has collected rare manuscripts and pictures from India, Nepal and Tibet. In Belgium, a priest has studied the works of Nagarjuna and has written a good work called *Le Traits de fa Grand Vertu de Saggess.* Stanislaw F. Michalski, a great distinguished scholar of Sanskrit in Poland, has founded the Oriental section of Warsaw Scientific Society and published books on the Gita, the Upanishads, the Ramayan and other Sanskrit classics. He has devoted his whole life to the study of Sanskrit and ancient Indian Literature.

In the twentieth century, the Theosophical Society and its presidents, Dr. Annie Besant, Dr. G. Arundale, C. Jinrajdas and N. Shriram have endeavoured hard through the centres of the society to disseminate the truths of Indian religion and culture. Dr. Annie Besant who had dedicated her whole life to the cause of social, cultural and spiritual uplift of India had diffused the knowledge about the Indian culture and expounded the religion of India through her books, articles, lectures, tours, etc.

Similarly, the works, discourses and tours of Swami Vivekanand, Swami Ram Tirtha (the inspired messenger of India), Rabindranath Tagore, Sri Aurobindo, Mahatma Gandhi, Dr. S. Radhakrishnan, Jawaharlal Nehru, etc., have spread Indian culture abroad. They have paved the path for building up India's spiritual empire in modern times. Exhibitions of Indian arts and industries and various Indian cultural programmes have been organized at many places in Europe and America. This has aroused abroad a keen interest in our culture and fine arts.

Now the west has developed a taste for Indian artistic works. As a result of the exhibitions of the paintings of talented artists, like Nandlal Bose, and the demonstration of Indian music and dance by the best artists like Udayshankar, Ramgopal and Radha Shriram the influence of Indian art is permeating in the west. Its glories and majesty are recognized there.

A large number of Indian poets, writers, journalists, novelists, essayists, critics and short story writers have written in English. Sarojini Naidu, Manmohan Ghosh, Rabindranath Tagore, Toru Dutta, Lalita Devi, H. Chattopadhyaya, Aurobindo, Mulkraj Anand, M. S. Iswaran, K. S. Venkataramani, Nehru, Humayun Kabir, Radhakrishnan, etc., are the distinguished literary figures who wrote in English. Consequently, there is rich luxuriant output in Indo-Anglican literature. The work of these have evoked loud appreciation from the west. Thus, the impact of the west was felt by us in the domains of religion, society, politics, literature nay, in every walk of life and after a violent shock we were awakened to our own inborn potentialities. But the west could not escape the effect of India's close contact. It not only realized anew "the glory that was Ind' but was raised into a higher and spiritual life of Divine Knowledge, Bliss and Harmony.

Bibliography

Agrawal, S.N. : *Indian Population*, APH, Bombay, 1960.

Ambhirajan, S. : *Political, Economic and British Policy in India*, Cambridge, 1978.

Aurora, G.S. : *Tribe, Caste, Class Encounters*, Administrative Staff College of India, Hyderabad, 1972.

Bagchi, A.K. : *Europe and Indian Entrepreneurship in India*, Oxford University Press, London, 1970.

Bali, D.R. : *Modern Indian Thought*, Sterling, London, 1989.

Balkrishna, R. : *Ancient History of India*, Madras, 1958.

Basu, A.N. : *Education in Modern India*, Brief Review, Calcutta, 1947.

Basu, S.K. : *The Managing Agency System in Prospect and Retrospect*, Calcutta, 1958.

Bayly, C.A. : *The New Cambridge History of India, Indian Society and the Making of the British Empire*, Oxford University Press, London, 1987.

Bell, D. : *The Coming of Post-industrial Society*, Heinneman Educational Books Ltd. : London, 1974.

Berger, P.L. and Luckmann : *The Social Construction of Reality*, Doubleday and Co., New York, 1966.

Bernier, F. : *Travels in the Mughal Empire*, MacMillan, London, 1891.

Beteille, A. : *Caste, Class and Power*, Barkeley, 1964.

Bettelheim, B. : *Dynamics of Prejudice: A Psychological and Sociological Study*, New York, 1950.

Bhatt, Anil : *Caste, Class and Politics: An Empirical Profile of Social Stratification* in *Modern India*, Manohar Book Service, New Delhi, 1975.

Bhattacharya, H.B. : *Cultural Heritage of India*, Calcutta, 1958.

Bipin Chandra : *The Rise and Growth of Economic Nationalism in India*, Delhi, 1977.

Bose, N.K. : *Culture and Society in India*, Popular Prakashan, Bombay, 1967.

Bourdieu, Pierre and L.J.D. Wacquant : *An Invitation to Reflexive Sociology*, University of Chicago Press, Chicago, 1992.

Broomfield, J.H. : *Elite Conflict in a Plural Society*, Oxford University Press, New Delhi, 1968.

Chopra, P.N. : *Social and Cultural History of India*, Sterling, 1979.

Chopra, Puri, Das : *A Social, and Cultural History of India*, Macmillan, Delhi, 1974.

Choudhury, R. : *The Evolution of Indian Industries*, Calcutta, 1939.

Cohn, B.S. : *Structural Change in Indian Rural Society*, London, 1969.

——— *India: The Social Anthropology of a Civilization*, Prentice Hall, New Jersey, 1971.

Das, M.N. : *Studies in the Economic and Social Development of Modern India*, Calcutta, 1959.

Dasgupta, Biplab : *The Naxalite Movement*, Asia Publishing House, Bombay, 1974.

Desai, A.R. : *Rural Sociology in India*, Popular Prakashan, Bombay, 1959.

——— *Social Background of Indian Nationalism*, Popular Prakashan, Bombay, 1972.

Durkheim, E. : *The Division o f Labour in Society*, Macmillan Company, New York, 1933.

Dutt, N.K. : *Origin and Growth of Caste in India*, Calcutta, 1931.

Farquher J.N. : *Modern Religious Movement in India*, OUP, New Delhi, 1914.

Gadgil, D.R. : *The Industrial Evolution of India*, Oxford University Press, New Delhi, 1942.

Garratt, G.D. : *The Legacy of India*, Oxford University Press, Bombay, 1967.

Gellner, E. : *Thought and Change*, The University of Chicago Press, Chicago, 1965.

Ghosal, U.N. : *A History of Indian Political Ideas*, Oxford University Press, Bombay, 1966.

Ghose, K. : *Agricultural Labourers in India*, Indian Publication, Calcutta, 1967.

Ghurye, G.S. : *Caste, Class in India*, Popular Prakashan, Bombay, 1950.

Habib, Irfan : *The Agrarian System of Mughal India*, Bombay, 1963.

Hagen, E.E. : *On the Theory of Social Change*, Illinois, 1962.

Hazlehurst, L.W : *Entrepreneurship and Merchant Caste*, Duke University, City, 1966.

Hutton, J.H. : *Castes in India*, Oxford, New York, 1961.

Joshi, P.C. and Damodaran, K. : *Marx Comes to India*, Manohar Book Service, New Delhi, 1975.

Kuppuswamy, B. : *Social Change in Modern India*, Delhi, 1985.

Lancaster, L.W. : *Masters of Political Though*, OUP, Calcutta, 1959.

Lokanathan, P.S. : *Industrialisation*, Oxford, New York, 1946.

Mairet, Philip : *Pioneer of Sociology: The Life and Letters of Patrick Geddes*, Lund Humphries, London, 1957.

Malhautra, M. : *New Century: Whose Century?* UBSPD, New Delhi, 2001.

Marcuse, H. : *Eros and Civilization*, The Beacon Press, London, 1955.

Marriott, McKim : *Caste Ranking and Community Structures*, University of Chicago Press, Chicago, 1955.

Mills, C. Wright : *Images of Man*, George Braziller, New York, 1960.

Mukherjee, R.K. : *What Will It Be?* The Macmillan Company of India, New Delhi, 1979.

—*Sociology of Indian Sociology*, Allied Publications, Bombay, 1979.

Mukherjee, S.N. : *History of Education in India*, Rajan Pub., Baroda, 1966.

Natrajan : *Century of Social Reform in India*, Popular Prakashan, Bombay, 1962.

Nehru, J. : *The Discovery of India*, Writer Views, Calcutta, 1946.

Nizami, K.A. : *Studies in Medieval History and Culture*, OUP, Bombay, 1966.

Oommen, T.K. : *Charisma Stability and Change*, Thomson Press, New Delhi, 1972.

Panikkar, K.M. : *Asia and Western Dominance*, MacMillan, London, 1953.

Prabhu, P.H. : *Hindu Social Organisation*, Popular Prakashan, Bombay, 1963.

Prasad, I. : *History of Medieval India*, Allahabad, 1925.

Prasad, N. : *The Myth of Caste System*, Khuda Baksh, Patna, 1957.

Prasad, R. : *Social Reforms: An Analysis of Indian Society*, Y.K. Publishers, Agra, 1990.

Raghaban, V. : *The Indian Heritage*, Sun Pub., Bangalore, 1956.

Rao, M.S.A. : *Urbanisation and Social Change*, Orient Longman, Delhi, 1970.

Rao, V.K.R.V. : *Education and Human Resource Development*, Allied, New Delhi, 1966.

Rawlinson, H.G. : *India-a Short Cultural History*, Surjeet Publishers, London, 1980.

Reisman, D. : *The Lonely Crowd*, Yale University Press, New York, 1950.

Revri, C. : *Indian Trade Union Movement*, Orient Longman, New Delhi, 1972.

Rosenthal, D.B. : *The United Elites: Politics and Government in Two Indian Cities*, Chicago University Press, Chicago, 1970.

Saberwal, Satish : *Towards a Cultural Policy*, Vikas Publishing House, New Delhi, 1974.

Schutz, A. : *On Phenomenology and Social Relations*, The University of Chicago Press, London, 1970.

Sharma, I.R. : *The Making of Modern India*, Orient Longman, New Delhi, 1951.

Shelvankar, K.S. : *The Problem of India*, MacMillan, London, 1940.

Singer, Milton : *Traditional India: Structure and Change*, Aldine Publishing Company, Chicago, 1968.

Smith, D.E. : *India as a Secular State*, Princeton, 1963.

Smith, W.C. : *Modern Islam in India*, London, 1946.

Thapar, Romila : *Past and Prejudice*, National Book Trust of India, Delhi, 1975.

Tiryakian, Edward A. : *Sociologism and Existentialism*, Prentice-Hall, New York, 1962.

Unnithan, T.K.N. : *Sociology for India*, Prentice-Hall of India, New Delhi, 1967.

Vidyarthi, L.P : *Conflict, Tension and Cultural Trends in India*, Punthi Pustak, Calcutta, 1969.

Weber, Max : *Essays in Sociology*, Routledge and Kegan Paul, London, 1952.

Weiner, Myron and Kothari, Rajni : *Indian Voting Behaviour*, Mukhopadhayaya, Calcutta, 1965.

Winch, P. : *The Idea of a Social Science*, MacMillan, London, 1968.

Zeitlin, I.M. : *Social and Cultural Life in India*, Appleton-Century Crofts, New York, 1973.

Index

T

U

V

W

❑❑❑